DOC BLAKELY'S PUSH BUTTON WIT

James "Doc" Blakely

Rich Publishing Co.
Houston, Texas 77070

To Kim,
who made my writing
what it is today—a joke

First Printed 1986
Library of Congress Catalog Card No. 85–61515
ISBN 0–9607256–3–6
Printed in the United States of America

Success

*To have laughed often
and loved much;*

*To have won the respect of
intelligent persons and the
affection of little children;*

*To have withstood the betrayal of false
friends and the approbation of
honest critics;*

*To look an old dog in the eye and know that
he likes you just 'cause you like him;*

*To have looked for beauty where they said
there was none and to have found it;*

*To have looked for the best in people instead of
the worst;*

*To leave the world a little better, whether
it's through a garden patch, a better
business or a redeemed social condition;*

*To know that even one life has lived a
fuller span or breathed a little easier
because you have lived;*

That is to have succeeded.

Edited by
Doc Blakely

Doc Blakely

**3404 Fairway drive
Wharton, Tex 77488
(409) 532-4502**

Contents

3. HOW TO DELIVER THE TOUCH   58

4. SITUATION HUMOR   87

PART III

JOKES: ONE-AND TWO-LINERS

PART I

Doc Blakely (right) receives the CPAE award, highest honor conferred by the National Speakers Association, from Bill Gove, former president of NSA. Only 3 awards were made in 1980: Earl Nightingale, Art Linkletter and Doc Blakely.

How This Book Will
Improve Your Humor Skills

1

Humor is a dynamite form of communication, capable of producing explosive laughter, blowing up in your face or fizzling out as a complete dud. Why do people say "stop me if you've heard this . . . ?" Because things that were once funny cease to be amusing if you know where the story is going from the start. That's because humor and laughter rely on surprise for entertainment value. A singer performs a number that everyone knows by heart and still the audience cries "Sing it again." But try telling an old joke and they'll say, "We've heard it."

This book will not only show you how to place the cap and light the fuse but also keep you supplied with enough new blasting material to blow the lid off of any speaking assignment. They won't be thinking "We've heard it" because with this fresh supply of quick wit, you'll be through with a thought in the time they take to think it.

Mystery of Humor Success

2

There is a simple basic key to producing laughter. Thoughts are probably racing through your mind like a pig in a python but if I told you now, you wouldn't get the point. It would be better for you to discover the key for yourself. It is not hidden, in fact it is repeated throughout every page in this collection. You have already been given the secret and may not have recognized it. The Chinese say one picture is worth a thousand words and since jokes conjure up vivid images, let me give you three picture perfect examples that will perhaps adjust your mental venetian blind to again reveal the secret.

My sister said morality is in a state of serious neglect and something should be done. My brother-in-law agrees and blames it all on the Homo Sapiens and the Lebanese.

A doctor cured a fat patient of overeating with a fear tactic, a question containing only 6 words. "Have you ever seen skin explode?"

A tough traffic cop gave me a ticket for parking illegally before I could get out of the car. I told him he should have given me a warning. He took out his pistol and fired once in the air.

The secret of good humor, riotous laughter, hilarious entertainment is on every page in this collection. You may discover it on the first page or it may not dawn on you until the last one but it is there and like a panther on a perch will leap out at you when you are truly prepared to receive it. Like any good picture puzzle, it is best if it is difficult enough to be challenging but once a few pieces are put together, the scene changes, grows, giving hints to further search. Like taking olives from a bottle, each one removed makes access to the whole a little easier. The first olive is to understand how this book is organized, the second is how to use it then perhaps the next one, the basic key to producing laughter, will release the whole lot and the secret to effective use of humor will come tumbling out.

Organization of This Book

Over one thousand entries are alphabetically arranged by subjects ranging from Ads to Women. A subject index is also provided. This permits selection of material for specific areas as easy as pulling the trigger on a jack hammer.

Furthermore, a special feature of this book is TIPS FOR THAT PROFESSIONAL TOUCH. It contains over 90 entries on the philosophy of successful humor usage from some of the nation's most popular professional speakers.

In addition to my own observation from almost two decades on the convention circuit, I have enlisted the aid of hilarious laugh getters, to share their philosophy and observations, on how they would use this material. Their names may not be familiar unless you attend a lot of conventions but their reputation is sterling, their advice golden and their speaking fees exceed five figures per speech. Examples are: Joe Griffith, formerly a professional actor and stockbroker, Dallas, Texas; Robert Henry, formerly a college dean, Auburn, Alabama; Newt Hielscher, formerly an insurance executive, Shreveport, Louisiana; and Jeanne Robertson, a former Miss America contestant, Burlington, North Carolina. All these people share a common bond—they were so funny and so good at making speeches that each gave up a very successful career in some other field to enter the risky arena of professional speaking where falling from favor, like a fluttering dove with a shattered wing, is as close as their judgment of the explosiveness of their material.

Wouldn't you like to have the advice and counsel of many of the top humorists in your brain trust? Well, you hold it in your hands or mind at this moment. These tantalizing tips are also listed with a brief description of the subject covered in the table of contents.

How to Use This Book

The humor in this collection is unique, compared to most collections, although there are many good quality books on the market. This is professional humor, devoid of the traditional writing style that sterilizes verbal usage.

It is of two types. First, there is the short, quick one- or two-liners like entry #5. Secondly, there is a condensed version, for example #9, of the standard joke. What makes the collection unique is that secret ingredient previously eluded to but not discussed.

Every successful professional has at least subconsciously sensed the secret and put it to use. The discovery of this magical revelation will come swiftly to some like the speed of a laser beam, to others it will be a gradual awakening reaching out with the soft touch of a rosy fingered dawn. Jack Benny knew the secret, Will Rogers was a master of it, Charlie Chaplin used it in visual form. They never tried to hide it. In fact, they practiced it before millions of people and probably marveled that so few could see the obvious. It keeps minds from wandering, keeps audiences on the edge of their chairs, and rivets full attention to the breastplate of your remarks. Without it, movies are dull and profitless, TV programs are turned off, sponsorships are dropped, fortunes are lost. It is used not only in humor but in every form of really effective communication.

Do you want it? Then read on if you dare. When you have dug deep enough, the secret, perhaps when you least expect it, will come bellowing out of the dark recesses of your mind like a crazed bull from a malt liquor can.

PART II

TIPS FOR THAT PROFESSIONAL TOUCH

1. HOW TO DEVELOP THE TOUCH
2. HOW TO DEDUCE THE TOUCH
3. HOW TO DELIVER THE TOUCH
4. SITUATION HUMOR
5. WHY DO WE DO IT?

A horse laugh is nothing new to Doc. He's a man of many convictions but fortunately has never done time for any of them.

How to Develop the Touch

Doc Blakely (left) and collegues Jeanne Robertson, Robert Henry and Joe Griffith make up *The Platform Professionals* © speakers group. Performing individually or in any combination they account for 500 speeches and seminars annually at conventions throughout the world. All 4 are recipients of the CPAE award from The National Speakers Association (equivalent to the Hall of Fame) and are listed by the Nightingale-Conant Corporation among the top 12 humorists in America.

It Starts with Self-Discipline

"I'd love to be a good speaker, but I know it's impossible. I lack the discipline." This is the common expression I hear from numerous people who see my profession as a glamorous experience. I see it as a glamorous experience also, but I agree that it takes discipline. It's difficult not to laugh when another speaker tells a good joke.

Imagine, for instance, if every funny person in the country decided to buckle down and get to work and started filling up the circuit with quality speakers. Why, we'd soon be up to our I.Q.'s in great jokes, for heaven's sake!

So you lack the discipline to develop into a full-fledged humorist? Well, good for you. Stick with it. I've got enough competition.

Ah, but for you, gentle reader, the situation is a completely different matter. You, clearly, are serious about your work. Haven't you purchased this book? Are you not reading it at this very moment? If that's not a commitment to the fine art of humor communication, whatever is?

Now for a couple of tricks of the trade:

1. Give humor-study top priority. A story in setting priorities is told of Charles Schwab, former president of U.S. Steel. An efficiency expert named Ivy Lee was interviewed by Schwab and asked if Lee had any quick suggestions for him. "Every morning," said Lee, "make a list of the things you have to do that day. List them in order of importance. Then concentrate on the first task until it's finished, without diverting your attention to anything else. Then go on to the second task, completing as much as you comfortably can in the course of the day." Schwab gave him a rather blank stare, and asked what he owed Lee for the suggestion. "Try it for a month," said Lee, "and then pay me what you think it's worth." Thirty days later, Schwab sent a check in the mail to Lee for $25,000.

The expert's advice is still good. If you want to pursue the creation of humor, dedicate yourself to a certain number of jokes to try, to study, to create each day. Put it in writing, establish your priorities, develop self-discipline, and don't be side-tracked until the day's commitment is completed.

2. Don't take yourself too seriously. Sometimes people try too hard to be funny, to create material, to deliver lines, and come off as a buffoon parroting some preconceived material. Learn to relax, to let go, to let the material flow in an adlibbed manner. Once your material begins to click, then you can worry about perfecting your delivery.

As an example, a young friend from the 7th grade came over

to my house one day when I was in deep thought. He walked right over to me, put his right hand on top of my head in a spread-eagle fashion. "Know what this is?" he asked. Without moving from my chair I rolled my eyes upward and replied, "What?" "A Brain-sucker," he answered, "know what it's doing?" "What?" I said. "Starving," he replied.

Many people that buy this book will do so with the hope they will be able to utilize some of the material and philosophy found within its pages. After awhile, negative thoughts will start to creep in and self-confidence dwindles. Well, you don't have to be a professional speaker or entertainer to make this material work, but you do have to believe in yourself and work at the art of communicating with good quality material. It takes discipline.

For example, Steve Martin got his start in television as a writer for the Smothers Brothers. "I just happened to be there with a hand full of poems," he says, "and they hired me because they wanted new writers. I worked in television for 5 years and it really taught me how to write. I'd never written anything before. I never knew how to be economical or to make a joke. I'd get a thought, but I didn't know how to make it into a joke. It was really good discipline."

So you can see how important discipline is to a guy who didn't even know how to be economical. In the last five years, his performances have grossed 150 million dollars. This funny man wrote a best selling book with the strange title of CRUEL SHOES. Now aren't you ashamed of yourself for rejecting that clever thought you had about your socks?

Gather Speech Material

One of the best ways to get material is by watching your fellow man. Study him, how he walks and talks, and love him enough to mimic him without hurting him.

If you are going to use derogatory humor, be sure to include a healthy dose of it directed at yourself. In fact, many successful humorists never tell derogatory stories on anyone but themselves. Here's an example from Red Skelton: "I played one town not long ago, and the audience was the most unusual I ever had. People came right up on the stage and picked me up on their shoulders. Then they carried me to the city limits and said, 'If you ever come back here again . . .'" According to Red, if you should ever be run out of town, put a little class into it. Make it look like you are leading the parade.

There are a lot of other clowns around and some of the funniest ones are never exposed. Keep your ears open for great remarks like these from the plumber, doctor, and other millionaires. Here's a great line overheard in a museum, "What kind of paintings are those? I can't make heads or tails out of them." "Five thousand wouldn't buy one like that." Someone in the group quips, "I'm one of the five thousand."

An elderly friend of mine told me that he starts every morning by crawling out of bed and reading the obituary columns. "If I don't see my name, I get dressed. My doctor won't let me have coffee, so I read a copy of Playboy to get my heart started."

The clowns are everywhere. All you have to do to test this philosophy is to go into any community and ask people who are the "characters." These people are naturally witty and material just seems to spontaneously flow from their minds. That's why they are so well loved. The "character" is just another name for a clown. Cultivate their friendship and listen to the wisdom they express in their most unique art form. They throw away material without thought of compensation, their reward being the laughter that it brings from their listeners. If you become a good listener and collect a few of these jewels from day to day, you will soon have a collection worthy of including in your own repertoire. To illustrate the point once again, here's a sample I recently heard in the local coffee shop. Two elderly people, a man and a woman, were trading quips. Both of them were local "characters." The woman, apparently in her 90's, was kidding the younger man, probably in his 70's about his youth. "Come along with me, sonny, and I'll show you a good time at my birthday party today. If we light all the candles, they'll have to call out the fire department."

"How old are you?"

"Not so fast, you sly devil. My age is *my* business."

"Yeah, well from the looks of things, you've been in business a long time."

The jesters are still holding court for all those who care to listen. Keep your ears open.

Collect Stories

Small communities make great places for collecting stories. Many times a city or county, or both, will have a museum that is operated by a volunteer "character." For some reason, museums tend to draw people who have a knack for remembering tall tales and relish repeating them to visitors. All you have to do to collect this kind of humor is just suggest something like, "I'll bet you know a lot of tall tales or funny stories concerning the history of this place." They will usually take it from there.

For example, here is a story related to me by the keeper of a museum: It seems a colorful lawyer from the past had agreed to take a piece of land as his fee for getting a defendant acquitted. According to court documents and old newspaper accounts, he lived up to his part of the bargain and successfully got a "not guilty" verdict. That same day he brought in a deed, duly signed. But shortly, his ex-client sued for recovery on the grounds that the deed had been obtained under duress.

The old lawyer indignantly denied the charge. He simply declared that the low down scoundrel had reneged on his agreement. "I just laid my pistol up against his head, cocked back the hammer and told him that if he didn't sign, I'd blow his brains out, and he signed then and there of his own free will."

A story like this is priceless, because it is true and hasn't made the rounds. Furthermore, it can be used to make a point. Suppose for instance that the mayor of your city or town had decided to resign rather than face all the bickering and pressure that mayors often have to put up with. A story like this could be used in a good natured way to illustrate that he had done a good job, but decided to give up the headaches of local politics. Only with humor could you express a sentiment in such a way that everyone could laugh with a great sense of relief and a mixture of truth and appreciation.

Study Others' Methods

Many people lament the fact that Vaudeville in the United States is all but dead. Vaudeville as we once knew it, for the most part, is gone, but the performers and associated occupations are still in existence. The difference is that the form has changed.

In years past, the Vaudeville circuit was the life blood for a number of comedians that traveled from city to city. Comedy acts were especially popular on the circuit and faced the same dangers that comedians and humorists face today. The first danger was an unresponsive audience, the second, perhaps deadlier than the first, was the presence of pirates who sat in the audience ready to steal material. Perhaps that is what killed the circuit altogether. One enterprising Vaudevillian was so proficient at stealing material and selling it to the new convention and association market that he could not utilize all the material he pilfered. He hired another comedian to do the material that he had left over.

Another comedian developed a technique which is in use today in modified form. Part of his act was to express amazement that his other competitors would be crazy enough to buy jokes from professional writers. He said the jokes weren't any good and would then tell a joke that Milton Berle or some other personality had paid big money for. The audience would howl with laughter as he went down the list of the guys who were dumb enough to spend good money on silly jokes. When he had finished however, he had developed a unique routine using great material, properly crediting those who had proven the material to be good, and had not spent a dime. This brings up a good point that is in use today. Most performers consider it ethical to use a joke or two from another speakers repertoire. This should be done sparingly and one should never take credit for the material themselves or act as if this material was originated by them. I'm talking now not about a line, but an entire monologue or a lengthy joke or routine that may be associated with some other speaker or well known personality. The reason for this is quite simple. There will come a time when you will be chastised for this theft and perhaps publicly humiliated.

That's the reason for works like this book. It is perfectly all right to use anything in this book in any way you see fit. You paid for it, it is yours. It's like having a writer at your disposal.

There are other ethical ways to continue developing material. One is to buy other humor books, another is to subscribe to services of comedy writers such as Robert Orben, 1200 North Nash Street, Arlington, Virginia 22209, who is well known for his prolific production of current one liners. Robert Orben, as you may recall, gained fame as a writer for Bob Hope and numerous other celebrities. He was, during the Gerald Ford administration, a comedy writer for the White House.

Another good source of material is a spin-off of the old Vaudeville days. A writer by the name of Madison produced material in a publication called Madison's Budget. The Budget cost $1.00 per issue and was a compilation of jokes and one-liners that Madison heard, read, and perhaps even wrote. Today's equivalent to that publication is Comedy and Comment, published and edited by Mack McGinnis, 448 N. Mitchner Ave., Indianapolis, Indiana 46219. Mack is a newspaper man and subscribes to newspapers and various other publications all over the country, keeping an eye out especially for humorous one-liners. Just as in the Vaudeville days, it makes good sense to keep abreast of the times by subscribing to good services such as these. Who knows, you may even accumulate so much material and do so well that you'll have to hire somebody to handle the excess. So times really haven't changed, have they?

Build a Humor File

You will note that the material in this book is organized and indexed liberally. You can expand this material in exactly the same way that I developed the original lines. Transcribe your jokes and stories on to 3x5 cards, make a list of all possible aspects of the humor, and cross-reference them building your own material or even making a supplementary edition to this one.

Then when it comes time for you to make that speech, you simply look in all the categories and the cross-references, even accumulating your 3x5 cards in little stacks so that they may be used under the appropriate subject heading.

Suppose you have to take an unpopular position on a subject and expect to be under fire from the crowd. You could open with a line like, "Somewhere I recall being advised to love your enemies—whiskey, tobacco, and women."

If you're discussing free enterprise: "We have the unusual opportunity to reverse a trend, to take from the common man and give to the rich. We are already half way to our goal—the rich have agreed to accept."

On physical fitness: "I told my company I needed a bodyguard. They took one look at my body and asked, 'What more could anyone do to it?' "

And finally, if you are chairman of the board of some large corporation: "As I look out over this audience and ponder the words of our corporate Vice President, 'These are the finest minds we can accumulate in the business.' I would like to start out this little meeting with a prayer."

Know What You Want to Accomplish

There's an old story about the expectant mother who was surprised with twins. She named the boys Pete and Repeat.

Although some of these points have been discussed individually, I intend to follow my own advice at this point and put together some tips on how to prepare a good speech:

1. Know exactly what you want to accomplish with your speech.
2. Learn as much as you can about your audience and try to see things through their eyes.
3. Anticipate questions they are likely to ask and know how to convincingly answer those questions.
4. Continually be on the lookout for supportive (grist) material.
5. Give the material some deep thought for a period of time sufficient enough to "jell" in your mind.

And don't be afraid to repeat or summarize on occasions. The audience will appreciate your efforts in most cases because people's minds have a tendency to wander.

For instance, one corporate executive was speaking to another large corporation as a guest. He kept stopping during his presentation to repeat the techniques he found so important to explain. During the question-answer session, one member of the audience jokingly asked, "You must not think we're very bright. Was that the reason you kept repeating yourself?" The exec said, "Listen, friend, I just hope there's a chance we can reach a few of you. We can't even get our own people to do this."

Choose a Central Theme

It will seem that no answer is ever forthcoming when you first begin to develop your central idea or theme for a speech. However, one day the light bulb will illuminate in your mind. In the same way, supporting material will continue to develop as you ask yourself the question of what do I want to accomplish, how do I want to say it, what reaction shall I advise the audience to take? The inventor, Peter Cooper, had a working slogan: "Eventually the answer comes." I know of one professional writer that has that line typed out and pasted on the front of his typewriter. It's comforting to know that if you continue to question yourself, the answers will come eventually.

Montaigne, the French philosopher, wrote "I hear some making excuses for being unable to express themselves, and pretending to have their heads full of many fine things, but, for want of eloquence, being unable to produce them; that is a sham . . . For my part, I hold, and Socrates makes it a rule, that whoever has in his mind a vivid and clear idea will express it. The matter seen, the words freely follow."

Does this work with humor? Of course. For instance, here's an example of a fellow who was answering a questionaire from a self-help marriage manual. The question was, "Do you and your mate follow very different religions?" He pondered the advice of Montaigne, and eventually the answer came, "Yes. We are both Baptists."

This philosophical treatment of material was made popular by Bill Mauldin who wrote, "Whatever rises to the top, hit it."

Make it Worthwhile

Whether you are going to make a short talk before a group of friends or a formal speech before a very large audience, you will want to know how effective you have been. This is not difficult for the purely humorous speaker, because the audience feedback will immediately determine whether you have been a success. However, most speakers, even humorists, want to produce a speech that can be developed into a book or booklet, get a standing ovation, make headlines in the press, win a Freedom Foundation award, and perhaps even be so magnificent that it will gain respect from your mother-in-law.

But, when you come right down to it, there is only one good way to judge your effectiveness. It's a good speech when it accomplishes its purpose.

Determine exactly what you want to accomplish with these golden words produced by your silver-tongued oratory, and you are far down the road to success. Add a dash of humor here and there, and you are soon outpacing the competition. Ask yourself these questions before launching off from the speaking platform.

What is the purpose of this talk? Why are you giving this speech?

What message do you want to leave with your listeners? What do you want them to do about it?

If there is a question/answer session, what questions are likely to be asked? How can you answer those questions intelligently, briefly, and convincingly?

The next thing you want to do is learn as much as possible about your audience, organization, their interests, problems, and needs. When you address them, you want them to feel that you are one of them and see things from their point of view. Then show them you are human by delivering a polished gem of wit and wisdom every once in awhile.

For instance, here is an actual example of a witty lay speaker I was privileged to hear speaking on the subject of success:

"Studies of people in business and industry who have achieved success show that four factors are almost always present. They are: 1. The ability to think, 2. An inner drive and love of work, 3. The capacity to assume responsibility, 4. The ability to lead people."

Then the speaker paused for two seconds and added, "Of course, there could be a number 5. That would read, 'A rich relative and inheritance laws may nullify all of the above.' "

Put Ideas Together

The really important thing in developing a speech is to think on the subject hard enough, deep enough, and long enough until it jells in your mind.

I have been on airplanes with numerous executives enroute to the same convention where several of us were to speak. The scene is a common one: Executives in three-piece pin-striped suits, sitting in first-class, scribbling notes out on a legal pad. They should be called illegal pads, because what they are about to do to an audience at the end of the plane ride is a crime against humanity. They are writing their speech, putting their notes together in some frenzied order to spew forth incoherent thoughts devoid not only of humor, but also of any meaning whatsoever.

The secret of putting together great ideas, good material, and effective humor is to gather the material on the subject well in advance of the meeting and then put it in your mind and "cook it."

It is not unusual for speech writers to spend an entire day coming up with a few well chosen paragraphs. They may start early in the morning and not write a word until late in the afternoon. It may appear that they are frantically beating a deadline, which they usually are, but the material had been "cooking" all day long. In the same way, a good speech may need several days, weeks, months, or even longer to be well done, or even rare.

Use Personal Experiences

The best subject matter to cover comes from your own experiences. Nothing quite compares to an incident that actually occurred—everybody loves nostalgia.

This doesn't mean that you can't use poetic license and improve on the story from time to time. As any truthful humorist will readily admit (that narrows it down quite a bit) a tale improves with the telling. How does this improvement come about? First, the humorist takes an experience that perhaps actually happened, then adds colorful material to "pump out a little more laughter." You can add flesh to a bare-bones experience by looking for material in this or other books that will expand an actual amusing experience to even greater proportions.

To illustrate, here's an actual case. I was employed as a speaker for a group of mid-west bankers. Another professional speaker, an advertising man, Murray Raphel, was planning a fascinating seminar on advertising. We had visited the night before and "talked shop" for several hours. The next morning at breakfast, Murray showed a note to me that was in his room. The note said, "I'm your maid. Have a nice day. Barbara." Murray explained to me that he was going to use this note in his seminar coming up in the next hour to illustrate an important point in advertising. To quote Murray, "I'm a nice guy, but I don't leave tips in the motel room very often. But, Barbara made me feel important by leaving this hand written note, it made me feel like I was somebody, that she had me especially in mind when she wrote this note. I left her a tip. Now, if she affects everybody in this motel the same way she does me, imagine what she is making just in tips. You see, my point is that it pays to advertise."

"I think Barbara just has a thing going with you," I replied.

"Why do you say that?"

"Because I've been here for two days and nobody's left me a note."

"Aha!, even a better point. Different maid. You didn't have Barbara!"

"How could I? She's always over in your room trying to get a tip."

This was an actual conversation and told fairly accurately as it actually occurred. I used this story on an audience because virtually everyone there had heard Murray and me at some time during the convention. Since they knew both of us and had also experienced the notes being left in their own rooms, it was a funny piece of material. It is also a classic because it actually occured. You will never have to be concerned about someone else telling this story before you go on. It is your experience, it has high interest appeal because you are able to recreate the humor in an actual situation. That does not mean it cannot be improved upon. It can. Now when I retell the story, I build up the suspense to finally meeting Barbara, describing what she looks like, how she sounds, what clever things she might have to say to put me down. Get the idea? And Barbara, frankly I'm glad you didn't write me a note. Otherwise, I never would have had this wonderful fantasy.

Build a Solid Foundation

Rudyard Kipling, was once asked how he was able to be so prolific as a writer. Kipling's answer was, "I have six honest servants. They've taught me all I know. Their names are Who, What, When, Where, Why, and How."

This is the basic foundation for all writing, reporting, speaking, and even joke telling.

When reading some of the short one- or two-liners in this book, you may be tempted to think, "That just isn't funny." That's because I have spared you all the journalistic mumbo-jumbo that usually precedes a joke, allowing you a push button punchline, but if you follow Kipling's advice, you can develop a story that will be distinctly your own. Here's an example. "If foreign car dealers were making so much money in the world, it would be my luck to get the Chrysler dealership in Cambodia."

Now, apply Kipling's method and convert it to a story. Look for the six honest serving men in the story and see if you can find them in this reconstructed version to illustrate my points.

Ralph Merriweather was walking along the freeway yesterday, looking for discarded aluminum cans to pick up a little extra income. He had his shoes off so he could feel for them in the grass. He stubbed his toe on a bottle, knocking out a cork, and a genie appeared before him. He was told he could have any wish he wanted. He said, "I've heard the foreign car dealers are really raking in the dough. So that's what I'd like to be." With that, POOF, he was enveloped by a white cloud of smoke. When he woke up, he had the Chrysler dealership in Cambodia.

Eat your heart out, Rudyard. I've got seven honest serving men or is it still six plus you?

Add Grist

In developing any speech you have to be on a constant look out for grist, pertinent facts and figures that can be used to brighten up your talk, support the points you make, add interest or a change of pace from time to time: illustrations, anecdotes, jokes, humorous lines, and suitable quotations.

The material in this book is just a starter. Look for items in everything you read, see, or hear. One method used by many journalists who grind out volumes of material in the form of editorials is to clip items for possible use, but rather than keep them filed by subjects put them altogether in one place. They are most often kept in a folder, with the most recent item on top. Whenever a new one is added, just look through the others that are already there to refresh your memory so that you will be able to find a particular item in a hurry when you want it. It's a simple technique, and although it sounds rather disorganized, it works.

What happens when the file gets so thick that it becomes unwieldy? Throw it away and start all over, if you can bring yourself to do it. That assures you of fresh material; besides, your memory bank will retain most of the things that are worth retaining.

I have done this for years. That's the reason my material is always new and fresh. I can never find anything, so I seldom repeat myself.

Add Spice

The minute you stand in front of an audience, you have crossed the line between business and show business. But make no mistake, you are in show business and the more you are aware of that, the more effective your presentation will be. The real dynamic communicators are those who can speak with force, in a well organized and interesting manner, and yes, even make the audience laugh. Once you have done that, your corporation, company, or self will be elevated to a higher regard. This isn't theory. It is a known fact. We concern ourselves with proper dress, neat grooming, and a high polish on our shoes when making an appearance, but we must not forget to put a high gloss on our words as well.

Some people may feel the use of humor is undignified, but there is a difference between a jokester and a raconteur. The jokester merely throws out one-liners, quips, and stories that are designed to purely entertain. The raconteur uses humor, but never loses sight of his or her reason for being there. Humor, thus, is a carrier for a more significant point.

In a recent talk where I spoke for 45 minutes, I closed my presentation by saying that my goal had been quite simply to make the audience forget its problems over the past 45 minutes. I illustrated that thought in a completely serious, deeply philosophical way, and added that humor had the power to heal like no other form of communication. Afterward a man came up and told me he had been against these "frivolous" types of presentations for the last three years. He said, "I was also against this one, until I heard your closing remarks and then it dawned on me just how important it is to have a sense of humor." Never again will he consider humor merely a form of foolery.

So where does one get material, other than this book? Of course, I'm biased and that is the reason I put all of this material together in the first place. I think it is a superb collection and use it myself. However, I realize that there are other sources of humor, other books—yes, even other great writers (note the sly humor).

You may want to go to a specialist in the field and get a page or two of jokes written by an expert on a particular subject. Professionals in this area charge from $500 to a few thousand dollars to do it. Doesn't that give you a little higher regard for this material now?

Of course, there is an alternative to custom written humor. It is called doing it yourself and involves expanding the collection of material you have already purchased in this book. But before you embark upon that journey, restrict yourself to mastering the material here and in other books. One precaution: You should not try to read a joke book like you read a novel. Fifteen minutes at a time, no more than 3 or 4 times a day is recommended. You will then be able to judge material with a fresh perspective.

I also recommend that you write in the margin of this book. When you find a story that fits the subject, simply make a note of it in the book, and you have expanded this piece of material. Here's an example. I was giving a talk one night, and a man and his wife in the audience, by the name of Mr. and Mrs. John Gay, were obviously enjoying themselves with hilarious reaction. Since I had already observed that they were great sports and good laughers, I remarked in the middle of a story with a sideline question, "Are you John?" "Are you Gay?" The crowd roared and he took it good-naturedly. Then he came back with a great zinger by saying, "Yes." And pointing to his wife, added, "So is she." It literally brought the house down. A member of the audience had topped the pro. Most pros would leave the story there, but the really innovative ones will retell the tale just as it happened to get even more mileage out of the situation. Therefore, humor becomes wholesale and retail and you need to work both sides of the street.

Choose the Right Joke

Three items are necessary to consider for selecting the right material. First, is the item funny? Secondly, are you comfortable using that remark in public? And, is it performable?

Many novice speakers hear a joke, think it's funny, and then use it without consideration as to whether it fits their needs or the situation.

Let's take the items one at a time. Is it funny? Something may be hilarious in one place and may never work in another. For instance, I was introduced at a meeting in which most of the audience knew me from previous performances. Jeanne Robertson, my colleague, a talented and witty performer herself, introduced me with a few lines, then added philisophically, that I had been described by another professional speaker, Bill Gove, as one who "let his little boy out to play." This was a completely unexpected comment and was the last line in her introduction. However, knowing that the audience would forgive me if this flash of an idea didn't work, I quickly dropped to my knees and walked out in front of the podium in a fashion similar to Red Skelton's "Mean Widdle Kid." This was funny. I thought it would be and I guessed exactly right. I would never try this again under any circumstances unless the exact situation came up using that exact line.

Secondly, are you comfortable using a line or story? Let's use the same example. Most normal people would be extremely uncomfortable as an adult trying a dumb visual stunt like the one just described. Who can get away with this? I was comfortable doing it and therefore had no problem with it. If you feel comfortable, don't be afraid to try. If you have the slightest idea that it would be embarrassing to you or to someone else, it's probably best to leave it to the professionals who have that sixth sense about material. Apply the old adage, "When in doubt, don't."

Thirdly, is a piece of material performable? Unfortunately, most material in joke books, and most humor in writing looks rather drab. Time after time, I have seen meeting planners and other non-professional speakers look at a line on paper and say, "Are you sure you want me to say that?" They simply do not think it is funny and consequently, are not able to perform. One of the most famous comedy routines in existence is Bud Abbott and Lou Costello's "Who's on First." It is absolutely hilarious when they perform it. Read it on the written page sometime, and you will wonder how they ever had the nerve to do it. These two geniuses simply recognized a piece of material as performable.

One final consideration is to draw all of this material together and make it applicable to the occasion. A little study in advance will help you fit the pieces of the puzzle together. For instance, I once spoke to the Mesa-Chandler-Tempe Board of Realtors in Arizona. I did a little background research and found they had abbreviated the names of this community board to initials M-C-T and because of the nature of the towns themselves referred to it as the "Mormons, Cowboys, and Teachers." In itself, that doesn't sound funny. But it so happens that Mesa has a high population of Mormons, Chandler is noted as an agricultural community and is loaded with Cowboys, Tempe is the seat of education for the University of Arizona. This will not appear funny on paper. In fact, it may seem very drab, but I can assure you it was a tremendous line for these people when I said, "I'm happy to be here at the home of Mormons, Cowboys, and Teachers." This was followed by a huge wave of laughter.

The next few lines got equally high grades when I said, "I can relate to two-thirds of that group. I was formerly a teacher, I am a cowboy, but the only thing I can't relate to are the Mormons because I don't belong to an organized religious group—I'm a Methodist." To me this humor fit the categories I have just discussed and I guessed exactly right. The item was funny. I felt comfortable saying it. It was performable.

Apply Building Block Techniques

While most humor is better left in a simple form, the occasional use of a "building block" technique may add the spice needed to keep variety in your speech. As previously mentioned, the mind loves a puzzle and it also loves to be fooled. That is the reason for the popularity of magicians who employ slight of hand. Word imagery can employ the same type of magic. For instance, a newspaper editor might employ the magic touch and the "building block" technique by stating that his newspaper has a staff of twelve people assigned to the sports section. Right away the mind visualizes a dozen employees. Then the editor starts building the image. "Five of our people say football is a game. (The mind immediately wonders what the others think of it). Five say it is a business (now the mind is wondering about the remainder). One knows that it is a religion." At this point the audience will usually laugh and be fooled into thinking that the punch line has been given, that all twelve people have been covered. After a split second, the mind will probably realize that the editor has only covered eleven people on the staff. That's when the editor adds the final block with the zinger "The twelfth one says, 'What's a football.' " This allows the puzzle to build with a series of blocks, fools the mind with a slight of hand technique and adds the final touch to produce the completed image as if by magic.

Sprinkle with Poetic Humor

Some years ago, I recall seeing Jackie Gleason on a television program recite the condition of his health in a hilariously funny form entitled, "I'm awfully well for the shape that I'm in." Gleason was the perfect pawn for this poetic humor. He laughed at himself for being out of shape, overweight, overindulgent in a variety of vices. For anyone who is getting on in years, suffering from disability, or numerous other qualities that lack that asthetic touch, this may be used to play upon the sympathy of the crowd in a most delightful way. It was originally published many years ago in the Washington Star under the title of "I'm really fine."

There's nothing whatever the matter with me,
I'm just as healthy as can be;
I have arthritis in both my knees,

And when I talk, I talk with a wheeze;
My pulse is weak; my blood is thin,
But I'm awfully healthy for the fix I'm in.

I think my liver is out of whack
And a terrible pain is in my back;
My hearing is poor, my eyesight is dim,
Most everything seems to be out of trim.

The doctors say that my days are few,
For every week they find something new;
And the way I stagger is a crime
I'm likely to drop most anytime.
I jump like mad at the drop of a pin,
But I'm awfully well for the fix I'm in.

I have arch supports for both of my feet,
Or I wouldn't be able to go on the street;
I cannot sleep night after night,
And in the morning I am a fright;
My memory is failing, my head's in a spin,
But I'm awfully well for the fix I'm in.

The moral is as this tale doth tell,
That for you and me who are not so well,
It's better to say "I'm fine" with a grin,
Or the other guy will tell you the shape he's in!

Willis Moreman is Executive Secretary of the Kansas Bankers Association. He has five secretaries and several assistants. A man with an obvious sense of humor, his attitude is "catching" among the other staff members. One year, Willis announced to the secretaries that they would be treated to a gourmet meal at a fine restaurant. They were told to take off an extra hour for lunch, order anything they wanted—just sign the tab. The boss did not go with them, but explained to them he wanted to do this to show his appreciation for their hard work.

In showing their appreciation, the girls got together and composed the following poem to show their appreciation to the boss. Note also that they ended the poem with a hopeful note of inspiration to continue the practice. The poem is entitled "Dear Willis."

Thank you for the gourmet meal,
It really hit the spot.
We're normally on diets
But today we ate a lot.

We talked of your thoughtfulness
   In picking up the tab,
But as for office gossip
   We indulged in *just* a dab,

To bring back two "doggie bags"
   Was planned for you and Bill,
But we ate every little scrap
   And drinks—we had refills!!!

Dining on fine French cuisine
   Outranked the Colonnade.
But what really made it great . . .
   We just signed—the bill was paid!!!

Thanks again for the great lunch.
   We want to make that clear.
(Can we start looking forward
   To a meal again next year?)

Mr. Moreman showed the poem to me shortly after it was written and said, in response to the last line, "You can bet, after reading that note, that there will be another next year." We both laughed and nodded in appreciation of a good piece of public relations work humorously done.

After addressing a very large crowd in Cincinnati, I was fortunate enough to meet Marie Brown of that city. She asked if I had seen a copy of a short poem that she produced from her wallet. While poetry is not often both funny and profound, this effort was. Marie was kind enough to pass along her personal philosophy of life. Although the author is unknown to both of us, we thought the effort should not go unappreciated.

He was a cautious man,
He never romped or even played;
He never smoked,
He never drank,
Or even kissed a maid;
And when he up and passed away,
Insurance was denied;
For since he hadn't ever lived,
They claimed he never died.

Where can you use this? Just about anywhere, but especially at any meeting pertaining to insurance, health, longevity, and safety.

Try a Touch of Shakespeare

Many people may not think of the great William Shakespeare as being a speech writer, but that is exactly what he was. His plays contain nearly 32,000 speeches, including more than 10,000 written entirely in prose.

A few tips from Shakespeare might be worthy of consideration, because he is as well known for his wit as his wisdom. Shakespeare believed that public speaking involved six factors: intelligence (wit), fluency (words), integrity (worth), gestures (actions), articulations (utterance), and style of speaking (power of speech).

The real trick in writing or speaking is to get the right combination of words together in as condensed a form as possible, to deliver them with great eloquence, and to have a lasting impact on the audience. Shakespeare was perhaps unequalled in this respect. In a remarkable 10-line passage from his play "Macbeth" are found the titles of nine books, including DUSTY DEATH, BRIEF CANDLE, TOLD BY AN IDIOT, SOUND AND FURY.

The humor of Shakespeare often comes out as light and breezy, at other times becomes stark reality, but it is the kind of humor to which one pleasantly nods in agreement, while a faint smile doth expand mind and mouth with truth. Take this example from the same 10-line passage, "Life's but a walking shadow, a poor player that struts and frets his hour upon the stage, and then is heard no more; it is a tale told by an idiot, full of sound and fury, signifying nothing." Who can take life seriously after reading that? Will, you're a real gas.

William Shakespeare also had a very deep philosophy about how humor may be best used and lectured to his audience through his characters against the use of dirty jokes, vulgar language, and profanity in public speaking. Although a lot of people might laugh, he knew that many would feel embarrassed or resentful and lose respect for the speaker of those thoughtless words and phrases. He let Hamlet speak his thoughts when this character said ". . . though it make the unskillful laugh, can not but make the judicious grieve . . ." At another point, another play, he chides "a jest's prosperity lies in the ear of him that hears it, never in the tongue of him that makes it."

The point is to choose your material well and make sure it is unoffensive. Then, use the Shakespearean method of speaking in language which is familiar to the audience of your day. Hundreds of years ago, this line probably convulsed audiences who came to hear Shakespeare's plays, "Well, niece, I hope to see you one day fitted with a husband." The niece delivers the punch line, "Not till God makes men of some other metal than earth." Today, that line is similar to, "Well, niece, you don't seem too thrilled about your date. Is there someone else?" The niece replies, "There must be."

To illustrate how Shakespeare can come alive today, I asked my good friend, colleague and fellow humorist, Joe Griffith of Dallas, Texas to contribute the following:

In my early days as an actor, I took about any "show business" job that came along. One time I was hired by the Dallas Shakespeare Festival to promote its new season by dressing up in Shakespearian garb and conducting a kind of "quiz show" aboard a Southwest Airlines flight between Dallas and San Antonio. My principal prop was a skull, reminiscent of the one in *Hamlet*. It was hollow, with a lid, and inside were slips of paper on which were typed questions pertaining to the Shakespeare plays. The idea was for me to stroll among the passengers and pass out play tickets in exchange for correct answers to my questions.

Needless to say, I was rather self-conscious boarding the plane. I took a seat next to a dignified looking gentleman already immersed in his *Wall Street Journal,* and as I strapped myself in, I said to him, "Perhaps I should explain why I'm dressed like this."

Without looking up, he said, "You don't have to. My son's in the band."

He was aware that people sometimes dress up in strange costumes and do weird things; but personally, he didn't want to get involved in such goings on. That's what he seemed to be saying. I thought it an interesting reaction. It gave me an idea for a comedy routine that subsequently proved very successful.

My platform version differs considerably from the actual experience. I suspected that trying to promote the Festival on board an airplane—one flying *away* from Dallas, at that—might seem illogical to an audience. Rather than waste time explaining all the whys and wherefores, I placed myself in the airport, greeting people coming into Dallas.

I paint the picture very carefully. The gigantic Dallas-Ft. Worth International Airport is alive with bustling travelers, and I'm in the middle of them, dressed in a white starched ruffled collar, a gaudy jacket, funny little knickers, leotards, and ballet slippers. My first encounter is with a man just getting off the plane from San Francisco. I say, "Pardon me, sir. I'll bet you can't guess what I'm promoting."

He looks me over, and says, "Gay Liberation?"

After awhile, I get discouraged. Nobody seems to recognize a Shakespeare outfit when he sees one. I stop one guy, and out of pure whimsy say to him, "Pardon me, sir. But my time machine broke down. Can you tell me what century this is?"

He glances hurriedly at his watch and says, "Sorry. This thing only gives the day and the month."

Next I go into the bar and harass a drunk into taking one of my questions. In a slurred voice, he reads, "A horse, a horse, my kingdom for a horse."

I say to him, "Now, sir, for a free ticket to the Shakespeare Festival, can you tell me who said that?"

He screws up his face and gives the problem his best mental effort. Finally his face lights up and he says, "John Wayne?"

That's not the routine verbatim. I've put in stage directions here—such as "in a slurred voice"—which in practice, I act out. But you get the idea, namely that personal experience doesn't have to lock you into a particular version. You can expand upon your original experience, condense it, embroider it, or whatever. Your platform version doesn't have to be objectively true—only "true to itself."

Keep Humor Positive

Although 80% of my work as a professional speaker is mostly entertaining, after-dinner presentations, the remaining 20% of my time is spent conducting seminars in human relations, communications, and salesmanship. Of course, it is obvious that I would be prone to use a great deal of humor in putting my points across. The power of humor is aptly illustrated in the following anecdote.

Conducting a two-day seminar for the giant Kaiser Aluminum and Chemical Corporation in Florida, I had the opportunity to impress upon my 30 or 40 hand-picked students the importance of positive humor. These fellows were all regional managers in charge of a number of sales people. Having risen from the ranks of salesman, as might be expected, this was a jolly lot. They had heard all the traveling salesman jokes and used a great deal of humor in their sales pitches and every day conversations. We met in a beautiful resort retreat near Howie-in-the-Hills, Florida. For two intensive days, we were thrown together and that gave us time to truly reflect upon the principles which I had been dispensing. Upon arriving at the resort, one of the first men I met was an outgoing, loud, lovable character, named Jim Mann. As soon as we met, he handed me a card which expressed his ideas about humor. The card read as follows:

I'm Jim Mann and I'm
TERRIBLE THANK YOU

| Oversexed | Overworked |
| Underloved | Underpaid |

For the next 48 hours, I continued to drive home my point that "beneath every wave of laughter, there is an underlying ripple of truth." We can use humor effectively in communication, but we must be very careful that the residual action produces a favorable result.

During the last hour that I shared with this wonderfully responsive group of men, I asked for an evaluation of the seminar and any personal comments they might have concerning the most important thing they had learned. For me it was the most rewarding part of the program, because of the feedback received from each of these professional people. Typical of the response was that of Jim Mann. He admitted that underneath his humorous facade he was a little bitter. As a collection agent for the company, he had heard every sad story in the books, and his business card simply reflected that negative attitude. On the surface, it came off as funny, but underneath, he realized that he was only compounding problems for the people with whom he came in contact. Since he was basically a very nice guy with a great sense of humor, he made a vow to simply change his angle of attack and start using positive humor. He handed me a card which had all the negatives scratched out and positives scribbled in their place. To show how serious he was about this change of heart, a few months later, he sent me a new business card, replacing the old attitude. The card is reprinted as follows:

I'm Jim Mann and I'm
TERRIFIC THANK YOU

| Undersexed | Underworked |
| Overloved | Overpaid |

Since that time, I've crossed paths with many of Jim's colleagues and each has expressed the thought that they have seen a remarkable change in the attitude of Mr. Mann . . . all for the better. Although he was always well liked because of his natural ability to use humor, he is now appreciated much more because of the combination of humor with an up beat attitude.

A good example of a business card that carries a great deal of humor in addition to a bit of advertisement is the card of Leland J. Glazebrook, a farm broadcaster from Sullivan, Illinois. Obviously, Leland is a character and this form of humorous self-deprecation is much appreciated by the rural crowd in which he most often mingles.

The front of the card reads—CORN-SOYBEAN NETWORK, Leland J. Glazebrook, Broadcaster, Writer, Speaker, 20 Cottontail Lane, Sullivan, Illinois 61951.

Note that this character even had the presence of mind to live on Cottontail Lane. However, the back of his card is the real "grabber" and nails Leland as a character who can be on the level or half a bubble off. The back side reads:

Warts Rubbed	Balky Horses
Chickens Culled	Oil For Wind Mills
High Yields Verified	Fly Swatter
Congressmen Called	Manure
Tax Men Lied To	Nails
Stock In Dry Oil Wells	Land
Shuckin' Pegs & Hooks	Garden Seed
Wrecked Pick-up Trucks	Home Made Soap
Plow Handles	

Preachin' & Lead Singing' at Range War Buryin's

Pursue Pure Intentions

As a speaker traveling the circuit, nearly everywhere I go, I am cautioned against doing certain things. One of the things that is most often mentioned by my clients is "don't say anything about the blacks." The other most common admonitions are "don't talk about religion" and "don't dwell on politics." If a client absolutely insists, I follow his advice, but usually try to get them to trust me. I continually use material in all three of those areas and have never had a bad reaction because the humor is used in the proper way, simply as a harmless form of entertainment.

Here's an example of how such humor can be used in an actual situation. I was in the first class section of an airplane leaving Atlanta, Georgia for Tampa. Seated on the outside aisle, I was intensely interested in reading something and not paying much attention to anyone around me. I suddenly sensed the presence of someone wanting to get around me to his seat and absent-mindedly pulled my legs up tight to allow the passage of my companion. Without a word, he sat down and appeared to be anxious not to arouse anyone's interest. I immediately recognized him as Julian Bond, the black legislator from Georgia, well known throughout the United States. It was rather obvious to me from his actions that he didn't care to engage in conversation, probably having been bored to tears by someone who recognized him as a celebrity. I thought for a moment that I would let him remain incognito, but then decided that it wasn't very good manners not to recognize a statesman of his prestige. So I turned to him with the typical, "Say, aren't you . . ." During the slight pause before I used a name, he appeared irritated and even rolled his eyes a little in the typical expression of those who think, "Oh, no, here we go again." That's when I changed my strategy and said, "Wait, don't tell me you're . . . Billy Carter." He let out a loud laugh and we shared a very pleasant conversation all the way to Tampa. The line was so absurd that he knew I had to be joking. That's the key to whites or blacks, politics or religion. Make sure everyone knows you are just joking, and be sure your intentions are as pure.

Choose Words for the Occasion

Toastmasters International has a nasty habit of calling on their membership for impromptu speeches. It can strip all the gears in your gray matter because you are most often called upon to speak on a subject about which you know nothing. The ones who pull it off and look well are those who talk about experiences in work, family, interests, sports, religions, awards, etc. In short they talk about their experiences or even secret ambitions. The experience can be rewarding if you remember to stick to the central idea, make a point, and back it up with one or more examples.

For instance, I was at a meeting one time where the emcee got carried away with his own importance, adding stories, jokes, quips, and other non-pertinent information to the program with irregular regularity. In other words, nobody knew when he was going to get through or what he might do next. Although it was only a fun-type meeting, the schedule had been bent so far out of shape that it was beyond straightening out the program. The emcee then announced to the audience that we were overtime and simply must get back on schedule for the coffee break. However, the featured speaker was at the head table and ready to spring into action. The emcee then did another 10 or 15 minutes of material, introduced the speaker in a long-winded manner, looked at his watch, and remarked, "Well, we've got time for a few words now from our main speaker." Here was a program that was headed for disaster. The audience realized the main speaker had only 3 minutes before the break. What could he possibly say in that length of time that would save the day? To his everlasting credit, here is what he said:

"A few well chosen words come to mind to fit this special occasion. They are not my words, but appropriately fill the bill for this occasion. Seven words uttered by Sir Winston Churchill exalting the British people to greater resolution in the face of tragedy, 'Never, Never, Never, Never, Never, give up.'"

That speaker became a hero. An accomplishment that the emcee could not match with several hours of patter. Why? Because he summed up the situation at a glance, experienced the pain and torment of an excessively long meeting, and an egotistical speaker. He knew exactly where he was, sensed the feeling of the crowd, scanned his memory bank for an appropriate experience to relate, used humor in the form of satire, expressed truth, and got the meeting back on schedule. Oh yes, an important point to remember is that he laughed heartily. So did the audience and yes, even the emcee. There is a thin line between humor and tragedy. If those same few well-chosen words had been delivered with an intent to be sarcastic, the humor would have evaporated and gloom could have descended upon the meeting. A good point to remember is never use satire if you really mean it.

Study Others, but Be Original

Dr. Charles Jarvis, a close friend and professional speaker from San Marcos, Texas, is not only a performer of great humor, but also a sound philosopher about its practice as well. Dr. Jarvis once wrote, "You will succeed as a speaker in direct proportion to the amount of original material you use." That is a profound piece of advice and separates the professionals from the amateurs as well as any recommendation I've ever heard.

So why do we constantly study other peoples acts, read the works of other writers, and search for other peoples ideas? The answer is that we need this kind of stimulation to be creative enough to be able to develop our own ideas. Just watching a creative performer can often plant the seed of an idea that will grow into something parallel yet completely different from what was observed.

In the days of Vaudeville, Orville Stamm had what must certainly be considered a unique and original idea. Orville billed himself as "The Strongest Boy in the World." His act consisted of an opening in which Orville played the violin with a huge bulldog suspended in a swing from the crook of his elbow on the arm manipulating the bow. Obviously, he chose a piece of material that required a lot of bow work to the amazement and delight of the Vaudeville audience. A series of other stunts were performed during the course of his act, but his closing must have been a real dandy. Orville laid on the stage and arched his back in a manner described as "bending the crab" by acrobats. When Mr. Stamm had thoroughly braced himself in the crab position, a small upright piano was placed on his abdomen, a pianist stood on his thighs and accompanied him as he sang "Ireland Must be Heaven, 'Cause My Mother Came from There." Those who saw it say it was sensational. Surely, it must have been original. However, it's such a great idea I'm surprised that nobody else is using it today. Why am I passing on this great idea to you? Because I can think of several hundred reasons why this will not work for me. Ahem, the chief one is that I'm much too original to stoop to stealing someone else's material.

Learn by Association

If you would use humor well, seek out the company of those who are gifted in writing or performing, listen to witty people, buy books, and cassette tape recordings of humorous speeches.

Through a study of great speeches—speeches that have lived—you will learn something about an effective speech and about how to construct your own.

It is extremely important not to pick favorites in the speaking field, because there is a real danger that you will begin to sound like one of them. Your thinking becomes colored by too much input by one artist. By listening and studying many types of speakers, with varying forms of delivery, one is able to educate himself and develop a style that has merely been influenced by great writers, great performers, and great delivery. By listening to others and picking up little tidbits of inspiration, the light bulb suddenly goes off in the mind to stimulate your own creativity. And keep in mind you can learn what not to do, as well as gain some great insight into what makes some performers popular. To illustrate, there is an old joke about a particularly boring speaker who ran way over his allotted time. When someone in the audience was asked for their reaction, his comment was, "The only way he could have said less would have been to have talked longer." Look for the good and the bad and resolve to modify your style accordingly. Strive for uniqueness, but do not be afraid to learn from the pros.

All forms of communication, including humor, in order to be really great, must grab the mind and heart. Demonthenes, a famous speaker who stuttered, put a pebble in his mouth and became one of the most famous speakers in the world. Demonthenes not only overcame a speech problem, but always made a magnificent point with his words. It was said of him, "When others speak, we applaud, but when Demonthenes speaks, we rise and go to war!"

But, sayeth thou, what hast this to do with humor? Just everything, that's all. It's just another medium of expression and must be studied carefully in order to be used effectively. Sir Winston Churchill was perhaps one of the best practioners of both eloquence and humor. For instance, it is reported that Sir Winston was making a speech to the Ladies Temperance League in England at the height of the great war. With eloquence that would have rivaled that of Demonthenes, he exalted the ladies to greater war effort. However, one of the ladies could not help taking a verbal shot at Churchill. During a question-answer session, she asked, "Sir Winston, is it true that you have drank enough brandy to fill this building to half full?" He pondered the question in his deliberate way for a moment, then replied, "Yes, madam, it is true. And as I look around me, it makes me realize just how much more important work is left to be done." Aha! A magnificent point made with humor.

Learn Then Earn

Earnest Bevin, an Englishman, was a poor boy who worked in the mines. He was a stutterer. Advised by doctors to learn everything he could about his subject, Bevin became an articulate spokesman for the mining industry. He developed new ideas and his interest was so intense that he was able to communicate these improvements to people that listened intently when he spoke. He became a top labor leader in Great Britain, bringing about many reforms in the dangerous mining industry.

The point is that if one knows his subject extremely well, it is much less difficult to convince even a hostile audience that your ideas have merit. Humor is just another way of expressing those ideas. Learn everything you can about the subject, and soon you will be articulate enough to bring about reforms in the dangerous comedy business. Dangerous? Of course, you can die in front of an audience. Melvin Helitzer, associate professor of journalism at Ohio State University, and a former professional comedy writer for Shari Lewis and Ernie Kovacs, says that all good jokes have 6 characteristics. Melvin has learned to use what he calls the HEARTS Theory—hostility, exaggeration, anger, realism, tension, and surprise. These are the ingredients in a good joke. So, learn to have a heart and earn the respect of your audience with humor. As Helitzer says, "You can't hate somebody you laugh with."

Doc Blakely clowns around in Washington D.C. with typical government official.

The Benefits of Laughter

Physicians cite research indicating that frequent laughter reduces tension, lowers pulse rate, and promotes good mental, as well as, physical health.

Laughter is sometimes described as a moment of concentrated euphoria. Laughter usually only comes about when we feel good about personal or world events. More physicians are recognizing and encouraging the use of humor to activate the body's own defense/health mechanisms.

One physician, using electromyogram recordings of his patient's facial muscles, was able to calculate a "feedback" between the facial muscles and the brain and determined it was electrical impulses that informed the brain it was having a good time. Thus, medical science collaborates the philosophy that a big smile or hearty laugh is health giving.

Researchers at Yale University further concluded that laughing inside was not nearly as stimulating to physical well-being as a vocal appreciation of laughing out loud.

Boston University research came up with the not too surprising conclusion that you can not be happy and sad at the same time. For instance, subjects were asked to view themselves in a mirror, smile broadly, and try to take themselves seriously. This resulted in several near hernias, but not one serious experimenter. On the other hand, people who frowned into a mirror were quite often able to produce unhappy feelings even when told to think happy thoughts. The admonition to "put on a happy face" is well advised. Research has shown that the simple act of smiling induces a happy state of mind.

Physicians are also experimenting with the use of humor to relieve depression in neurotic patients. Many of the differences between depressed, unhappy, neurotic people and well-adjusted persons involves how they deal with frustrations or stress. Some psychiatrists recommended relief from this stress by outbursts of anger. This has worked in the past, but anger is not the only emotion that is incompatible with depression. More and more, psychiatrists are recommending laughter as a recognized alternative. As one patient said, "When I get up in the morning feeling depressed, I now have a choice. I can laugh or I can cry. Laughing is a lot more fun."

Laughter and Health

Many people may take this book to be a flippant attempt to escape reality for a few moments. That is not the case at all. It is an attempt to escape reality for lots of moments. Why? Because good things happen to you when you laugh. For example, you inhale and exhale in short bursts, thus increasing the amount of oxygen taken into your lungs and into your blood stream. Your heart beat is increased (of course, you can get the same effect by watching cheerleaders at a football game). If you have low blood pressure, laughter will make it rise. If you have high blood pressure, laughter will make it decrease. These therapeutic values are not often discussed, but they are facts nonetheless. So have a good laugh, it could be the healthiest thing that has happened to you all day.

Here's a therapeutic medical story to illustrate. A young foreign man came to this country and immediately started studying the language. A prospective employer told him to go to the local clinic for a physical. By this time, he was very proud of his new mastery of this strange language. The busy doctor rushed into the private room and told the young man to strip to the waist, then rushed out. When the doctor came back, he found this guy standing there with his pants off.

Laughter is a foreign language. Although we don't completely understand it, we know that good things can happen to you when you exercise it.

The Power of Laughter

Before his first cancer surgery, John Wayne, was called "a big phony macho." This criticism was leveled at "The Duke" because of his strong stance on military preparedness, his life long use of guns, and his unabashed support of military preparedness. The Harvard Lampoon dared him to "appear in the most radical, the most intellectual, in short, the most hostile territory on earth" to defend his political and philosophical views.

The result was that, surprisingly, Wayne accepted and Harvard was never before assaulted with such a mixture of aggressive humor. In a frontal attack, John Wayne rode a tank from the airport to the campus, walked on stage carrying a toy rifle, and used this opening line—"Coming here is like being invited to lunch by the Borgias." Humor was used to completely win the crowd to his point of view, and in this bastion of hostility toward his philosophy, the personal triumph was obvious when the crowd ended by standing and shouting, "Duke, Duke, Duke."

Amidst the laughter and good natured kidding there was also a great message and understanding from a younger generation of the nerve and dedication to a cause. That's where humor can be so helpful in putting across a point. If the Harvard audience had not been loosened up by a great line, a lot of self-kidding, and a great performance, they never would have opened their minds long enough to hear the great philosophy of John Wayne. Just a bit of his thinking comes out in this quote attributed to him. "There's a lot about life, but I think tomorrow is the most important thing. It comes to us every midnight very clear, perfect when it arrives and is put in our hands. It hopes we've learned something from yesterday."

Have Fun with a Purpose

As a former classroom teacher, at the college level, I became very aware of the dull, drab way in which education was expected to be carried out. I became a maverick, pumping my classes full of humorous anecdotes, quips, jokes, and descriptive humor to make it entertaining. The result was that I had a good time and so did my students. I only spent 10 years in the classroom, but it was long enough to see some of my students go on to become research scientists, doctors, veterinarians, teachers, some of them even got jobs and went to work for a living.

Is there a correlation between good humor and success? The magazine, Highlights, thinks so. It is a magazine designed for young children, even preschool readers. It is filled with great factual information, entertaining stories, and yes, even jokes. But does this have anything to do with success? I think it does and has some support in at least one survey taken by the University of Michigan in which their students were sent questionaires to determine their relative success in chosen fields. The only common denominator that the computers could attribute to successful attainment of accomplishment was a sense of humor.

Being Funny Is a Way of Life

Did you ever wonder what makes people funny? Most often, it has been my observation, that humorists are those people who have suffered some type of injustice, either mental or physical, or both. The message might be if you want to be funny start looking for some way to punish yourself. Then start looking for some way to cope with the painful situation without going berserk. Art Buchwald, the noted newspaper humorist, admits to having a very unhappy childhood and running away from home at the age of 16. However, humor became a way of life with him. He blames it all on the service and the U.S. Marine Corps. In coping with the discipline of that prestigious military organization, he learned to smile a slight grin similar to a Cheshire cat. "I always had a grin on my face," he said. "They always thought I did it." It all has something to do with the way Buchwald sees the world around him. He has a talent for seeing the mirth in virtually any situation that surrounds him. "You can look at a situation and either laugh or cry," he said, "It's a matter of survival for me." When addressing a large college crowd, where the president had reportedly been in hot water, he is reported to have said, "I have a great deal of respect for your president. In fact, I worship the very quicksand he walks on."

Turning to inflation, he remarked, "It's now cheaper to borrow money from the Mafia than the Chase-Manhattan Bank."

And the high price of Arab oil? He blames it all on the Harvard Business School . . . "if they hadn't taught the sons of Arab sheiks how to be capitalists, oil would still be $3.00 a barrel."

Think Funny to Be Funny

My friend and colleague, professional speaker Joe Griffith, has some great ideas on the practical application of humor. These ideas revolve around the observation that escapes some people. For instance, Joe advises, "Some words are funnier than others. Motorcycle is a funny word, so is Winnebago. When I'm in Oklahoma I talk about Ponca City. It's funnier than Stillwater or Muskogee. Cleveland is funny, but say Chicago and nobody laughs. The difference is knowing that Cleveland is funnier than Chicago. Words with X's, L's, and K's are funnier than other words. Six has a rhythm to it that 8 doesn't have. Innately, you've got to know that." Now when you use the material in this book, look a little more closely for the funny words in it. Experiment with substitution to make them not only applicable, but perhaps even funnier than the original line.

Griffith is not only an observer of the use of words, but is also a master of the adlib. Because he "thinks" funny, he often comes up with a real jewel that can be used in other situations. Once while he was speaking, a waitress proceeded to clean the dishes from the head table as if nothing important was going on. The instant the audience seemed distracted by this, Joe simply gave her a quick take, smiled, then leaned outward toward the audience in an intimate fashion and said, "Have y'all met my wife." There was wild, hilarious laughter, applause, and cheers. Then he added, "We work as a team, I talk and she cleans up."

Is this situation ever likely to happen again? No, but if it does, there would be a great line. If you "think funny," you probably have figured at least one way to use this. Stop reading this right where you are and creatively try to think of a way to use the line, then I'll tell you the simplest and most direct method to apply it in the next paragraph.

Give up? It is so simple, it is disgusting. The really creative, lazy mind would simply hire a waitress to come in at the appropriate time to set up the scene. Expensive? No, just check with any of the waitresses in charge of catering the meal. A couple of dollars will usually do the trick. You may have to ask more than one, but rest assured that one of them will be thrilled by the experience, and have something to talk about for the rest of her life.

Anatomy of a Laugh

What is laughter all about? "No one knows," Dr. Delmar Solem reports. "Many books have been written about it, but no one really understands it."

Dr. Solem is a Professor of Drama at the University of Miami and at one time, was the only person in the country teaching a comedy seminar. Now a former student of his is also teaching the course akin to it at the University of Virginia.

"I think it's intellectual. To appreciate comedy, you must have an intellectual bent to discover the incongruities, the contrast between what is and what seems to be, between what's true and what's false."

Frank Leahy, Director of Drama at Palm Beach Junior College, explains, "Life is a comedy to people who think and a tragedy to those who feel."

In 1905, Freud himself delved into the subject of humor in a book titled, JOKES AND THEIR RELATION TO THE UNCONSCIOUS. He concluded that "a joke often expresses something the individual himself is unable to express, and does it in an abbreviated form." In simpler terms, a joke may liberate one from inhibitions.

Dr. Ronald Schenberg, a Florida psychologist, reports, "Some people carry themselves lightly. They're relatively accepting of themselves. They have a greater sense of ease and generally have the ability to appreciate all things in life, including various kinds of humor."

So why is it one person will fall out, doubled over with laughter, and another will merely smile, if he does even that much? Who knows? We cannot even determine what is laughter. But, perhaps the reason some smile and laugh in spite of everything is that they are the ones who know best what Yeats meant when he wrote, "We must laugh and we must sing, we are blest by everything."

What's in a Laugh?

What causes a smile or a laugh? There's no answer, of course, that is part of the fun. Some believe it is the sudden transformation of a strained expectation into nothing; failing to get what you want or getting what you don't want.

A person laughs when there is a conflict between what a thing is supposed to be and what it actually turns out to be. A person falling in the swimming pool in a bathing suit is not funny. A person falling in or being thrown in fully clothed is another thing. Mostly it is the unexpected, like Fred Allen's story about the glass blower with the hiccups who blew 200 percolator tops before he could stop.

Charlie Chaplin defined humor as playful pain. Here's an actual example. The chairman of a meeting I was attending had just announced the next meeting would be on the second Friday of the month as always, May 1st. This irrefutable fact had already been printed in the program, so it had to be so. The vice-president, who happened to be seated in the audience, raised his hand and called for a point of order. "I'm sorry to say, Mr. President, that can not be. The second Friday of the month is May 8th, not May 1st." Then the president said he didn't know exactly what to do since he was sure the speaker for the next program had been secured, but now he didn't know whether he was coming May 1st or May 8th. In a painfully, playful way the vice-president quipped, "Why don't you call the speaker and find out."

"Thank you for your advice, Mr. Vice-President," replied the president. In the very next item of business, the president became painfully aware that he had another problem for which he had no answer. He playfully turned to the vice-president and asked, "I need some more advice." The vice-president rose to the occasion when he shot back, "I only give advice. I can't do anything about dumb mistakes."

Playful pain? Chaplin would probably agree, twirl his cane, whirl on his heel, and disappear in a burst of laughter.

The Social Aspects of Humor

The power of laughter can be used for both good and evil. Among the Eskimos of Greenland, there is an established practice of duels of ridicule. Two angered parties, instead of fighting it out with guns and knives, stand before each other and hurl insults. The contests take place in public before the bemused tribal community. To the accompaniment of drums and songs, the duel is carried out until the level of laughter and obvious sentiment from the spectators determine the winner. The bouts are taken quite seriously, but the laughter has been so intense on occasions that the loser goes into exile.

One of the primary forms of discipline of Japanese children is to be warned by their parents that if they behave in certain ways, they will be laughed at.

Among the Pygmies, being laughed at is one of the most dreaded forms of ridicule and punishment.

Even in our society, we must be careful to use humor in such a way that the individual or group of individuals are not singled out to be laughed at.

On the positive side, it is not too difficult to laugh with individuals or groups of individuals. Remember in Grammar school when someone started giggling for no reason? Soon, another picked up the giggle, then another, then the entire class. Often, no one can remember what started it. Psychologically, this can be used to advantage as a speaker if you can get one or two individuals "rolling." Work on them, play to them, but do not humiliate them. They are your best friends and serve as a source of contamination to spread laughter throughout the rest of the audience. If you doubt that laughter is infectious, just get a group of preschool children together to play "belly laugh." Have them lie down on the floor with their head on a participants belly. By having them arranged in a circle, there will soon be treated to a mini-epidemic of laughter through the simplest of remarks like, "Don't anybody laugh now." Soon, somebody starts laughing and there is a continuous wave that spreads around the circle. The contagious aspects of humor are that way in many other social situations.

How can we make use of this contagious epidemic? Simple, if you have a choice, place the audience as close to the speaker as possible, put participants in a crowded room, get the audience in the lap of the speaker, and soon the speaker will have them in the palm of his hand. And everybody knows that laps in contact with palms can produce belly laughs.

Tickling the Audience

The Romans used tickling as a form of cruel punishment. Having listened to a lot of poor comedians trying to tickle an audience, I can understand how much torture that would be. Maybe that's where the old Southern expression, "tickled to death", came from. It is interesting to note that if infants are tickled by a kind and loving figure (such as a mother or father), they respond with giggles and merriment. However, if a stranger tries the same approach, the result is often just the opposite—baby cries. This happens with an audience. If they perceive you to be a kind and loving character, they will laugh at your material. If you are not it is an entirely different story.

Sometimes, the stage can be set in your favor by the way you react at the cocktail party or pre-meeting functions. Once while speaking in California, I was attending a cocktail party which included 500 or 600 people. I had been pumped up quite high in the publicity material and a few of the "old sages" resented my publicity. One boldly approached me, martini in hand, and asked, "Are you the guy who's speaking here tonight? Say something funny." I've been around long enough to know that this is a no-win situation, so I proceeded not to use the tickle-by-torture method. I simply smiled my warmest, friendliest smile and said, "You look like an entertaining fellow. I'll bet you've got some great stories. How about telling me one?" He then launched into 15 minutes of stories to which I patiently listened and heartily laughed in all the right places. Every time he finished one, I bragged on his delivery and pleaded for more material. When they flicked the lights to signal the end of the cocktail party and time for the meeting to begin, somebody passed by and asked him, "Hey, Charlie, is that the speaker?" Charlie replied, "Yes, and does he ever have some great material. You're gonna love this guy." The fact was that I had hardly said anything, but simply listened. Everybody in this audience knew Charlie was hard to please. But since Charlie was on my side, the whole crowd got off to a great start, and the meeting was a snap. Why? I think in this instance it was because the audience was responding to a loving figure who was trying to tickle them in the right kind of way.

When Is it Funny?

Joe Griffith is a former investment counselor and stockbroker. His speeches are, surprisingly enough, about 90% humor. Recently while reading an old newspaper clipping about Joe, it dawned on me just how funny things can be with the change of time.

Griffith is a real professional and updates his material to keep pace with current trends. One of the lines he was using in 1979 would get almost no response today, but at the time, it was a biggie. The line was, "If Betty Ford had a drinking problem, how come President Ford was always falling over?" The joke was funny then because Mrs. Ford had admitted she had a problem and the world in general believed it to be cured. Of course, everyone remembers the stumbling antics of Gerald Ford and the fact that he was a genuinely nice fellow with a sense of humor.

That's a very old example which illustrates the thin line between offense and gales of laughter. A more current example would be this actual occurrence in a local Rotary Club. A lovable character in this club was genuinely liked by everyone in town. He was a good sport who realized he had a tendency to talk too long when he got interested in a project he was promoting. Because he did such a good job of administration, he was given one project after another, always explaining at length and in very serious fashion how the project was to be coordinated. Then one day he was asked to give the invocation. Surprisingly, it was one of the shortest prayers on record. Shortly thereafter, a member asked for the floor and said, "I think we've stumbled on a way to get shorter reports out of Fred. Ask him to say the prayer more often." Because of the thin line between offense and humor, this line brought howls of laughter. Of course, Fred gave the club member his famous frown and stare routine, which made it even funnier. When the laughter died down, another member jumped to his feet and added, "I've got it, next time he has a report to make, let's just have him pray it." More laughter, more stares. Then in a low, but loud voice, a seated member remarked, "Ought not to pick on a man his age." With the ball still rolling, humor was maintained throughout the meeting. Everyone had all but forgotten about Fred until a visiting guest remarked that "he loved to come to the club because he always heard so many one-liners." That's when another joker struck with a remark, "Yeah, not to mention one of Fred's 20-liners."

This whole meeting was made much more enjoyable because of a routine observation that one of the members talked too long. Even when he did the opposite and talked too short, the members still poked fun at him about his reputation for verbosity. By picking up on these character traits of some members in the audience, selecting the right kind of material to point out these traits, you may be able to also walk the thin line successfully. The key is to simply make sure the person is a "character" and enjoys being in the limelight. This is the basis for the famous "roast" routines, simply used in another format.

Everybody Wants a Sense of Humor

Someone once described a sense of humor as being similar to the desire to own a Porsche. Not everybody has one, but everybody wants one.

A group of pollsters surveyed two colleges to determine if students ranked themselves as average, below average, or above average in a sense of humor. Although the entire student body was surveyed in both colleges, less than 2% at one college and less than 6% at the other were willing to sign themselves a lower than average sense of humor.

The result of polls like this indicate a growing acceptance for the sterling qualities of an appreciation of humor in polite company. There are some places of course, such as church, where humor is still considered inappropriate. Even the Bible warns "A fool lifteth up his voice in laughter, but a wiseman doth scarce smile a little."

Why was humor formerly cast in an unfavorable light and why is the attitude changing? It is probably because humor in the past was often cruel, vicious or degrading. Formerly, humor was used to turn others into ridicule and to congratulate ourselves on being above their defects.

Humor today, in the hands of a skilled practitioner, is more often used in a therapeutic manner to observe the nature of man, including faults that are common to both joker and jokee. Basically, we have learned to laugh with one another instead of at one another to a point where a sense of humor is now appreciated and ranking mirth on a level with intellect.

How to Dissect Humor

"Humor can be dissected as a frog can," the essayist, E. B. White said once, "but the thing dies in the process and the innards are discouraging to any but the pure scientific mind."

True, but a few insights can be gained from some true professionals. Richard Pryor is a genuinely funny man. Try to tell some of his jokes and you may fall flat on your face. Why is Pryor so funny? One reason is because he can produce scenery for the mind in a wink of an eye. When Pryor talks about standing in a long line, for instance, he actually makes you see that line, simply by standing in place and looking questioningly all around him.

Purely by chance (I happened to be in the right place), I was invited to visit in the home of Erma Bombeck who now lives in

Phoenix, Arizona. I found her to be a very witty woman, but more than that she was a very nice person. It was obvious that she was not trying to entertain the three of us who were invited to share coffee around her table, but she never suppressed a line that popped into her head. Equally impressive was the fact that she never failed to appreciate a good line that was obviously an adlib connected to the conversation. She has a hearty laugh and obvious appreciation for humor. Her husband, Bill, is a very quiet, hospitable man with an obvious cast-iron core of self-esteem. Bill sort of blends in with the wallpaper and people have a tendency to forget he is even there because of Erma's fame and popularity. After a half hour of coffee conversation, we politely excused ourselves although at no time did we ever feel as if we were intruding. As we were leaving, I privately whispered to Erma, "You'll never know how much I appreciate the opportunity to visit in this home and meet someone who has been my idol for many years . . . Bill Bombeck." Did she laugh? Of course, because that line followed Erma's line of reasoning that "in humor, you start with the truth, an unpleasant or frustrating situation, then exaggerate it, and take it a step further to absurdity."

To follow this line of reasoning, Red Skelton advises "don't take short cuts and use dirty words to get a quick, cheap laugh. To develop your talent, watch your fellow man, notice his quirks and mistakes and love him enough to mimic him without hurting him."

Even those of us who have an intense interest and use for humor cannot completely explain it. And we never tire of its application. A reporter once asked Red Skelton if he intended to retire and he readily admitted he had no plans for that "because that's like packing up your soul and putting it away."

Do Jokes Get Old?

Believe it or not, there is an international conference on humor. Mostly composed of psychologists and scholars in behavioral disciplines, these scientists concern themselves with trying to discover new uses for humor. It is a rather frustrating business, because jokes have changed little since the beginning of time. There is a new interpretation, however, of material, and this is where the challenge lies today. For instance, practical joking can be traced back even to now extinct civilizations. One tribe of Indians in Argentina delighted in rushing from their hut while entertaining guests, to demolish the visitors canoe. When he was able to control his uproarous laughter, the host would then produce a replacement canoe he had built before his guests arrived. A smash hit in Hollywood is the comedian, Gallagher, whose main claim to humorous fame is demolishing a watermelon with a large mallet. Humor just doesn't get old. To quote Rodney Dangerfield, "If something's done well, it's not outdated. Wives are still around aren't they." Here's a couple of Rodney's jewels: "I asked my daughter what she wanted to be when she grew up. She looked at me and said, 'Single.' " "My wife's a lousy cook. In my house, we say prayers after we eat. I don't think meatloaf should glow in the dark."

Humor doesn't grow old; it just gets recycled.

The Serious Side of Humor

The study of humor is much more serious than most people realize and not easy to analyze. In one university experiment conducted by the University of Tennessee, a psychology professor conducted a series of scientific experiments indicating that laughter depends not only on the source of amusement, but also on the mind of the laugher, the environment, and the audience composition. One of the experiments suggested that a collection of strangers would not laugh at abrasive, insult comedy material until they had a chance to know each other better and thus feel more relaxed.

A gentle humorist who poked fun mainly at himself and his past experiences was better accepted in the experiments by all classes of people. It made almost no difference to the audience whether they knew each other or not in their response to a gentle form of humor.

On the other hand, only an audience that was intimately acquainted with most of the individuals in it were responsive to an insult type humor where members of the audience were singled out as the butt of the joke.

The conclusion of this experiment, of course, is that one way to analyze humor is to analyze the audience. If it is a group that is homogenous, where everyone knows everyone else, it is possible to single out individuals and still expect the crowd to react favorably. On the other hand, if it is a group of strangers, it may be dangerous, from the standpoint of laughter response, to use anything but humor of a more gentle persuasion. If the audience is a group of strangers, they are more likely to underreact to a more acid, personal form of humor. They would be more apt to respond, without feeling laughed at, to the type of humor which is non-specific. In tailoring your humorous remarks, keep the angle of attack in mind in order to get the best possible reception for your remarks. Don't be afraid to use acid type humor, but know where it has the best chance of succeeding.

Good Humor Carries a Message

The first regular column in the New World appeared in the Boston newspaper, New-England Courant, in 1722 under the byline "Mrs. Silence Dogood." The writer was actually young Benjamin Franklin. Humor has changed a great deal since then. A typical Dogood/ Franklin remark needling Harvard for turning out budding scholars describes them "as great blockheads as ever, only more proud and self-conceited." Well, humor back then was a bit different and probably seemed funny at the time.

Mark Twain began his humorous columns in the 1860's for the Territorial Enterprise of Virginia City, Nevada. The columns were not intended to be funny, merely an amusing tale which occurred to Samuel Clements. Clements (Twain) overheard somebody laughing at his first column and decided to write more, which earned him an enviable reputation as one of America's greatest humorists.

Until 1979, journalism's highest award, the Pulitzer Prize, had not been won by a writer considered basically a humorist. Russell Baker captured the attention of Pulitzer judges with his humor. Interestingly enough, the columns for which he won the prize dealt with tax reform, shorter life spans of trends, inflation, the difference between serious and solemn, loneliness, fear, dying, a boyhood summer, Norman Rockwell, and the death of a magazine. How could these subjects be classified as humor? The thin line between something funny and a serious message has been incorporated by Russell Baker in newspaper humor by turning it into literature—funny, but full of pain and absurdity. He merely reports what we have all seen or sensed, but didn't realize we observed it until he points it out to us. For instance, in a recent column, he commented that he simply refused to buy a car that cost more than the house he grew up in, $6,000.

Sincerity in Humor

Sincerity is not often thought of as an important element that can be expressed through humor. However, once the mastery of humor is complete, it can be used under extremely delicate situations to express appreciation of others and reduce tensions under unbelievable circumstances.

For instance, when an assassin tried to carry out his plan on President Ronald Reagan, the President had the presence of mind to use humor in a delightful way to express his sentiments to those who were less than calm over the distressing events which had just occurred. President Reagan, by now famed for his Irish wit, is a masterful actor capable of delivering lines that can disarm the most alarming situation. When it was discovered that the President had a bullet lodged in his lung, the entire nation held their collective breath. Mrs. Reagan was immediately rushed to his side with the knowledge that he had been wounded. His disarming comment to her was "Honey, I forgot to duck." When doctors frantically prepared him for surgery and hovered over the operating table, President Reagan is reported to have lifted his head slightly, smiled at them, and quipped, "Please tell me you are all Republicans."

This form of light-hearted sincerity is one of the most important elements in communication and can be used most effectively in a life-threatening situation or in eloquent speech.

Philosophy and Humor

This may come as a surprise to some students, but humor can be very philosophical, very entertaining, and very meaningful in the hands of a skilled practioner. Abraham Lincoln is a good example of one who used it expertly. One day when Lincoln was walking along the road toward Springfield, Illinois, the capitol, he flagged a man down in a carriage and asked if he would take his coat into Springfield. The man agreed to do so, but then asked how Lincoln would get to town to pick it up. Lincoln replied, "I intend to remain in it."

Lincoln survived many tragedies, including a nervous breakdown and numerous political defeats through his philosophical humor. As one philosopher once humorized, or is it a humorist once philosophized, "Comedy is an escape, not from truth, but from despair; a narrow escape into faith . . . in tragedy every moment is eternity; in comedy, tragedy is only an instant far removed."

Inspiration in Humor

Most people don't think of humor as a form of inspiration, but it can be used to great advantage to those who understand its power. Another example from the near tragedy of the assassination attempt on President Reagan's life is his comment to doctors who marvelled at his fast recovery that "If I had received this much attention in California, I never would have left Hollywood."

On another level, perhaps someone you have not even heard of has used humor to inspire others. One of the persons who comes to mind is Pete Strudwick. Although Pete is well-known in some circles, he is probably not a familiar figure to most Americans. Pete's story is an inspiration in itself. Born in Germany, approximately 50 years ago, he was smuggled out of that country into the United States by his mother. The reason for the hasty departure was because Pete was born without feet and hands and was marked for extermination by the Nazi regime. With a sense of humor, he refused to accept his limitations and went on to achieve a relatively normal life. If running the Pike's Peak Marathon can be considered normal, he fills the bill. Because of his unusual athletic abilities, Strudwick has been retained to train Marine recruits in San Diego, California. He not only jogs with the trainees, but provides classroom instruction, inspiration, and humor. His feet are more like stumps and he runs with specially prepared shoes that approximate the size of a shoe heel. He explains the sensation to others as "like strapping a couple of beer cans to your heels and jogging off into the sunset." When asked how he could possibly compete in the toughest marathon of all, the Pike's Peak Marathon, he replied, "I don't lean backwards." And you thought inspiration had to be serious business, didn't you? Well, just as there is a thin line between comedy and tragedy, humor can be a double-edged sword.

The Well Placed Adlib

It's always a good idea to have a comment or two thought up in advance for something that could possibly go wrong in making a presentation. One example of this is in the music field. Floyd "Red" Rice and his family orchestra plays for dances as well as concerts. "Red" works out of Oklahoma City, but travels nationally. Playing a concert in San Angelo, Texas with the San Angelo Symphony Orchestra, "Red" kept the audience pleased with some sing-a-long songs and a dance-a-long daughter. Another daughter and a wife rounded out the troupe of professional entertainers. It so happened that this night the airconditioner went out and the temperature was near 90°. The audience was kept entertained, despite the drench of perspiration covering the entertainers, by such lines as "It was so hot here this afternoon I saw a robin pulling a worm out of the ground, and he was using potholders." When his dance-a-long daughter did a dance and high-kick routine while playing the bass fiddle, he remarked, "That was the Fifth of Beethoven. Right now, I'd settle for a fifth of Gatorade."

During a lively rendition of a classical song by Red's wife, Lou

Ann, her electric keyboard failed. During a momentary pause to switch to an auxiliary system, "Red" quipped, "I was afraid that might happen. You see, on the way down here from Oklahoma, somebody shot an arrow through it."

Of course, "Red" is an old professional and most likely could come up with numerous adlibs that were truly thought up on the spur of the moment. However, it is most likely that these kinds of comments come from the experience of having the same thing happen before. With a little forethought you can anticipate what might go wrong and have a quip ready to fill in for those precious moments when attention might otherwise be lost. Certainly no performer looks forward to hot nights without airconditioning or a power failure on the electric keyboard, but when it happens, it can produce some of the most memorable moments if the performer is prepared with a few well-chosen push button remarks.

The Layman Jokers

Too many people think that humor is developed only by professionals. There are many lay people and some of the funniest ones are not doing it for a living, at least not as their major occupation. Take the example of football coach, Lou Holtz, formerly of Arkansas: "Our bowl preparation to play Alabama yesterday wasn't much different than any other death march."

"Personally, I would have rather played New Hampshire."

During the season Holtz said: "If this is supposed to be a rebuilding year, we need urban renewal." "Coaching is nothing more than eliminating mistakes before you get fired."

"I've seen a lot of great running backs and Alabama certainly has had its share. John Capelletti, at Penn State, was one of the best. When I was at North Carolina State, he bounced off our tacklers like Ethiopian spears off Mussolini's tanks."

"When things are going wrong, you hope you're a bad shot, because that's when you consider suicide."

So take heart, friends. As a layman, surely you can appreciate another layman approaching perfection even by professional standards.

Pulpit Humor

Going to church as a child, I got the definite impression that I was a miserable, rotten, no good sinner and that church was a form of punishment—a preview of what was to come unless I repented of my wicked ways.

To this day, this feeling has been ingrained in the minds of many people. As a humorous banquet speaker, I used to dread speaking in the basement of a church, which I often did. Church is Holy ground and laughter and applause, the opium of the humorists, seem inappropriate. Then one day, I was invited to a Methodist church by a friend. I was simply astounded when the preacher told a joke from the pulpit, the congregation laughed—actually laughed, heartily, unashamed, as if they were enjoying themselves. It was a joyous place, with much merriment, even applause. Could it be that this method has actually been responsible for winning sinners to salvation? Laugh, if you will, but for whatever reason, the United Methodist Church is one of the largest Protestant denomination in the United States today.

Of course, the Methodists do not have a monopoly on the use of humor in religion. A 45-year old Southern Baptist preacher, Grady Nutt, now deceased, sprang from the pulpit to the convention circuit to a star of the television show, Hee Haw. He was known as the Prime Minister of Humor. "In church," said Grady, "I try to keep people off balance with humor for the three or four times I want to hit them between the eyes." He believed that "in the guise of humor, you can say things that need to be said. People listen differently. You can coax them in the direction they need to go." Yet, Grady admits that "if all I do in church is entertain, then I have let you down. I'm dead serious about trying to convey something crucial—truth. Truth is the broth, humor the cup I put it in." There may be those who criticize ministers for the use of humor, but for the unusually gifted minister, it may be the way to reach his congregation. "Most people do not relate humor and religion together too well," admits Grady Nutt. But, he was not like most people. "The second "T" is important in the name Nutt. Without it, I'm just like the rest of you!"

Comics and Preachers

"The function of the best comedians, whether on stage or in literature, is very similar to the great preachers of old," according to Robert Polhemus, Stanford University English professor. The professor maintains that transforming death into transcendence is akin to a joke, standing reality on its head. While that may sound irreverent, it is not meant to be. Consider, for instance, this parallel: "I will play with and make ridiculous fear, loneliness, smallness, ignorance, authority, chaos, nihilism, and even death. I will transform for a time woe into joy."

The deeper implication that the professor is pointing out is that there has developed a "comic faith" in this country, "a tacit belief that the world is both funny and potentially good." The main purposes and uses of religion which Polhemus said comedy now fulfills are: "To reconcile people to their fates; to smoothe out social enmity; to make people feel important and part of a 'chosen group' to institutionalize ways of getting rid of guilt; to allow people to identify with righteousness; to release hostility in good conscience; and to lift them out of themselves and become freer of spirit."

Could it be that the modern congregation is the audience that crowds an auditorium to view a comic performance? While the pure comedian may not have this deeper goal, most humorists do feel a deep commitment to the higher use of humor for lifting the burden of life's absurdities and predicaments. For instance, imagine this scene: A hell fire and brimstone evangelist, pointed a boney finger skyward, yelling, "When the roll is called up yonder," then likewise gestured between his wide spread feet and whispered, "I'll be there."

Epinephrine, Chlorpromazine, and Amusement

Humor is generally regarded as a clearly psychological and emotional reaction, but from the journal of *Abnormal and Social Psychology* comes a fascinating experiment. Three groups of people were given injections of epinephrine (a stimulant), saline (water with a little salt in it), and chlorpromazine (a major tranquilizer).

The results were most intriguing because epinephrine, which increases physiological stimulation, should have no result on psychological appreciation. The three groups were shown a funny film and asked to rate it according to the level of funniness. The epinephrine group rated it most humorous, the saline group gave it an intermediate rating, and the chlorpromazine group failed to appreciate the humor at all. A practical application of this information means simply that the body and mind must be in tune in order to appreciate or to perform humor. It may also explain why it is so easy to bomb in front of a drunk audience.

Educational Jokes

Classroom banter helps school children learn more and score higher on tests according to Tel Aviv University psychologist Dr. Avner Ziv. Dr. Ziv tries to persuade teachers to brighten up their lectures with a joke or two, because his research shows that students will remember the cracks along with the reading, writing, and arithmetic.

"The idea's in humor, which are crazy ideas, gives you the inspiration and courage to be creative," Ziv said. "And laughter makes you less aggressive and more receptive."

Six years of study have convinced him that the pleasure associated with comedy and laughter reduces the anxiety students feel over trying to master difficult subjects. Professors participating in the research delivered the same lectures with or without jokes. The result was that the students exposed to jokes remembered the material and scored higher on exams. One precaution is that, according to Ziv, "The jokes have to be good and related to the subject. Otherwise, it's distracting."

"Why study laughter? Well, nobody ever comes to a psychologist and says, 'I've got a good sense of humor. Help me,' " Ziv explained. "And, psychologists are so serious, like teachers, that they're afraid to study or use humor because they're afraid of not being taken seriously." This scientist is not trying to revolutionize education, but he does admit to "coming up with a few ideas and having a few laughs doing it."

It is so important to repeat at this point one of the things that research has discovered with humorists "that the jokes have to be good and related to the subject. Otherwise, it's distracting." This is a key point. After all, didn't the study group that was exposed to humor score higher than the others? Actually, all this proves is that acting like a dummy can sometimes definitely prove you aren't one.

Dark Humor

I was once interviewed on a radio program in which my host asked the unusual question, "Is there humor in everything—even death?"

Surprisingly enough, some of the wittiest remarks in the world are found in cemeteries. These are epitaphs, parting shots given by the deceased or given in his/her memory. Few have used this form of dark humor any better than the hypochondriac buried in a Georgia cemetery who had chisled on his tombstone, "I told you I was sick!"

In Moultrie, Georgia there is the epitaph: "Here lies the father of 29. He would have had more, but he didn't have time." A sheep thief was caught and hanged in Bletchley Bucks, England. His epitaph read: "Here lies the body of Thomas Kemp, who lived by wool and died by hemp."

A widow in Atlanta had the following inscription carved on her adulterous husband's tombstone: "Gone. But not forgiven."

An old maid's epitaph in Scranton, Pennsylvania: "No hits, no runs, no heirs."

At Cripple Creek, Colorado, an epitaph to a man who died by accident: "Within this grave, there lies poor Andy; bit by a snake, no whiskey handy."

If handled in a very light-hearted manner, dark humor can be some of the finest forms of communication. For instance, a community leader, such as mayor, might explain to an audience that he is leaning favorably toward a certain proposal through the use of this story. "A fellow had two wives, Millie and Tillie, both of whom preceded him in death. He left word that when his number was up, he wanted to be buried equidistant between his two beloved ladies. He wanted the world to know that he loved them both dearly and showed absolutely no partiality. But, confidentially, he remarked, off the record, to his friend, the undertaker, to "tip me just a little toward Tillie."

Rebellion Humor

The authority figure is always a good target for rebellion humor. It can be used by enlisted men to joke about their officers, or it may be used by officers to joke about the light in which officers are seen through the eyes of the enlisted men. It can be a strange mixture of admiration and resentment. Two examples perhaps will explain the theory better than more philosophy.

A general calls his headquarters and an enlisted man answers the phone. When questioned about some order, the enlisted man replies, "Who knows what that fat headed general will do next?" The voice on the other end barked," Do you know who this is?" "No, sir," came the reply. "This is General Smith." Without a moments hesitation the non-com shot back, "Do you know who this is?" "No." "So long, fathead."

Now this kind of rebellious nature can be admired by both sides in this story. An Army general, a Navy admiral, and a Marine general were arguing over who had the bravest men. To prove his point, the Army general took his two companions up on a parachute jumping exercise, told a private to jump without his chute which the private promptly did. As he disappeared below, the general remarked, "THAT'S a brave man."

The admiral said they hadn't seen anything yet. He took his two companions to a large battle ship, told an enlisted man to dive into shark infested waters which he promptly did. As he disappeared beneath the oceans waves, never to be seen again, the admiral bragged, "Now, THAT is a brave man."

The Marine colonel said that was for sissies, just come with him. He drove up to a base with his two companions and was promptly challenged by a Marine recruit who levelled a rifle at the three. The admiral was indignant and told him to stand aside. The recruit, since he had allegiance to both the Navy and the Marines, looked to his superior officer first and asked, "Pardon me, general. I'm kinda new at this game. Who do I shoot first, you or the admiral?" As the car backed out of the gate, the Marine colonel turned to his two companions and said, "Now, THAT, gentlemen, is a brave man."

How to Deliver the Touch

3

The question often asked of Doc is "Do you always laugh at your own jokes?" His answer, illustrated here at the California Mortgage Bankers Association. "You'd laugh too if you were looking at what I'm looking at. . . . A good audience is the best show in town."

No Business Like Show Business

Last year it was estimated that 300 million dollars was devoted to business showmanship in meetings in the United States. These meetings are becoming progressively more show business oriented through the use of professional entertainers and speakers. Productions may sometimes be as lavish as a Broadway play, often including full-size orchestras, movie stars, television personalities, and professional speakers who may not have name recognition but are extremely well prepared to deliver a profound message in the most entertaining way.

Just setting up a few chairs and having a meeting is a recipe for boredom. People today have spent 25 years watching television, listening to stereophonic sound, and now using personalized computers in color. They expect more than a boring talk or a stale slide show. Think of the methods used in television, such as Sesame Street, to get messages across to our children or television ads used to reach consumers. Think of TV sports—the same guy who watches the NFL games, complete with interviews and warm ups, comes to a sales meeting. He is not going to listen long unless you can grab his attention and hold it. That is not an easy thing to do, but the humorist usually has the greatest chance of success as a solo entertainer. For that reason, many humorists are used in various capacities from keynoting a convention to the after-dinner, luncheon or banquet fun.

The most important function of business entertainment is to hold the attention of the audience, to excite them, to affect them emotionally, and to give a message that will be more memorable. Businesses keep doing it for one reason. It works.

Many of today's conventions are rewards for good service and you can't stop giving rewards because your employees are the ones who are bringing in the money that makes the company successful.

As an example, the Best Western Motel chain has an annual meeting that includes extensive projections of corporate goals for the coming years. These extensive plans often take three hours of explanation, viewing charts and graphs, and using all the latest audio-visual materials. However, Best Western discovered that many of their audience was losing interest because of the rather boring statistical nature of this type of talk. So, they created a character known as Willy B. Preposterous, a comical puppet that is supplied with a live voice and trades banter with the chief corporate executive. Willy, of course, takes a comical view of nearly everything explained and usually gets his point across with comments like "Now, let me see if I understand this." Of course, Willy never does understand it, which makes it a hilarious session, which the audience loves because they could not get away with saying some of the things that Willy does to the chief executive even though they would like to. By the time the session is over, the crowd has been thoroughly entertained, but even more important is the fact that issues have been brought out, examined, allowing Willy B. Preposterous to play the devil's advocate. The corporate plan has thus been thoroughly digested and entertainingly presented so that the audience has given its highest attention to some very serious points but in a light-hearted manner.

Speculation is that the entertainment element of business will become more important within the meeting, because it's there that the message is delivered. In other words, the business show and show business will go on.

Reading Is Hum-drum

Don't read your speech in a hum-drum fashion. This is the worst thing to do and the quickest way to kill enthusiasm. It is also the most common way of delivering a speech, because the person making the remarks wants to be absolutely sure that these words are not misinterpreted. Business meetings are notoriously dull on this account. However, you can learn a great deal by watching the anchor men on nightly newscasts. Try to imitate the mechanics of what they do. Although they have a written script in front of them, they only glance down at it on occasions. It's obvious that these TV speakers can not remember the script word for word. It merely serves as a guide, and they have a tendency to adlib a lot. You can do exactly the same thing.

If your speech concerns some very serious material, and you absolutely do not wish to be misquoted, it may be acceptable to read your speech word for word, but your audience will certainly appreciate it if you can adlib sufficient bits of humor to make it palatable. Be like the TV weatherman who lost his script and adlibbed, "Tonight, it will be partly dark, turning to dark, followed by partly light, turning to light. And the weekend weather is expected to be followed by Monday."

Rehearse for Confidence

Don't let anybody see you doing this, because if they do, they may "take you away," as Jonathan Winters used to say about his strange redman character, "to live in funny teepee." It may even be a bit embarrassing to you to do this in your own presence, but it is a dynamite tool that has been proven to work for people who are serious about being funny. After you have written your speech, polished it, rehearsed it, tape recorded it, and listened to it several times, it is time to get in some skull practice. Athletes do it all the time and nobody thinks they are weird, do they? Skull practice simply means getting mentally prepared to see yourself in action, knowing the game plan, ready to win.

Here's the way it works. Get a good sized, full-length mirror, a podium, a little scotch tape, and lots of pictures of people. Tape the faces of people, crowds, anything you can get your hands on that represents a dummy audience. Tape them on the sides of the mirror, along the wall, anywhere that will give you the visual impression that you are speaking before a large audience. Then deliver your speech, and watch yourself closely in the mirror. You will learn a lot about yourself and your material. One precaution—if the audience laughs, turn pro immediately. You won't even need an agent.

Psych up for Effect

Here's a little tip that may save your hide in front of an audience. Your words and thoughts may be as pure as the driven snow . . . but it depends on what it is driven through. If you are being promoted as a truly happy person and snap at the waiter, the message comes through. In effect, what you are speaks so loudly that we may not hear what you proclaim.

A traveler in England listened to a world famous theologian preach at All Saints Church in Oxford. Even though it has been decades since the traveler recalls the experience, he remembers perfectly after all these years the expression on the speaker's face in the pulpit. He looked very unhappy. His subject? "Gratitude."

So if you intend to use humor, practice not only the art of communicating that humor, but the practice of living a happy fulfilled life. Don't let yourself be surrounded by a polluted atmosphere. As one wag explained after hearing a particularly dull, gloomy speaker, "A cloud so thick and black follows him around that if he shot an arrow into the air, it would stick."

Conquer the Opponent

You remember the game we used to play as kids, "One for the money, Two for the show, Three to get ready, Four to go?" Then everyone would tear off in a foot race or some other sort of competitive game. Speaking is a similar type of competition except that you are usually competing against yourself. Leaving out, for the moment, debates and organized speaking contests, the public speaker is pitted against a most difficult opponent to conquer—himself or herself. It is not honest to let a fit of depression, headache, or any other non-life threatening disturbance interfere with your performance. All that must be blocked out. "Three to get ready" is a time to go over your game plan, mentally rehearse your material, see yourself running this race, and winning.

The confidence you will build through this meditation may surprise you. Contrary to popular opinion, it does not have to be silent meditation. During the time you are eating, conversing with companions at the head table, let your mind drift back on course at every opportunity. Concentrate on your opening lines, summarize the material you will cover; concentrate again on the close of your talk, and above all, concentrate on the audience being won to your side. There have been many instances of great humorists and orators who were able to "get up" for a speech even under the most difficult circumstances. Senator Hubert Humphrey exhibited tremendous oratorical poise, wit, and courage while battling a terminal illness. He knew, the audience knew it, but all "got up" for the occasion and won.

Avoid Rejection

There is no question that more people fear speaking than any other form of public appearance. This is basically a deep seated fear of rejection. Yet, there is also a deep seated hope for acceptance and that's why the fantasy of being applauded before a group of people holds such universal appeal.

Why do we do it? Here's a great tip from the actor, the late Pat O'Brien. When asked why he continued to punish his body, at his age, with road trips, suggesting that "he didn't need it," Pat explained, "Well, I do need it. There's some altruism involved; you're bringing enjoyment to people who need it. But it's selfish, too—there's a lot of fun in making people laugh. You get a different audience every night, and each one has different reactions. You lose a laugh one night, then you try to get it back the next time out."

That statement was made in an interview on Pat O'Brien's 80th birthday, which goes to prove the fact that a good laugh can keep you going long after you should have been gone. And, as the old

Chinese proverb states, "A bit of fragrance always clings to the hand that gives you roses."

Overcome Stage Fright

An unusual but highly effective way of overcoming stage fright is to practice speaking to yourself. Not the same words you will speak to your audience, however, but words of encouragement that you are going to do well. One successful ventriloquist speaks to his dummy back stage and says something like, "Look, we have nothing to fear, the audience will love us because we love them. We look good and we know our material perfectly. But even if something should happen, we'll just wing it, maybe we'll find something new. Now, let's get out there, get our laughs, touch this audience, and have fun." With enthusiasm, the two dummies did go out and "wow" the audience.

The best speakers also seem to be having an extension of a conversation rather than giving a speech. Maybe that's a big secret in being relaxed. As a performer, I always feel like I am in a higher gear and really pouring on the coal. Yet, time after time people tell me they enjoy my presentation because I appear so "relaxed." William Jennings Bryan gives this advice which is appropriate for humorists or anyone else: "Eloquence consists of being tremendously enthused about worthwhile things concerning which you are thoroughly informed. You've got a story to tell and in the telling of the story, you render a service."

Just in case you lack a little confidence, here's a cheap trick that can be used and the audience will never be the wiser. Write a few key words on the palm of your hand with a ball point pen. If you have overcome stage fright and your palms are not sweaty, you will be able to read this without any problem. Then simply take the finger of one hand and count off point number one, etc. The audience will think you are a real whiz who is able to speak without notes and after a little rehearsal, you will be. Mark Twain used to write on his fingernails with a quill pen. This was back during the days when they used real ink. When he finished a point, he would simply take the thumb of the other hand and erase the mark from his fingernail. Apparently the way he did it, it seemed very natural as if one were merely utilizing the hands in a manner typical of people who examine their hands and fingers while they talk. You've seen the type. At any rate, the old cheater must have done pretty well. Besides, he always claimed to be a writer, not a speaker.

Be Yourself

One of the fears most of us have is letting people see us as we actually are. For that reason, when we approach the platform we usually turn on a type of character that we perceive is a little better than what we actually are. Some years ago I was on a television program with a man who had a wide following for his TV show because of his jolly, joking, carefree nature. He was pudgy, folksy, and in general, appeared to be the Friar Tuck type who had nothing but jokes and good things for everyone. This man was periodically in front of the camera and off to the side because his guests were also entertaining. The most disappointing observation to me was that this jolly, rotund jokester was a riot in front of the cameras, but immediately upon stepping out of range, he changed into a difficult, bitter person. He snapped at the camera crew, assistants, and guests. What happened to him? I honestly don't know. He simply faded from sight. Although he fooled the public for awhile, this man could not be true to himself and was doomed to failure.

I have said this before, but it won't hurt to say it again. Be yourself. If you don't like being yourself, then change, but survey the scale of individuality and find a place that will allow you to break through your barriers, accumulating partial successes one by one. As you strive to make yourself a better person, you also become a better speaker. Audiences sense this true, honest character in your personality and will beg for your instruction, inspiration, encouragement, and even relief through the cleansing powers of effective humor.

Get Attention in 30 Seconds

The first 30 seconds of a speech are extremely critical. Generally, the audience has not made up its mind about you and will probably not give you much of a chance to make an impression if you take more than 30 seconds to do so. How do you gain favorable attention? It can be done with a clever statement, a one-liner, a rebel yell, blowing a police whistle, ringing a bell, doing a magic trick, and countless other ways to gain immediate attention of the audience. One English comic I know always starts his program with a pratt fall. The instant he is introduced, he bounds to the microphone and looks down as if searching for his spot on the stage. He backs up a quick step and falls through the curtain to a gutter (walkway) below. He always emerges with only head and elbows protruding from behind the curtain. The audience howls and invariably he is a smash hit no matter what he does after that.

It is a fairly well accepted fact that 10% of the people will love you no matter what you do, 10% will dislike you regardless of what you do unless you're extremely good, and 80% of the people are neutral. Therefore, it is important to gain the attention of the 80% and perhaps win the majority of the 10% that does not impress easily. This calculates to at least 90% of the audience being on your side if you can gain favorable attention in the first few seconds. That's the reason all of this material is short, to the point, and designed to create push button wit in a favorable light. Oh, in case you haven't guessed, a one-liner is much less dangerous than a pratt fall or some of the other techniques previously mentioned.

You, We, or Me

One of the rules that is widely taught in public speaking is to never start off talking about yourself. Instead of saying, "It's a great pleasure for me to be here . . . ," it is recommended that you say something like this, "You people in this room know more about our subject than any other group in America." That's theory, good logic, and good advice for most forms of speaking. The exception may very well be in the use of humor. You can start off talking about you and get away with it much to the delight of the audience. The key is to degrade yourself. Start off letting the joke be on you and the audience will generally love you for it. Start off by letting them be the butt of the joke, and all theories may fly out the window.

An example of someone using humor to start off talking about himself is the case of the Texas columnist doing an after-dinner talk. After a flowery introduction, he remarked, "I did not work on the student newspaper at the University of Texas when I was a student there, and I carefully avoided lab assignments on that paper as well. I attribute whatever writing skill I have to those two facts."

If you really want to get in thick with the crowd, talk a little about you, a little about me, and a lot about we. If you can figure a way to relate your position to their's in any way and convince them that "we have a job to do," the battle may be won.

Forget or ignore this rule consistently, and you may find yourself in the position of the Lone Ranger, on top of a hill, surrounded by 20,000 wild, screaming Comanches. The Lone Ranger turns to Tonto and says, "What will we do, Tonto?" Tonto gave him that dull stare and asked, "What you mean 'we' . . . white man?"

Put on a Happy Face

More than one professional speaker has told me that the best way to present a speech is to be fully prepared, and put on a happy face to let the audience know you are really glad to be there. When it shows that you are happy to be there, the audience is also glad to be there. The audience listens with interest to what you have to say. They are stirred, motivated, entertained, influenced, and get something out of your presentation.

There is an old saying that, "The show must go on." Speakers accept this same philosophy and regardless of their personal mood, stress or other unusual circumstances, they are invariably able to block out all interference to perform in a professional way. This becomes a way of programming your biocomputer to strive for this high level of professionalism. Don't ask me how, but it works. I think the philosophy resides somewhere in the computer adage, "Garbage In, Garbage Out." That simply means that if you put bad thoughts and vibes into your brain, you can expect only bad to come out. On the other end of the scale, good input means good output.

I have seen speakers, on occasion, so ill that they had to lie down backstage before being introduced. From the looks of them, you would not think it would be possible for the show to go on. However, these speakers have learned to conserve their strength and muster every bit of energy at their disposal for the period of time when they are performing. I have experienced similar situations and have been amazed at the outcome of what might otherwise be a very serious situation. Once when stricken with laryngitis, I left my home to present a talk in Florida within 8 hours. You might ask why I would bother under those circumstances. The answer is that I had an inner faith that assured me I would be able to speak by the time I arrived. By saying absolutely nothing during the intervening hours, I arrived at my destination and only minutes before I was introduced did I feel my voice beginning to heal. I put on a happy face, made the crowd aware that I was glad to be there, and the program went off without a hitch. Strangely, only a few minutes after I finished the talk my vocal cords constricted again, and I was unable to speak for another day or so. Don't ask me how it works; all I know is that my biocomputer was able to reschedule my body until I had time to have this inconvenient illness.

My friend and fellow writer, veterinarian, Dr. Baxter Black, who writes a column entitled "On the Edge of Common Sense," poetically points out my philosophy with this beautifully constructed piece of wit:

Life Beyond Fortran

There's a natural resentment
When we don't understand
For technical advances
Attributed to man.

Now I'm learning evolution
And positions of the stars
And why it is, that wives, most times,
Don't like you in the bars.

But the greatest of inventions
That I have ever seen
Is the flashing phosphorescence
Of a C.R.T.V. screen.

For those of the unknowing,
It's part of a computer
That makes us all seem wise somehow,
Smarter and astuter.

But I guess the thing that chaps me
Is it never makes mistakes!
It's always human error,
Power surges or earthquakes!

It's what you put into it
That determines your reward.
Like dealin' square with strangers
And givin' part back to the Lord.

Commandment number seventeen
Is what it's all about;
Computin's just like livin',
Garbage in and garbage out!

By Baxter Black, D.V.M.

Relax to Enjoy

When you deliver a speech, be as relaxed as your personality will allow. The world is not coming to an end. You have probably seen speakers who have a rather mundane quality about their voice or mannerisms in person, but when they ascend to the stage, they lower their voice and take on a completely different personality. With few exceptions, this never works. Think of actors like James

Stewart and Gary Cooper. They didn't really have to act. Except for a change of roles, scenery and situations, they played themselves. Most successful speakers are this way.

Now don't overreact to this, and decide to become the relaxed type of speaker, if you are so nervous you could thread a sewing machine with it running. Imagine Rodney Dangerfield trying to imitate Gary Cooper. As Rodney would say, "Someone told me I reminded them of Gary Cooper. I said, 'He's dead.' The guy replied, 'Yes, I know.'" The message is don't be a dead head or a live wire unless you really are. Be yourself.

The Eyes Have It

Strive for eye contact with the audience. That's what you're there for. Among goose hunters, there is an old rule of thumb that you are never within range of a goose flying overhead unless you can see their eyes. When you can, you have a much better chance of bagging your game. The same holds true with an audience. Don't look at those people in the back of an audience if they are so far away you can't see their eyes. Make your speech come alive by striving for contact eyeball to eyeball. It is especially important to pick out those friendly faces with the crinkles about the eyes, a smile on the face.

By the same token, don't let some sourpuss mesmerize you by giving you the old "stare routine." This character is usually hoping you will fall flat on your face, and that's the only thing that gives this kind of person any inner joy or satisfaction. By watching crowd reaction, you will also learn when to inject more humor by watching the audience's eyes . . . especially if they are closed.

There Is Drama in Movement

The physical action of the hands and body combine to create drama in physical movement. Abraham Lincoln once said he liked to see a preacher give a sermon and act like he were "fighting a swarm of bees." Actors who get "inside" a character often take on characteristics different from their own. Red Skelton, Sid Caesar, Tim Conway, are all extremely talented in the area of pantomime and physical drama.

I have worked with Bob Richards, former Olympic decathlon champion, on several occasions. One of the reasons for his great popularity is his extreme concentration and the utilization of the drama he is able to create not only with his voice, but with his body movements. Before Bob goes on the stage, he can be seen in various forms of intense concentration back stage. One of his characteristic warm-up positions is to be seated in the "thinker's" position. With the one fist pressed against his forehead, eyes closed, Bob shuts out the entire world around him for a period of time just prior to his introduction. He is completely motionless and still backstage, but the moment he steps on the stage, he is transformed into a wildly, enthusiastic, dramatic speaker with great natural emphasis on body movements. To quote Bob, "If you yearn to magnetize your audience, you yourself must be magnetized. No race is won by the biggest athlete. It is the size of the fight in the dog that counts, never the size of the dog in the fight. Plato described people of influence who, once magnetized, believing they can be winners, are thus able to touch others and pass on that magic gift." This is a key point to remember. No amount of calculated body movements will ever make you appear natural or improve your delivery in using humor. But if you become magnetized with the power of communication in this form, believe that your material is good, practice, and get "inside" the story, the drama in physical movement will come about in a natural way.

Speak to Be Heard

A weak voice is a sign of fear, lack of confidence, or both. My earliest recollection of awareness that I had a gift for making people laugh was when I was in grade school. Because our class was very small, I was forced to take part in a drama presentation in the school play. There simply were not enough people to fill all the parts otherwise. Since the teacher knew I was an unwilling participant, she gave me only a small part and convinced me it would be easy to memorize the part and the lines. It was a swashbuckling play about ships and pirates. I decided to make the best of a bad situation and threw myself into the role with a great deal of enthusiasm. Even during rehearsals, everytime I would run out on stage and yell, "Hark, I thought I heard a pistol shot," the spectators would break out in uncontrollable laughter. Here I was trying to be serious and all these ding-dongs were laughing at my effort. Quite by accident, I discovered one of the keys to good comedy. If you speak in a loud, clear voice, fling your arms about, and exaggerate a good bit, it excites an audience.

Here's another key point I have learned since then. Don't worry if the audience laughs or doesn't laugh. If they do, then you are a sure-fire hit. If they don't . . . just pretend you're serious. In either case, speak up loud and clear, you can't lose.

Use Your Voice for Effect

This sounds almost so simple that it shouldn't be mentioned, but I am amazed at the number of people who have not learned this extremely important lesson. So often when amateurs deliver humorous stories or lines, they do so in a monotone. Study the great entertainers and you will notice, with few exceptions, that they all use voice inflection to a very high degree. Think of the screechy voice of Flip Wilson's Geraldine, the hilarious antics of loud mouthed Carol Burnett, and who can forget Red Skelton's "Mean Widdle Kid?" The point is simply this, when the occasion calls for a loud mouthed delivery, do it justice. If a scream is in order, don't be afraid to try it. On the other hand, if a meek character is being portrayed, he should be one with a mild, perhaps mumbling voice. A drunk will slur his words and suspense can often be created with a whisper just prior to the punchline.

Voice inflection may be more humorously illustrated by the thought of a character like Ted Baxter on the Mary Tyler Moore Show. Upon entering a quite sound stage, Ted shouts in a rather loud baritone, "What's going on here?" Someone immediately rushes up and says, "Lower your voice." Ted gives that familiar look and in a deep bass voice repeats, "What's going on here?" You see, humor was created with this situation using only voice inflection.

Gestures Enhance Visual Impact

I once heard a dynamic speaker say, "The audience really has to see me in action in order to get the full impact of my presentation." He was inferring, probably correctly, that he used a lot of facial expressions and gestures to enhance his speech. However, this should not be a concern of the lay speaker in the beginning. It is advisable to structure your speech so that the humor comes across as well on tape or just listening to a speaker with your eyes closed as it does in the total sense of seeing, hearing, feeling. One good technique that some speakers use in developing material is to tape record their presentations without any audience whatsoever. Then listen back to the remarks made and try to visualize the weak points from a purely auditory standpoint. Once this has been made as strong as possible, then you may concern yourself with the second step, that of adding the necessary visual effects. This point was driven home very clearly to me recently while traveling in an automobile. I was tuned to a radio station that carried only the auditory portion of a television show. Even though the visual interpretation was completely imaginary, the program was just as enjoyable to me because of the clarity of the material involved. The media has done an excellent job in this respect. Television writers are well aware that many people may be out of the room during a television show but still do not miss any of the content if they keep their ears open. If you doubt this, just turn your television set on sometime and listen to your favorite program without watching the action. You will find, as I have, that the auditory portion has been presented in such a professional manner that very little, if any, is lost when you are not viewing the picture. Then imagine how much more pleasant it can be, and usually is, when you are able to add another sense to your arsenal of humor. Learn to structure your humor this way, with a firm foundation of material that has supplementary visual gestures to enhance your total performance. A good case in point is the famous Amos 'n Andy radio show which aired for thirty years during 1929–59. The show was heard by an estimated 42 million people on a regular basis and was so popular that movie theaters would stop a film to pipe in the program. The power of the well-structured comedy routine is undeniable. It is the power of the word.

Depend on Listeners

Look to the audience for help, win their sympathy, empathy, and approval. An eloquent senator, William E. Borah, stated it plainly, "The effectiveness of a speech is determined largely by the inspiration, or the assistance, which a speaker receives from listeners."

You have probably already observed that it is extremely easy to speak to an audience that is already on your side. For instance if you should happen to be an officer, say, in a district service club at the annual convention, the crowd will make you feel like a king before you ever approach the platform. That is because everyone present has something in common. What do you do when you do not have anything in common with the audience? "Knock and the door shall be opened, ask and ye shall receive." It may be up to you on occasions to provide the atmosphere and win a hearing in spite of the audience.

How do you do this? Here's one way. As a touring speaker on the Knife and Fork Club circuit, I was faced with addressing over 250 clubs throughout the nation with whom I had little in common.

These were black tie affairs, often very reserved and stuffy as far as the atmosphere is concerned. I quickly decided that if this was to be an enjoyable experience, I had to know more about each audience. My plan and policy was simple, but even more effective than I had suspected it might be. I got into the banquet room as early as they would let me. There was always a few people, early birds, who were seated at their favorite tables. I made a habit of approaching each table in a systematic order, starting with those up front because you want the front lines on your side. The line I found most effective in building a public relations program involved a subtle bit of humor; "Hello, I'm Doc Blakely. I'm not running for a thing, and I'm not selling insurance. I'm a speaker here tonight and just wanted to stop by and say 'hello' before we get started. When this meeting is over, I know you folks are going to scatter like a covey of quail and I may never get a chance to personally thank you for coming out tonight."

This bit of humor invariably broke the ice of formality and most everyone opened up their hearts and minds. I can't count the number of times someone came up to me after a meeting and said something like, "Of all the speakers we have ever had at this meeting, you are the first one who has ever come out into the audience and showed that he cared for us." The point is quite simple. If you want to win the support of an audience, seek it out. Knock and the door shall be opened.

Stimulate Memory with Visuals

My friend, Murray Raphel, who owns his own advertising firm in Atlantic City, New Jersey is also a professional speaker. Although his seminars and speeches mainly revolve around advertising and communications, Murray has a great creative imagination, especially with the use of humor. His business card is both the most eye-catching and the most humorous I've ever seen. The card is folded over and when you open it, a tiny cardboard typewriter unfolds. This is appropriate for an ad man, one who makes his living communicating through the written word. However, the most creative part of this typewriter is that inside the carriage, another pop-up appears. It is a tiny sheet of paper that stands erect just like we have all seen so many times in the business office. Upon close examination, I was startled to find that I could actually read the tiny words written on the paper in the tiny typewriter. By using all lower case letters he created a piece of visual humor that was sheer genius. It reads:

am i the typewriter you've been looking for?
i type ads, direct mail and speeches. i even give speeches.
now when's the last time you saw a talking writer type? (or a talking typewriter?).

Murray Raphel

These cards cost several dollars each, but through the skilled use of creative thinking and visual humor, nobody that receives one is ever likely to forget the man that gave it to him. With a little imagination, a few lines from this book, and this clever idea, you may be able to capitalize on visual humor in a way that neither of us imagined.

Show and Tell

As a speaker, I am always aware of the reaction of an audience even when I'm a member of one. Once while a member of the audience at my local Rotary Club in Wharton, Texas, we were privileged to have a group of visiting Englishmen from Rotary International. Each one was a guest of a Texan Rotarian. Each was expected to say a few words to the club. Each Englishman approached the platform to be introduced by his American host. The first three speakers were typical—"Bring you greetings . . . nice to be here . . . wonderful hospitality . . . friendliest chaps . . ." When the last pair came up to the platform, it was evident from the very beginning that this was going to be something different. The Texan was wearing a cap reminiscent of Sherlock Holmes (checkered, ear flaps, a bill front and back) and the Englishman was wearing a 10-gallon hat. Both were witty in their remarks and caustic in their humorous barbs thrown out toward each other.

This was a bit of show and tell magic which "set up" the crowd for good humorous lines and stories. Both these men had visited previously in England and now it was the American's turn to play host. Both were very short by English or American standards. In his cowboy hat, the Englishman, Roy Clark, commented on his first glimpse of his companion, Les Kincaid. You must now imagine a very short Englishman, wearing a huge formal English medallion around his neck, topped off by a blue cowboy hat. "When we first heard the Texans were coming, my wife and I went down to the station to meet them. Now keep in mind, neither me or my wife have ever been out of England. When the Americans got off the train, they were all wearing these huge hats, all with cowboy boots, all smoking big cigars . . . and looking like they were about to spit. They were supposed to stay in our home and we were to pick out a guest. My wife turned to me and said, 'I'm not havin' one,' and left." Roy continues, "So there I was, walking around, looking up at all these gigantic people, when I bumps into this little short fellow who hits me just about the chest. It was Les." He went on to explain about the medallion around his neck, called a gong, which signifies his rank as president of the Rotary Club in England. "We're very stuffy over there you know, but Les Kincaid certainly helped to take a bit of the wind out of our sails. We went to a wedding party, dressed in our formal attire, with my official medallion and all. At the precise moment when a hush fell over the entire reception party, Les said in a rather loud voice, Wouldn't it have been a lot less embarrassing if you had brought a present?"

There's a great lesson in communication, showmanship, good humor, and show and tell. It's a lesson you can use as well. Next time you are to do a humorous presentation, simply consider all the possible items that could be used to visually illustrate some of your points. It could be a brochure, pens, pencils, cards, checkbooks, a claw hammer, the list is endless. One speaker friend of mine, Dr. Don Newbury, uses a variety of visual gags. One of the most sophisticated is a battery operated telephone which he conceals on his person. In the middle of his presentation, the phone rings. He keeps talking until about the third ring and finally turns to the audience and says, "Is anybody going to answer that phone?" When it rings again, he reaches inside his coat, pulls out the receiver, says, "Hello," turns to the audience and says, "Oh, it's for me." Then he launches into a hilarious routine about someone calling from a massage parlor for some prominent member of the audience. Without "show," it is doubtful if the "tell" part of this brand of humor could be pulled off as effectively.

Avoid Common Pitfalls

There are many pitfalls to avoid in speaking, but three are especially important and should be kept in mind for the humorous presentation.

First, never apologize to an audience. The only exception would be if you were late for an engagement. Even then, it is best to try to humorize the situation and make light of it. Audiences don't want to hear if you are not feeling well, not qualified, not prepared, or let's face it, not going over well. You can only be responsible for doing the best job possible, the audience must be responsible for themselves. An apology is dull and boring and detracts from your image as a carefree, fun-loving performer.

Secondly, don't be too general in your comments. It is better to get down to specifics, usually two or three points, some think even one is best. Jack Benny was always stingy, Rodney Dangerfield never gets any respect, Dean Martin always has booze on his mind (although occasionally, he could be distracted by girls). Even to this day, girls and booze are about as specific as Dean cares to get.

The third pitfall to avoid is never to close your speech with a meaningless "thank you." This is the most common mistake made on the American platform today. If you have truly done your job, the audience should be thanking you. Also since humor is doing the unexpected, give them something for their money. Red Skelton ends with a "God Bless," Walter Cronkite used "That's the way it is . . .," Paul Harvey uses "Good day." If you are a man addressing a group of women, you might try closing with an unusual quote like the one from W. C. Fields, "Ah yes, it was a woman who drove me to drink . . . and I never even wrote and thanked her for it." That's a clever way of saying thank you to the ladies, but avoiding the pitfall of using the old cliche.

Stick to Time Schedule

One of the worst sins on the American platform today is talking too long. Many amateur speakers fear that they will not be able to fill up the time allotted to them, but shortly after the "bug bites" and they start liking this experience, it's amazing how time flies. The result is that often a speaker, even a good one, over stays his welcome.

It is best to find out exactly how long the program is supposed to be before you accept the invitation to speak. Have a clear under-standing with your client or person extending the invitation exactly how long you are to take on the program. Then, just prior to the meeting, double check with the meeting planner to make sure the schedule has not been changed. It is a very common experience among professionals to have a meeting planner lean over and whis-per to you during your introduction something like, "We are behind schedule. Please cut your remarks down from the 1 hour we talked about to 15 minutes." Be prepared, be sensible, be professional enough to be able to do this. This is where pride can enter in and mar your relationship with someone who has invited you to speak.

It is an all too common occurrence for a speaker to decide "I was invited to speak for an hour and I'm going to take an hour." You can not win under these circumstances. Everybody will be uncomfortable . . . especially you.

Then again, you may never be rushed for time. It is a good idea to establish personal limits on your own to detect when you have been on long enough. Some speakers can go for hours and not tire the audience. Others fall far short of this mark and realize that is the case. One speaker I know always spoke exactly 30 minutes. You could almost set your watch by his performance. I asked once why he never spoke any longer than that when the audience was obviously begging for more under time favorable circumstances. His answer was, "Because I've never been criticized for talking too short."

Use Audience Jargon

Gene Perret, a friend of mine, is head writer for the Bob Hope specials. One great lesson in comedy I have learned from Gene's creative genius is to search for terms that will give you inside jokes with an audience. For instance, he once visited me in my home town of Wharton, Texas, population 10,000. Since this is a small town, everybody knows everyone else and their business. Gene very quickly picked up on this and asked a few questions prior to addressing the local Rotary Club at lunch. He asked me for the name of the smallest town in close proximity to Wharton that would be recognized by all the members. I gave him the name of Glen Flora, population probably less than 100. His opening line to the local Rotary Club was, "Great to be here in Wharton . . . gateway to Glen Flora." Also aware that everyone in town knew of my profession as an after-dinner humorist, his second line was "It's always a pleasure to be back in Texas, to see Doc Blakely, and visit my old jokes."

This is a great lesson for all of us to learn. When dealing with any audience, ask your contact what terms are used frequently by the attendees and what is general knowledge among them that they might be surprised to learn you are also aware. Why is that funny? Simply because you are using their inside terms. Two basic ways of accumulating this inside information are recommended by Perret: Ask and listen. What are hot topics among the members? What terms do they use? If it is strictly a local audience, ask questions about the area. One word of caution: Before depending upon local references, check with several in the audience to make sure that they are aware of the inside nature of such a remark. It is deadly to speak to a large audience and tell an inside joke that only the head table can understand.

Listening to conversations, particularly at cocktail parties, is a great way to pass the time in a very interesting manner and also to come up with some great ideas. Using Gene's technique, I overheard conversations during the happy hour preceding dinner for a large corporation where I was engaged to speak. One group, District 11, had engaged in a particularly wild escapade the night before. It seemed the whole district had partied far too much and wound up the night in a burlesque house called "The Body Shop" immediately across the street from the hotel. By listening, I discovered a disturbance had ensued, police were called and a few of the members narrowly missed a ride in the paddy wagon. My opening line was, "What a pleasure it is to address this distinguished group . . . in addition to District 11." That line brought hilarious laughter from District 11 and wild applause from the rest of the crowd. Then I added, "the only district I know of that has two headquarters . . . The Body Shop and the Police Station." More laughter, more applause, and we were off to a beautiful start that never ceased to flow in a hilarious direction. These two lines can probably never be used again. But they were exactly right for the situation at hand. They stunned the audience, because of the inside nature of the stories known to an outsider and the use of jargon that is characteristic to a specific group of people. Humor can be a valuable tool for any speaker. Ask the proper questions and keep your ears open to make that big response not only possible, but probable through the use of inside jargon.

Be Genuinely Nice

One of the first rules in using humor is to remember that the old adage "nice guys finish last" is absolutely untrue when speaking from the platform. It is important to project a likeable image from the lectern. It is more important to be a genuinely nice person at all times. Former astronaut, Frank Borman, and former Miss America, Marilyn Van Derbur, are notable examples, in my opinion, of nice persons who have earned the respect of their audience both on and off the stage.

Frank Borman had just returned from a trip to outer space. He spoke to a very large convention, and much to my surprise, appeared at a reception afterwards at some distance from the hotel. At the time, my two small boys were accompanying my wife and me, but had remained at the hotel in the care of a babysitter provided by the convention. I remarked to Frank Borman that I wished I had known he was going to be here because my boys would have been thrilled to meet him. Then I added, "But I bet you're not going to stay very long, are you?" He replied, "Well, as a matter of fact, I was just getting ready to leave. How long would it take you to go back to the hotel and get the boys?" I apologized, "Thanks for your thoughtfulness, but it would probably take an hour in this traffic." Without hesitation, he replied, "Why don't you go ahead and get them and I'll delay my departure until after we've had a chance to visit." Upon returning to the reception with my small children, I was impressed at the time that astronaut Borman spent with them, speaking on their level. Not once did he tell them what a great man he was or what he had accomplished. Instead he asked if they had any questions about outer space, and when those had been satisfied, proceeded to ask them questions about what they intended to do, what interests they had, and as much as possible, philosophizing about life in general through the eyes of a six and eight year old. Believe me, from that day on to this day, Frank Borman has my full attention when he speaks, either as an astronaut, as President of Eastern Airlines, or as a nice guy.

Another example is the female image projected by Marilyn Van Derbur. I first met Miss Van Derbur shortly after she had won the title of Miss America, when she appeared at a social reception prior to a speaking engagement. Again, I did not expect her to appear at the reception because of her celebrity status. At the time, I had not even considered becoming a professional speaker myself, but was merely interested in hearing her remarks as a member of the audience. Therefore, I had no professional or personal credentials to impress her with. She has always had a radiant personality, and I was standing around like so many others just hoping to get a glimpse of this famous beauty to see what all the fuss was about. To be perfectly frank, I was not terribly impressed until it came my turn to say some niceties like, "Nice of you to come . . . You're sure pretty . . . A credit to your sex . . ." But when she looked into my eyes, it was as if there was two steel rods joining our pupils together only about two feet apart. There was a beautiful, radiant smile and an intense concentration in those eyes as if she could look right through my skull into the jello where my brain used to be. No matter how many people tried to get her attention during "my time," no matter how much distraction was going on around us, her gaze and attention was strictly focused on me. Rather than tell me about herself, she asked very pertinent questions about me. She seemed genuinely interested in my answers. When it appeared that she was completely satisfied that I had no more questions or remarks to direct toward her and had taken my leave, then, and only then did she turn to the next person in the crowd surrounding her. Needless to say, when Marilyn spoke that night, if I sensed it was a laugh she was looking for, I gave it to her. If she wanted someone to cheer, I'd gladly be the first one on top of the table. We have since worked together on rallies and at conventions, but my initial impression has never changed. I am still one of her most devoted fans; the same can be said for Frank Borman. As the old saying goes, "If you would have a friend, be one." Nice guys . . . and girls . . . do finish first in this business.

Build Suspense with Words

A serious speaker friend of mine once described the thrill of speaking as "observing the hush that falls over an audience when I go for their souls." You can create the same kind of atmosphere through appropriate suspense building just before a humorous zinger is used to burst the bubble of tension that you have created.

Here's a way to create some high interest and tension. Simply pause, crane your neck outward, and take a good hard look at all the exits in the room where you are speaking. Then in hushed tones, ask your audience, "Are all the doors closed?" If they're not, suggest somebody close them. Then announce, "I have been trying to decide whether or not I should tell you this." Allow a second or two to elapse, then continue, "I think this city (town, association, etc.) is ready for this. Please don't let this go any further than this room. This is a secret between you and me." Don't you see how the tension has already begun? I sometimes use this technique by adding an additional comment like, "Are there any newspaper reporters here?" It's amazing to me that invariably newspaper reporters will slump down into their seats and I have never had one announce that he is there. But, you can bet your bold type that you have everyone's attention from the newspaper reporter on. "If there are any reporters here, please don't print this in your paper."

Now the crowd is on the very edge of suspense. They don't know if you are going to divulge some great secret, spread gossip, or start a scandal. All they know is they want to know what you have in mind. That's when you hit them with a line like, "Charlie Smith wears dirty underwear." This will be especially funny if Charlie Smith is well known and has a good sense of humor. Most people will think that this is the punch line. It isn't. It is a pre-punchline. The follow-up is "I know he wears dirty underwear, because I heard someone say he had been coming to these meetings for 20 years and in all that time, Charlie had never changed."

As I have so often said sometimes material on paper looks rather drab. If you doubt that this piece of material will work, just try it somewhere. Use the method I have described word for word (except change the name of Charlie Smith . . . wise guy) and you'll see. It works.

Use Smooth Transitions

It is important to know how to get from one joke to the next without getting lost in the process. Getting from one line or joke to another line or joke in a speech is an art. The vehicle for this transition is usually called a segue.

Select any two jokes or any two lines that appeal to you, that you feel are funny. Then use a segue to go from one to the other. A segue is just any smooth logical transition from one scene to the next. Suppose you have a funny routine about doctors and another about religion that you wish to incorporate into a talk. A logical segue at the end of the medical material might be something like. "A doctor is a skilled practioner (now the segue); in many ways, he is similar to the Pope. Both think they are closer to God than the rest of us. Now don't you Catholics get offended. Religion can be a very healthy experience too. . . ." The audience doesn't realize you have taken them from point A to point B. It is obvious that this transition is not easy, it will require some deep thought on your part, but if it is done right, it is a joy to segue your journey through to a successful completion of a humorous speech.

Apply "Senses" with Humor

Too many speakers rely on only one or two senses, like the sense of sight or sound. On occasions, it is a good idea to throw in another sense or two to add variety to your presentation. For instance, the sense of odor could be appealed to with a line like, "I had to scold my wife recently for opening a perfumed letter sent to me by a businesswoman. I told her that in the first place, she's not supposed to read my letters, and in the second place, she's not supposed to smell my letters. That smell was addressed to me." Search for other stories that appeal to the other senses and you'll add the spice that is missing even from the speeches of many seasoned speakers.

Make them feel the cold, hear the crash, touch the thorns, smell the roses.

There are some jokes that border on the absurd. One such example almost defies verbal explanation but I think you will get the picture in the following example. Suppose you have just had a rotten meal at your local club and you are to present the program. The audience is in a foul mood because of the slow service and poor food. You can gain the sympathy of the audience as well as their forgiveness for the situation through the use of humor. Even if the people responsible for the meal are in the room, you can still get away with a pungent jab and very probably save the day with a comment like, "Some of you may have noticed that the roast beef was dry, the service left something to be desired but personally I found the whole meal to be a delightful experience except for one thing. The coffee was too hot." Then lift your coffee so that only the cup is visible to the audience. Turn it slightly to the other side to reveal a spoon. It's handle dropping down the side as if melted but actually only bent to give the impression. The tension may just evaporate into smiles and grins. Someone will laugh. It is the perfect visual joke—absurd, yes, but a brilliant contrast of rebuke and relief. Above all, it is kind. Humor has saved the day and put you off on the right foot in an otherwise difficult situation.

Work with Emcees

Occasionally, you may work with a naturally witty person as a master of ceremonies who sets up the audience in a delightful way. This is always a real pleasure because the Emcee "warms up" the audience for your presentation. On occasions, it works in the opposite manner and it behooves you to be ready for this possibility. Listen carefully while the Emcee is working, and try to play on something he has said or done during the course of introducing people in the audience or introducing you. I worked in Chicago once at an after-dinner banquet celebrating the annual district conference for District 645 of Rotary International, the birthplace of Rotary. This was a tremendous affair and a great Emcee really had the audience in stitches. He had the unusual gift of putting things in rhyme and introduced all of the people at the head table in this manner. People on either side of me leaned over with words of encouragement like, "How on earth are you going to top that?" It wasn't going to be easy, but I was determined to find a way. Then I began to notice a trend. When the rhyme material first started, it was extremely funny, but it was carried on just a little bit too far, and began to drag; not much, but just enough that everyone was ready to drop it. To the Emcee's everlasting credit, he did exactly that. Then, he launched into my introduction and gave me a great, witty, stinging intro. He had asked in advance if I minded and I readily encouraged him to do exactly that. The audience had almost forgotten that the rhyming mechanism was about to get on their nerves, but I quickly brought it back with my opening line: "Jim, we have listened to your poetry as fresh as a breeze. If you ever live your life over again, live it overseas." The result was a deafening roar from the crowd and an equally appreciative Emcee. We had both capitalized on the spur of the moment. Will the line ever work again? Yes, if the situation ever arises again—which may be never. Then again it may happen tomorrow.

Comfort the Uncomfortable

Many times people are uncomfortable using humor because it puts them in an embarrassing light. This is especially true of a reserved, dignified person. For some reason, it is uncomfortable for them to act the part of a buffoon even if it is only acting it out in words. However, these same people often are quite comfortable telling about some silly dream they had because this gives them an easy way out of an embarrassing situation. Everyone knows no one is responsible for what they dream.

This is a great way to use an imaginative piece of material. Simply tell it as a dream on yourself. In fact, there are even jokes about dreams. Like the truck driver who went to see a psychiatrist and told the shrink that he was worn out because he kept dreaming every night that he was making a long run to Denver. The psychiatrist told him to simply concentrate before he went to sleep on calling his psychiatrist who would gladly volunteer to drive his truck to Denver. The plan worked beautifully, and for several weeks, the truck driver got much needed rest. Then one day he appeared in the office again complaining that he was worn out now because in his dreams, he had Dolly Parton and Angie Dickenson coming over to his house and keeping him up. The doctor asked, "Why didn't you call me as usual and I would've come over and helped out?" The truck driver replied, "I tried, but every time I called, they said you were in Denver."

Think on Your Feet

Steve Allen is a master showman, a quick wit, one who is able to think on his feet. If you do any amount of speaking, you will eventually develop the ability to be creative in this way also. Once you discover something by accident that works, it is merely a matter of recreating the scene and making it work again. Steve Allen had as one of his sponsors in the early days of the Tonight Show a manufacturer of Fiberglass. Allen's commercial consisted of nightly slamming the Fiberglass chair with a hammer, thereby demonstrating the strength of this strange, new material. One night as spun glass is wont to do, the chair breaks—absolutely shatters into a dozen humiliating pieces. Looking up from the wreckage, never skipping a beat, Allen smiles, "That's right, ladies and gentlemen, this HAMMER is made of Fiberglass."

This experience has since been recreated in many different ways with Steve's personal appearances. The next time something goes wrong with one of your presentations, even if you didn't think up a great line, think about what you could have said. It may be the beginning of a brand new piece of material.

Adapt Like a Pro

There are approximately 500 young comedians in the country today making a fairly decent living. The average age is in the early 30's, and although these humor merchants make large salaries and are able to work Las Vegas nightclubs, they usually are far less effective on the convention circuit. That's one reason you don't see many of them there. It's not that conventions can't afford their fees, the truth of the matter is their form of humor is directed toward a different type of audience. Strangely enough, the people who are most effective on the corporate convention circuit, conventions, associations, service clubs, and other business meetings are the older speakers. So if you find yourself in the over 35 category, take heart; you may be just entering your prime as a purveyor of mirth.

The older you get, generally the funnier you get. Some say we get wiser, and the wise speaker realizes that age does funny things to many parts of us. If we not only look funny but act funny, just think how much more entertaining that is to a crowd than some young, good-looking kid standing in front of an audience who has to make do with only raw talent.

Here's another great difference. The average comic on the nightclub circuit can work New York or Los Angeles with 12 good minutes and get booked on the talk shows if they have 9 CLEAN minutes. In all probability, you will not have the luxury of developing such a short routine. The world in which we find ourselves demands much more. You must make humor a constant study and discipline your true companion. The older, wiser speakers are the only ones who can compete in the business market. Want to know how you get older and wiser? Here's how. I was speaking to the West Virginia Realtors Association in Parkersburg, West Virginia. I had been invited to make the keynote address at the opening session, which began at 9:00 a.m. My instructions were to speak for one hour. This was to be followed by a two-hour break allowing the convention participants to view the exhibits before the noon luncheon. As the flags were being presented in the opening ceremonies, someone rushed a note to the president, who anxiously read it, pondered the message for a few seconds, then leaned over and whispered to me, "We're afraid that too many people will leave during the break and may not attend the luncheon. We've just received word that the Governor will be able to speak at the luncheon and we want to have a capacity audience for him. How about talking until 11:45 before you let them go?" That's just one hour and 45 minutes longer than I had anticipated speaking. Without any visible emotion, I smiled, nodded politely and said, "Drop dead." It didn't work. The president expected me, as a professional, to be able to perform under any circumstances. Fortunately, because I have a depth of material and am used to conducting seminars lasting up to many hours, it was not an impossible task. During the necessary preliminary remarks and introductions of important people, I was able to collect my wits and mentally lay out a plan to fill the two hours and 45 minutes with meaningful material and lots of humor. Now I know what they mean when they use the term "Old Pro." What is the point? Keep studying, keep learning, you'll never know when you'll be called upon to do the unusual. And above all, keep your sense of humor, you may need it. It's like the old lady being interviewed on her 100th birthday, who answered the question, "How did you live to be this old?" She answered, "By not dyin', you clown."

Practice and Polish for Payoff

The ancient philosophers were convinced that orators were great people. Why? Because a person speaks not only with words, but with all that he or she has, and a bad person could simply not be an effective speaker. Philosophically, we would all agree with that, but it is only fair to note that Mussolini and Hitler persuaded millions and their reputation is a bit on the tainted side.

For the most part, however, it behooves us to be the kind of person who would work for good rather than evil, who would polish his or her life in a way to create the most beneficial impact of total personality. Simply stated this means that if you would shine in the light of a good performance, polish your techniques by living the standards that you profess to support in public.

As Quintilian wrote, "It must be allowed that learning does take away something, as the file takes something from rough metal, the whetstone from blunt instruments, and age from wine; but takes away what is faulty; and that which learning has polished is less only because it is better."

So, practice and polish your best efforts to shine through like a pro. Here is a good example of polished, condensed humor: a journalist received a letter from a doctor in Oklahoma who found exception with an article the journalist had written. The doctor demanded an apology for what he considered an offensive article, and stated, "You have insulted the President and every intelligent citizen of Oklahoma." The Texas journalist wrote back, "I'm sorry for insulting the President of the U.S. and every intelligent citizen of Oklahoma. Please convey my regrets to both of them."

While that is great humor, it may not be good philosophy. Follow these suggestions and your speeches will come alive. Speak on what you believe in. Let yourself feel the full importance of what you say and how you say it. Respond emotionally to your thoughts and words as you deliver them. Never alienate your audience.

From Hobby to Career

Many professional speakers started their careers by promoting their businesses or their hobbies as a lay speaker. They simply enjoyed what they were doing, were enthused about it, became good at it, and were faced one day with the choice of remaining in business or going into a new one. Whether this may eventually be the case with you or not is immaterial, but don't think you are going to become a great lay or pro speaker overnight. Don't get discouraged either, but keep plugging away. Most agents say it takes about 2,000 talks before you really get good at it. If you happen to fall into that category, you may one day replace people like the late Jessica Savitch, of NBC who, in addition to her job, did 365 speeches per year. Author Isaac Asimov, science fiction writer, earns $10,000 each for his estimated 200 annual appearances. In his spare time, he has also written 201 books.

This information should encourage you, not stand in your way as a barrier. Find a subject you are interested in, think of a message, jot down every idea that comes to your mind, and you may be able to capitalize in your business, writing, or who knows, you may be competition for the professionals one day . . . and soon. Quintilian explained it this way: "To become a great speaker, you first become an outstanding, knowledgeable person who speaks well."

Talk Ain't Cheap

To gain a greater appreciation of the value of the spoken word, perhaps it would be good to look at a few of the better known names in the business and the value placed upon their chosen words. Ralph Waldo Emerson's fee was $5 plus his dinner. My, how times have changed. Parade Magazine reports the fee of Bob Hope is $30,000 plus expenses, Art Buchwald gets about $3,500, and most lesser known professional humorists are somewhere around Buchwald's range. It is reported that Ralph Nader earns a total of $800,000 per year speaking, but it's doubtful that anyone can match his brand of humor . . . or would want to.

So, why would a meeting planner want to spend that kind of money for a professional when so many people are willing to do it for free? If you've ever been to a really important meeting and heard a truly poor presentation, you'll understand the old adage: "Talk ain't cheap and free speakers may be overpaid." The changing times demands good material and confident, polished performers. You have in your hands some great raw material, but it is up to you to make it shine through practice and additional study.

Situation Humor

4

Doc Blakely addresses the WesPac Investment group in Honolulu. Standard attire in Hawaii is native and casual. Just what the Doctor ordered.

A Heart Attack—Never Again

As a former member of the Board of Directors of the National Speakers Association, I have participated in nearly every convention since the NSA was formed in 1975. However, I have developed a reputation among the attendees, not as a performing humorist, but as a teacher of techniques. We have plenty of performers who are gifted in the art, but it always seemed to be my gift to teach concepts to the newer members, and hopefully to some of the professionals. I spend a lot of time on these programs and try to make them not only entertaining, but as meaningful as possible. I have always taken a great deal of pleasure in creating original programs and when I was asked to conduct a seminar on "What To Do When The Lights Go Out and Other Calamities," I was flattered to have been assigned such a meaningful subject. I was told by the Program Chairman to cover the subjects of poor PA systems, bad lighting, hecklers, and anything else I thought worthy of mentioning. The training session was designed not only to present problems, but to offer answers to them.

One of the subjects I wanted to cover was what to do when someone in the audience has an emergency medical condition—the most obvious emergency being a heart attack. I have actually had this emergency arise while speaking and several of my friends have had experiences where the condition was fatal. Needless to say, the speaker is in a very difficult position, but also one of responsibility since he has the microphone and if he is quick witted, can give directions and perhaps even save a life.

With this original thought in mind, as only a small portion of the total program, I decided that my audience would never realize the importance of the actual occurrence unless they saw it happen in person. I decided to stage a heart attack in the audience. I spoke to no one about this idea because I was quite sure that it would be rejected by all those in charge of the program. I selected my good friend Bob Jansen, a fellow speaker from Wauwatosa, Wisconsin, intuitively knowing that he would not turn down my request. Bob is the perfect type for this ploy. Although he is in robust health, he is at the age which no one would doubt the occurrence of a heart attack. He is rotund, jolly, and lovably loud enough so that nearly everyone at the convention knew him.

Only six people in the audience of 400 knew that this heart attack was going to happen. They included Bob, me, and the person on either side of Bob. Without ever mentioning medical difficulties, I had Bob keyed in to put on his act right after I had told a joke and the laughter had died down. With perfect timing, Bob keeled over in the audience and his friend, Dottie Walters, also with perfect timing, screamed, "This man's having a heart attack."

What occurred after that even amazed me. I had never seen such shock and pandemonium sweep over an audience before. The aisles became clogged, several medically trained people were making their way to the front, crawling over others to get there, and a general uncontrolled atmosphere prevailed. It was even more dramatic than I had hoped for. Quickly taking the initiative, I maintained control of the audience with the microphone, asked the people to be seated, remain calm, keep the aisles clear, and almost in the same breath, asked if there was an EMT (Emergency Medical Technician) in the audience. A friend who had also been asked to play the part of an EMT rushed forward, examined the patient, and pronounced "We need an ambulance, quick." Still maintaining control of the audience, I calmly asked the person in charge of the room, stationed at the door, to step outside and call an ambulance. This was also a set-up. She disappeared, but did not follow through with the phone call. By this time, the audience had calmed somewhat and were cooperating beautifully, but still obviously very concerned. Their eyes were still riveted on Bob Jansen who was slumped across a couple of chairs.

I detached the microphone and walked over to Bob's prostrate form. I turned to the audience and said, "Folks, you are going to see one of the most miraculous cures you have ever seen in your life. Bob Jansen, I now pronounce you healed. Stand up." Then, I explained to the audience that he had been acting out the part and so had I in order to show them, rather than just talk about what you should do when there is an emergency in the audience. There was great relief, applause, a lot of laughter, and appreciation initially. Later on, a lot of the members began to worry about what could have happened. Many of them, after thinking it over, wanted to kill me.

It was a calculated risk on my part. The pandemonium was so severe that I realize now a heart attack from some other member could have actually been stimulated because of my creative bent toward showmanship. Although nothing did happen, and I defended my position with this philosophy, I do not recommend it to anyone else and can personally promise that I will never try it again.

Having dramatically made my point, however, and achieved many accolades for the manner in which I did it, there was an extra bonus which neither I nor Bob had anticipated. Unknown to the rest of us, Bob Jansen had confided, afterwards, that he had never felt very popular at these meetings. Although he was a "laugh a minute," he did not have the self-esteem that he would like to have had in knowing that people really and truly cared for him. Bob became an instant celebrity and spent the rest of the convention shaking hands with hundreds of his fellow speakers. To quote Bob, "The workshop ended, but not for me. People stood in line to tell me how relieved they were that I hadn't had a real heart attack. One woman even cried. . . . For the first time in my life, I felt that people had a genuine interest in me. They were glad it was only a hoax and said so. The sun shines a little brighter for me now. I'm standing a little taller. I've had a look into what might have been. I feel privileged to have had the experience (But I would never, ever do it again)."

Response to a Comedy Writer

My friend, Gene Perret, comedy writer, previously mentioned, called one day and said he would like to visit. We had a wild and wacky couple of days and during that time, he mentioned that his personal style of writing humorous one-liners was to write 30 lines about one subject before going to another. Most writers stop at 20 to 25, but Gene said his best material often came from those last extra lines.

Keeping that thought in mind, note how I tried his philosophy and let him know he had impressed me with this technique, without directly mentioning that I was using it. Gene wrote a very witty book entitled HIT OR MISS MANAGEMENT and was kind enough to present me with a signed copy as a memento of our visit. Here is the letter just as I sent it. Note how humor can be used to appear cutting but actually show appreciation. Notice also the end of the letter reflects the technique of a "switch" or joke.

October 2, 1980

Do Not
Read In
This Space

1. The quality of your book will never be questioned. In fact I predict it won't ever be mentioned.
2. Hit or Miss Management—I thought it was a novel about a beauty contest run by the Mafia.
3. This book is a work of art comparable to the Venus de Milo. She has no arms. Perret has no taste.

4. I laughed and laughed. Then I laid this wonderfully funny book down and read yours.

5. A word to the wise is sufficient. The word is underwhelming.

6. Where else but in America could such equal opportunity exist? Both Blakely & Perret are writers. Of course, it's like saying Phyllis Diller & Dolly Parton are the same sex.

7. Some writers seek greatness, some achieve greatness, and some merely have greatness thrust upon them. In all three categories, you have no place.

8. Your book will make managers wiser. They won't buy your next one.

9. Chapter 3 on decisions was a turning point for me. I decided to skip it.

10. HIT OR MISS MANAGEMENT provided an evening of entertainment at our recent dinner party. It was just the right number of pages to straighten up the dining table.

11. Your writing style reminded me of Hemingway—Hemingway Garcia, he writes only in a foreign language.

12. Your style is hefty—garbage surrounded by plastic.

13. Take away the ink, the promo, the glitter and glamor, and what do you have? Perret's philosophy.

14. I predict your book will make the best-seller list. The margins make a dandy place to make the list.

15. The book has drama, pathos, and suspense. Everything but humor.

16. Other writers will be jealous of this work. Then they'll read it.

17. Mark Twain, Will Rogers, and Gene Perret share a common characteristic. Their brain no longer functions.

18. A TV writer who has time to write a book on management will stimulate management to see that he doesn't have time to manage that again.

19. This is a book about the good, bad, and ugly. Employees play the good, management plays the bad. Gene plays himself.

20. The contents of this book will soon be on the screen. I'm gonna throw it through a window.

21. I use my copy to hold down important papers. It's on top of the Charmin'.

22. I was impressed that you could think of that many words. Then I discovered your secret and wasn't all that impressed. You used some of them twice.

23. Technical writers have a wealth of resources and informa-

tion to draw from. What really amazes me is a writer like you who can fill 186 pages with beautiful writing and not say anything.

24. The jacket is well designed with darts hitting well off the mark. Prophetic perhaps, since darts are just miniature bombs.

25. The author appears to have a receding hairline and a beard. Either that or his photo was printed upside down.

26. Books like this are a strong deterrent to crime. All inmates should be forced to read it as punishment.

27. When I read it, my spirits soared like the Titanic.

28. Only a fool would read it and not laugh out loud. Yes, friends, only a fool would read it and not laugh. Well, I may exaggerate, but only about the laughter.

29. The book is as funny as can be . . . and so is Gene Perret. Neither will ever improve.

30. With this book, Gene Perret deserves another Emmy . . . for acting . . . like a writer.

Thought this would be a chance to try your philosophy. It was fun and so were you. You've given me a whole new dimension into the writing business. We thoroughly enjoyed your visit and your presentation to the Rotary Club, but most of all, we just enjoyed getting to know a really pleasant fella' with a wonderful gift and a lot of talent.

Of course, you know that you make me crazy, but I shouldn't mention that because otherwise, you probably would never have noticed.

"Doc" Blakely

By the way, if you are interested in keeping current on comedy writing, techniques in humor, and good information on the comedy writing trade, write for a sample copy of the newsletter *Gene Perret's Round Table, P. O. Box 13, King of Prussia, PA 19406.*

Hunting for Humor

Kent Hill is a close friend, a full time good humor man, and part time lunatic. For several years, we have hunted deer together on the same lease. Having shared the frustrations of cold, wet, miserable hours in search of fulfilling some primeval instinct, we often also share a good laugh over being outwitted by the simple creatures that share our leased domain.

In spite of our complex, sophisticated machinery and equipment, we often yearn for a better way. The following is a remarkable piece of humorous literature sent to me by my partner.

The Deer Hunter

Friday—

Midnight	Leave bar drunk
12:10 a.m.	Stop for breakfast
12:25 a.m.	Throw up
12:45 a.m.	Arrive home
12:50 a.m.	Pass out
1:00 a.m.	Alarm clock rings
2:00 a.m.	Hunting partner arrives, drags you out of bed
2:30 a.m.	Throw everything except kitchen sink in the camper
3:00 a.m.	Leave for the deep woods
3:15 a.m.	Drive back home and pick up gun
3:30 a.m.	Get speeding ticket trying to get to the woods before daylight
4:00 a.m.	Set up camp—forgot tent
4:30 a.m.	Head for deep woods
6:05 a.m.	See (8) deer, take aim, and squeeze trigger
6:07 a.m.	"CLICK"
6:08 a.m.	Load gun while watching deer go over the hill
8:00 a.m.	Head back to camp
9:00 a.m.	Still looking for camp
10:00 a.m.	Realize you don't know where camp is
Noon	Fire gun for help, eat wild berries
12:15 p.m.	Ran out of bullets—deer came back
12:20 p.m.	Strange feeling in stomach
12:30 p.m.	Realize you ate poison berries
12:45 p.m.	Rescued!
12:55 p.m.	Rushed to hospital to have stomach pumped
3:00 p.m.	Arrive back in camp
3:30 p.m.	Leave camp to kill deer
4:00 p.m.	Return to camp for bullets
4:01 p.m.	Load gun and leave camp again
5:00 p.m.	Empty gun on squirrel that's bugging you
6:00 p.m.	Arrive at camp, see deer grazing in camp
6:01 p.m.	Load gun
6:02 p.m.	Fire gun
6:03 p.m.	One (1) dead pickup truck
6:05 p.m.	Hunting partner returns to camp dragging deer
6:06 p.m.	Repress strong desire to shoot partner
6:07 p.m.	Fall into fire
6:10 p.m.	Change clothes, throw burned ones into fire
6:15 p.m.	Pack pickup, leave partner and his deer in the woods
6:25 p.m.	Pickup boils over—hole shot in radiator
6:26 p.m.	Start walking
6:30 p.m.	Stumble and fall, drop gun in the mud
6:35 p.m.	Meet bear
6:36 p.m.	Take aim
6:37 p.m.	Fire gun, blow up barrel plugged with mud
6:39 p.m.	Climb tree
9:00 p.m.	Bear departs, wrap gun around tree
Midnight	Home at last
Sunday	Watch for wild game on TV while slowly tearing license into little pieces, placing into envelope and mailing to game warden with very clear instructions on what he can do with it.
Monday	Go to archery shop and buy a bow!

Lick 'Em or Confuse 'Em

My friend, Tom Curlee, with Central Power & Light Company, in Corpus Christi, Texas has a great sense of humor and appreciation for anyone else with the same quality. When the Light Company was called upon to justify the need for an increase in their rates, Tom's colleague, L. E. Sheppard, Jr., was singled out by the opposition in a hearing. Mr. Sheppard dazzled the opposition with a strange combination of facts, figures, and wit. The opposition could not get a straight yes or no answer, but also could not offer counter evidence that would prove their position. The result was that the hearing was thrown into complete chaos, and although the rate increase was not granted, the opposition was set back in their efforts for a hasty defeat of the proposal.

With that bit of background, you will appreciate the humor involved in this official certificate of appreciation presented to him by his boss, Tom Curlee. The certificate was done in Old English lettering, and as soon as I saw it and inquired about the history, I requested permission from Tom to share it with you. The certificate is presented to L.E. Sheppard, Jr.—for his unique contribution as a rate case witness. It reads:

> *"You did not succeed in answering all your questions. Indeed, we felt you did not completely answer any of them. The answers you gave only served to raise a whole set of new questions. In some ways we felt that there was as much confusion as ever, but the confusion was on a much higher level, and to the extent that the intervenors had cause to regret asking the questions in the first place."*

This is a great example of humor being used to appreciate humor. The tough job of fighting for economic survival for the company was made a little more pleasant in this manner.

Humorous Jurisprudence

Most people would think that legal battles are serious enough that they would be completely devoid of humor. However, one notable exception has come to my attention. Some years ago, the state of Texas claimed the oil rights to offshore drilling which was disputed by the Federal Government. A legal battle ensued between lawyers for the Federal Government and Austen Furse, then Assistant Attorney General for the state of Texas. Some highlights of the case were sent to me by Mr. Furse. The federal district court claimed offshore oil finds for the nation. Texas claimed them for the state and they battled it out in court. Although millions of dollars were at stake, surprisingly both Mr. Furse and his opposing lawyers were able to maintain an air of levity in their legal correspondence and memorandums.

Although only a portion of these memorandums are reported here, it is fascinating reading. The Federal Government maintained that the oil reserves were in the actual possession of "Davey Jones," in whose locker it remains stored. However, this argument, unlike the locker itself, will not hold water.

"Admittedly the Trustee has been unable to retain actual physical possession of the property. The Trustee has been in office for nearly three years, and the world record for staying under water is only thirteen minutes and forty-two and one-half seconds. (Guiness Book of World Records, 1974 edition, p. 51). While the Trustee may have been in hot water at times, he is confessedly not amphibious."

Attorney Furse replied to this memorandum, in part, with the following:

"Trustee's Memorandum, on file herein, having plumbed the depths of salty legal argument, has provoked this reply on the part of Respondents.

It seems that the Trustee in this case, not being endowed with the buoyancy of the Carpenter of Nazareth, *Matt.* 14:25; *Mark* 6:49, insists that he is exercising the only dominion over the property in question of which it is susceptible. None of his divers employees are divers, and he has no merpersons or naiads on his payroll. As for himself, he eschews immersion in the res, and leaves it to his attorneys to be all wet."

Austen made his point that visitation to the area by the Federal Government did not constitute possession, especially of the sub-surface. He closed his memorandum with the following poem:

> "Roll on, thou deep and dark blue ocean, roll!
> Ten thousand fleets sweep over thee in vain!
> The driller's bit must take its gaseous toll,
> The custodia legis to maintain."

A government lawyer responded to this memorandum in proper legal terms but also tendered addendum which reads as follows:

> Water, water everywhere,
>   The drilling rig did sink;
> Water, water everywhere,
>   The lawyers cease to think.
> The issues, like the res itself,
>   Are deep and do perplex us;

> The counsel's rhyme, in maritime,
>   Would drown the State of Texas.
>
> The verse of Furse could be much worse;
>   His Brief remains adrift.
> Through legal sands and sea-filled lands
>   This landlocked Court must sift.
>
> Day after day, night after night,
>   We grapple with this Motion,
> As slippery as a drilling rig
>   Upon the Texas ocean.
> The legal sharks make deadly marks
>   With voices loud and strident;
> But when it's through, the Texas crew
>   Is hoist upon their trident."

Austen Furse continued to represent the State of Texas in a lighthearted manner, using humor to drive home his legal points. Although he was up against stiff competition, both from a legalistic and a humorous standpoint, his strength of purpose and sense of humor eventually prevailed. The State of Texas persuaded a judge to rule in their favor, bringing millions of dollars direct to the state.

Those Accursed Awards

Everyone has been to the local Chamber of Commerce banquet and seen the Citizen of the Year Award presented. These are notoriously dull awards and I'm convinced that there is a contest held to find the person who can do the worst job of keeping the secret a secret until the very end. Invariably, people in the audience will begin to look at one another, raise their eyebrows, and in general, signal to their friends that they have already guessed who the recipient of this award is. Usually, they are exactly right. This is a very difficult assignment, even for the professional.

As a member of my own Chamber of Commerce in Wharton, Texas, I was so vocal about this travesty of justice that I won the contest and was allowed to introduce the Citizen of the Year. The award was unknown even to the recipient. I not only wrote the material based on factual information, but also made the presentation. All through these introductory remarks, I saw people in the audience nodding their head as if they had already guessed who the recipient was. In my humble opinion, this is an excellent example of the use of deception, mild humor, truth, and a great surprise withheld until the very last moment. Imagine you know all the possible recipients, be honest with yourself, and see if you could possibly have guessed the identity of the Citizen of the Year. The idea is original with me, but I think you will find it so good and so simple that you will be able to use it in a similar situation:

The 1981 Citizen of the Year award goes to a most outstanding candidate. She came to Wharton in 1940 in a management position with one of the leading businesses in Wharton County. Under her leadership, the numbers of employees were expanded by 150% over a period of 40 years. She served on the committee to form Wharton County Junior College during the post-planning fever that swept the country and was instrumental in the formation of the Wharton Country Club. She has served on virtually every standing and special committee in the Chamber.

This outstanding citizen was one of the original incorporators of the Wharton Industrial Foundation which has had such a tremendous influence on this area. Over 29 acres and seven businesses with 1½-million dollars in improvements and over one million dollars in payroll can be traced back to her efforts and involvements in this outstanding, progressive achievement.

Although not as famous as the aviatrix, Amelia Earhart, she was directly involved with the building of the airport and has assisted the efforts of the Wharton community through her 14 years of involvement in close cooperation with the City Council. She has been a member of the Board of the South Texas Girl Scout Council and as an equal opportunity developer, also a major office holder in the Wharton County Boy Builders Association. This outstanding citizen has quietly, unassumingly served as president or on the board of 18 prominent foundations or associations for Wharton and Wharton County.

Always a patriotic, freedom-loving citizen, she enlisted during the bi-centennial year in the Wharton Navy, entering with the rank of admiral. Perhaps this association has lead to her often salty description of also having "worked like Hades on state and local politics."

Always a colorful character, this gracious individual has more recently found time to be a charter member of Ducks Unlimited, a patron of the Wharton County Museum, and a life-time member of the Texas Exes Association. Although few may remember it now, in 1970, she was awarded the Jaycee designation as their Citizen of the Year.

Although a strong defender of the University of Texas, this year's outstanding citizen was broad minded enough to send two of her four children to Texas A&M, so at least "someone in the family would have an education." She is married and a member of the St. Thomas Episcopal Church, naturally serving on the Board as administrative layperson.

By now some of you may have guessed the identity of this year's outstanding Citizen of the Year, but I doubt it. The Citizen of the Year recipient is not Superwoman. Even though all of the achievements are true, I have lied about the most important point. The Citizen of the Year is not a Superwoman, but a Super . . . Man . . . Ham Rugeley.

Never too Old

A few years ago, I began to receive material in my mail box from L. M. Blair. It produced a rather vague recollection every time the advertisement crossed my desk. Then one day I stumbled on to the fact that L. M. Blair is a woman. Alone, confined to a wheelchair, in her 80's, L. M. Blair had every right to turn inward, become bitter, and reject the world. She did just the opposite. She began to listen to cassette tapes of motivational, inspirational, and perhaps most importantly, humorous speakers. As a result, she accumulated many thousands of cassette tapes and expanded her mental horizons to such a point that she wanted to share this information with others. Working out of her home and using direct mail, she rents the world's greatest minds for only $1.00 per cassette. Of course, you can purchase the cassette of your choice from L. M. Blair, but, as might be expected of one with a sense of humor, why not just rent a brain for a buck and send it back when you've gleaned the most important ideas? (Discovery Cassette Exchange, P. O. Box 105, Richmond, Missouri 64085). LaVon Blair spreads a little ray of sunshine everywhere she goes whether it is via telephone or by direct mail. She has been confined to a wheelchair for 20 years, but that hasn't stopped her love of life and desire to improve the quality of life for others. LaVon also promoted the Sunshine Diary, a publication for children, which encourages them to write down the happenings every day that make them feel loved, comfortable, important, proud, or happy. Children are encouraged to find at least 3 good things to record, even if the day is a disaster. To quote LaVon, expressing her thoughts to children, "Focus on every little ray you have—be thankful for it and it will grow and grow! You see, sunshine really is magic!" So is laughter, LaVon . . . so is laughter.

Getting it Read

Michael Brown, Arlington, Texas, formerly a Dallas television talk show host, now a professional speaker is a very witty friend. We both belong to the National Speakers Association and have occasion to meet once or twice annually. As usual at these busy meetings, everyone is trying to impress everybody with their wit and charm. For weeks afterwards, we are busy sending notes to each other saying the usual trite things, "glad to see you, etc."

While I always enjoy and appreciate these courteous, thoughtful notes and letters, Michael Brown sent one that got my attention. Original, humorous, satirical, it impressed me in a way that few others ever have. The letter is reprinted below exactly as I received it. This is the kind you don't throw away.

AUG 2, 198_0_

Dear _"Doc"_,

Just a _personal_ note to say how GREAT it was seeing you recently at the _N.S.A. CONVENTION_ in _NEW ORLEANS_

I also enjoyed talking with you in _THE ELEVATOR_. Your warm _HUMOR_ just always seems to shine through, as I hope my _SINCERITY_ does, and I'm glad we can correspond like this on a _PERSONAL_ _LEVEL_.

I think it's important that we as members of _N.S.A._ can share _IDEAS_ by _PERSONAL_ _CONTACT_ such as this letter.

So what if it takes _$10-15 POSTAGE_ to write to the hundreds of my personal friends in _N.S.A._.... isn't it worth it to know we've become such close friends, ~~BILL~~ _DOC_?

Well, I have to run now...I have a lot of other _CLOSE FRIENDS_ that I want to send a personal note to.

SINCERELY,
Michael Brown
Michael Brown

P.S. Won't you take the time now to pre-enroll for my upcoming seminar on _EFFECTIVE_ _COMMUNICATION TECHNIQUES_? Request a brochure and send _$200.00_ cash, in non-sequentially numbered _$10.00_ bills. We'll look forward to hearing from you, ~~JACK~~ _DOC_ ...I'd have to say you're one of my best friends!

Inviting Humor

Robert Henry, professional speaker, colleague and friend, Auburn, Alabama, is a truly witty man. Not only does he look, talk, and act funny, he thinks funny. Here's a case in point. Robert and his family had just built a new house. Since we live many miles apart and we both travel so much, he was reasonably sure I wouldn't be able to attend his house party but he verbally asked me anyway. When I explained that, regrettably, I would be speaking to a convention in Honolulu on that date, he said, "I thought so. You're never gonna make the bigtime if you don't quit taking jobs in out of the way places."

Just to show that his heart was in the right place, Robert sent the following invitation anyway. It's a jewel.

Congratulations!

You have just received the toughest invitation to get in Auburn, Alabama. Because you have received it, you are certified as either: charming, witty, clever, beautiful people, great conversationalist, singer of country songs, "Red Man" tobacco chewer, have a home on Lake Martin, do not care who the hell the next football coach is, any combination or all of the aforementioned. Most importantly, the Henry's think you are very special people.

Therefore, you are invited to the famous Henry's New Year's Eve Party. Produced, catered, directed, and starred in by Robert and Merrilyn Henry. It will begin @ 8:00 p.m. and last until Robert goes to bed. It will be located @ our home in Bent Creek subdivision @ 331 Graystone Lane.

Years from now, when your granchildren are talking about this party, you will be able to say, ". . . child, I was there!"

R.S.V.P—Regrets Only
Phone: 821–2415

The crowning point of humor was driven home even further when I looked at the post mark. It was mailed 3 days after the party was over.

Why Do We Do It?

5

Want to draw a crowd? Use a Platform Professional. (Society of Real Estate Appraisers, Chicago).

Creed for the Laughmaker

The question "Why do we do it" is often asked of the humorist. It does seem like a senseless occupation to spend one's life acting the buffoon. Of what worth is the heart of a clown? Perhaps the "Creed for the Laughmaker," attributed to Merritt K. Freeman, is a fitting tribute to these closing thoughts. It reads:

"Oh Lord, give me this day the ability to make someone laugh. Lend me the power to bring a smile to someone's lips. Grant me the ability to banish misfortune and troubles from the minds of others through the medium of a smile. Give me the power to clown and laugh—to see the laughing eyes of children at all ages. Cast my reflection with an ever-wearing smile so none weary of my presence. Bring to my lips the quips that help me cast joy amongst my fellowmen. Give me the power to share joy with all, the rich or poor, young or old. And lastly, one last favor, give me the right to eavesdrop so that when the final curtain comes down, I can hear someone say: 'He made me laugh.' "

PART III

JOKES: ONE- AND TWO-LINERS

Body language is very important. This shot was taken on a very windy day.

Ads

1. Saw some swell ads in the paper the other day. "Young man, Democrat, would like to meet young lady, Republican. Object: third party!" HENNY YOUNGMAN

2. Ad in The Wisconsin State Journal: "Wife wanted, must have farm experience and own tractor. Please send picture of tractor."

3. In the help-wanted section of a newspaper, this ad appeared: "Wanted, executive, age 22 to 80, to sit with feet on desk, watching other people. Must be willing to take a 20-minute coffee break every afternoon and play golf at least two afternoons a week. Starting salary $1,000 a week. Please understand, we don't have this job open, but we thought you'd like to know what everyone is applying for."

4. A rancher in Texas had to confront the new federal statute prohibiting job classification by sex. He finally ran the following ad in the local newspaper: "Cowperson wanted. Applicant must use profanity and share a bunk house with four male cowpersons who seldom bathe."

5. "Advertising is what makes you think you've longed all your life for something you never heard of before." EARL WILSON

6. "Trash & Treasure Sale" Notice: "Good chance to get rid of everything not worth keeping, but too good to throw away. Bring your husband."

Age

7. Statistics show that three-fourths of all women are secretive about their age. The other fourth lie about it.

8. To keep yourself young, think like a young person. To get old in a hurry, try acting like one.

9. At a New Year's Eve party, an attractive matron asked a younger man to guess her age. "You must have some ideas," she said as he hesitated. "I have several ideas," he admitted with a smile. "The only problem is that I can't decide to make you 10 years younger because of your looks, or 10 years older because of your charm."

10. The old man stroked his chin slowly with the back of his gnarled hand and looked passively at his friends. "Wal," he said,

"to tell you the truth, there was so much goin' on down to the depot I never did get up to the village."

11. A course of solarium treatment had been recommended for an elderly lady. To dispel her nervousness, the consultant told her, "Why, a few weeks of that, and you'll be ten years younger." "Oh, dear," wailed the old lady, "it won't affect my pension, will it?"

12. "In Texas, men are men and women are women and I defy you to improve on a situation like that." Aging single girl: "I don't want to improve on it. I just want to get in on it."

13. A man who had reached the age of 100 was being interviewed on TV. "Mr. Jones," began the announcer, "how do you account for your longevity?" "Toadstools," was the reply. "Toadstools! Really?" "Yup," said Mr. Jones. "Never ate 'em!"

14. An old timer said: "Times are shore getting hard. Pinto beans are 90¢ a pound, smoking tobacco 40¢ a pack and the fish won't bite. If things get any worse, I'm going to have to line up a few more lawns for my wife to mow."

15. An old timer from the Irish hill country took his first trip to a large city. Walking into one of the skyscrapers he saw a doorman standing by a special kind of door. An old woman stepped in, a light flashed red, and she was gone. A few seconds later the elevator descended, the door opened and a beautiful young lady stepped out. "Begorra," said the old man, blinking his eyes. "I should have brought me old lady."

16. With her fortieth birthday approaching, a lady sought advice from her grandmother. "Is it true that life begins at forty?" "Begins to what?" asked Grandma.

17. "How did you live to be 100 years old, Grandma?"
   "By not dying, you clown."

18. Those who reach the century mark sometimes give their formula, such as no liquor, no cussing, no unusual excitement, and hard work. Who wants a hundred years of that?

19. Young people sow oats and old people grow sage.

20. A governor told the Associated Press News Council that a certain aged and manly political colleague was sure to live to be 100 years old, at which time, if he died at all, he would only do so to run for a higher office.

21. A young reporter asked a silent screen siren if she'd mind telling her age. "Not at all," she replied with her famous smile, "I'm plenty-nine."

22. Uncle Fred insists that men and whisky improve with age: "The older I get, the more I like it."

23. When you're young, you do your own thing. When you're old, you send it out and have it done for you.

24. It's the old story. Climb the ladder of success, reach the top and you find you're over the hill.

25. Aunt Edith doesn't waste years; everything she subtracts from her own age, she adds to her sister's-in-law.

26. There's no fool like an old fool. Ask any young fool.

27. The prime of life comes at a point between 16 and 65, depending on the age of the person talking.

28. Bob Hope says: "Well, I got to tell the truth . . . when a girl flirts with me in the movies, these days I figure she's after my popcorn."

29. It's amazing what some coeds can get away with and still keep their amateur standing.

30. You're only young once—during which folks try to make you behave as if you weren't.

31. For every man who lives to be 85, there are seven women, but, of course, by that time, it's too late!

32. Remember when we used to save for our old age instead of for April 15th?

33. You're an old timer if you remember when buying on time meant getting to a store before it closed.

34. You're old when everything hurts—and what doesn't hurt doesn't work.

America

35. "In America, there are two classes of travel: first class and with children." ROBERT BENCHLEY

36. It was a dramatic meeting in the jungles of Tanzania. The trails had crossed and two American explorers, with their parties,

practically collided. As they sat around the campfire that evening, one of the explorers explained his reason for being there. "The urge to travel," he said poetically, "has always surged through my veins. I'm the kind of a fellow who wants to see what's on the other side of the hill. City life nauseates me. The sounds, the filth, the man-made monsters—they're not for me. I seek the companionship of nature—the flutter of the birds, the prattle of the animals, the beauty of the verdant foliage. Now tell me, why did you come?" The second explorer replied, "Creditors."

37.   A marine sentry was on guard duty late one night in a combat zone. He had been warned about some enemy infiltrators who spoke flawless English. Marine sentry: "Halt. Advance and be recognized. Recite the second verse of the Star Spangled Banner." "The second verse? Man, I don't know the second verse!" "Pass. . . . American."

38.   American education is special. What other country teaches calculus and Russian in grade school and remedial reading in college?

39.   The trouble with America's relations back in the old country is that so many of 'em are broke, dead or dead broke.

40.   After years of studying, a European couple finally passed their citizenship exams. When the papers arrived in the mail, the husband rushed into the kitchen with the news: "Maria, Maria, at last we are Americans!" "That's great," she replied, whipping off her apron, "now you can wash the dishes."

41.   America is a great country. We can say what we think and, even if we can't think, we can say it anyway.

42.   The Declaration of Independence is a magnificently written document in America which carried to King George III a simple two-word message: DROP DEAD!

43.   Americans are putting up Christmas decorations so early, I saw a turkey in a pear tree.

44.   I think the anti-litter drive in America is having some success. More and more people are looking in the rearview mirror before they toss trash out of their cars.

45.   If America is a free country, how come I can't afford to live here?

46.   It's ridiculous how expensive modern packaging has become.

Do you realize the average American buys $10 worth of gas and has to take it home in an $8,000 container?

47. Twenty-five percent of Central park is covered with trees and the rest by muggers.

48. At the USO Ball, Bob Hope flew in to honor Chicago Bears founder George Halas, 85. . . . Predictably, Hope had things to say: . . . "How about Don Rickles as Ambassador to Iran? I can see him walking into the Ayatollah Kohomeini and saying, 'Look, hockey puck . . . you need a new flea collar!' But I really thought Carter was big when he called and said, 'Is there anything I can do for you?' Reagan said, 'Yeah. Run in '84.' And how about that Billy Carter! I had an uncle like him. When he died, they cremated him and his liver burned for three months."

49. There is a new electronic game out called "Public Utility." Turn on a switch and it asks for a rate increase.

50. By 1999, judging from predictions of economists, the average American will be making twice as much as an Englishman, three and a half times as much as a Russian, and half as much as he needs.

51. If it wasn't for Russia, how would America know whether we are ahead or behind? (HUGH PARK in Atlanta Journal)

52. The average consumer is like a dog chasing its tail. We're both trying to make ends meet.

53. America would be a lot better off if the pilgrims had landed in Saudi Arabia.

54. We're great believers in the two party system—one on Friday and one on Saturday.

55. A friend declares what America needs is a good five-cent bumper sticker remover.

56. The American way of life is to dawdle away an hour drinking instant coffee.

57. Late humorist Will Rogers in October, 1931, wrote: "The trouble with us is, America is just muscle-bound from holding a steering wheel. The only place we are calloused from work, is the bottom of our driving toe. . . . We are the first nation in the history of the world to go to the poorhouse in an automobile."

58. Ours is the only country in the world where we pay $150,000 for a house and then leave it for two weeks every summer to go sleep in a tent.

59. Only in America will a man jog five miles, then take an escalator to the mezzanine.

60. In a country where we're trying to legalize marijuana, you have to go to a pusher to buy saccharin. And we're the only country in the world that locks the jury up at night and lets the prisoner go home.

61. The blonde heard that the average American is $2,000 in debt, so she rushed out and did a lot of shopping. She hates to be below average.

62. Somewhere in America there's a factory making nothing but square wheels for grocery carts.

63. We do have something in common with teenagers. They listen to rock groups and we listen to economists—and neither one of us understands a word they're saying.

64. These days by the time you get it all together, there's no gas to take it anywhere.

65. A survey in America shows that the girdle business is holding firm. This, of course, is based on last year's figures.

66. When the white man discovered this country, Indians were running it. No taxes, no debts, women did all the work. And white man thought he could improve on a system like that?

67. "America—where we pay $1 a gallon for gas, $4 for a pound of coffee, and $3 for a pound of hamburger, then turn on TV to watch 'The Price is Right!'"

Animals

68. Dog is not man's best friend. Ever try to borrow money from one?

69. Did you hear about the psychotic owl? He goes Why? Why? Why?

70. I hate horses—they are uncomfortable in the middle and dangerous at both ends.

71. Know how to keep a horse from slobbering? Teach him how to spit.

72. That a dog is smarter than people has long been known to man. The dog sleeps when he is tired, eats whenever food is available, does his philandering away from home, and is man's best friend because he wags only his tail, not his tongue.

73. "I got three deer and a potfur."
    "What's a potfur?"
    "To cook the deer in!"

74. The zoo keeper saw a kangaroo jump over the top of his ten-foot cage and hop out of sight. "What happened?" the excited zoo-keeper asked a lady standing nearby. "I haven't the faintest idea," said the lady, "all I did was to tickle him a little with this feather." "Well, lady," said the zookeeper, "You'd better tickle me in the same place. I'm the one who has to catch him."

75. "I hear you bought your wife a mink."
    "Yeah. And it only cost a hundred dollars, including the cage."

76. Looking around in a pet shop, a lady wandered over to a parakeet's cage. "Can you talk?" asked the woman. "Sure," replied the bird, "can you fly?"

77. A woman who had been bitten by a dog was advised by her physician to write her last wishes as she might soon succumb to hydrophobia. She spent so long with pencil and paper that the doctor finally asked her whether the will wasn't getting to be pretty lengthy. "Will!" she declared. "Nothing of the kind! I'm writing out a list of the people I'm going to bite."

78. Anybody who doesn't count his chickens before they're hatched probably doesn't raise poultry.

79. A sow's ear may not make a silk purse but a good calf does wonders for a stocking.

80. With my luck, if I had been a dog on Noah's Ark, I'd have ended up with both fleas.

81. According to legend, when the Biblical flood came and Noah loaded up his ark with a pair of all animalkind, the old scow sprang a leak and threatened to sink. At the moment when the situation was most critical, the two dogs plugged the leak with their noses. That heroic act saved the ark, but it left the dogs with noses that

never have warmed up. Despite the valiant efforts of the dogs, the hole in the ark grew larger and one of the women passengers volunteered to stick her foot into the breach, thus accounting for the fact that women's feet are always cold. In the end, however, one of Noah's sons saved the ark by sitting over the leak, and that's why to this good day men always stand with their back to the fire.

82.   Fred Allen used to tell of the scarecrow that scared the crows so well that they brought back the corn they'd stolen two years before.

83.   An old Indian proverb. Never anger an alligator until after you've crossed the river. That was a prerequisite for becoming an old Indian.

84.   "Did you ever notice, no matter how much a chicken eats, he never gets fat in the face?" SOUPY SALES

85.   Does acupuncture work? Of course, you never see a sick porcupine, do you?

86.   My wife asked me to haul off the cat. I put it in a basket and tromped through the woods for seven to eight miles. "Did you lose the cat?" asked my wife. "Lose it," I replied. "If I hadn't followed it, I wouldn't have found my way home."

87.   A mother mouse and her little ones were suddenly confronted by a cat. The mother mouse braced herself and said, "Bow wow!" The cat turned tail and fled. Then the mother mouse turned to her children and said: "Now you see how important it is to know a second language."

88.   A dog, returning from obedience school, was asked by his owner, "Did you learn how to add and subtract today?" The dog shook his head. "Did you learn how to write?" The dog again shook his head. "Did you learn how to read?" Once more he shook his head. "Did you learn any foreign languages?" Then the dog replied. "Meow!"

89.   A male elephant sees this good-looking shapely female elephant. "Wow!" exclaims the male elephant, "that's what I call a real body—3,600, 2,400, 3,600."

90.   Letter to Bob Sylvester from John F. Conte, public info department of the U.S. Postal Service: "I am informed that recently a postmaster had to hurry first aid to a carrier with a dog-bitten

leg." "Did you put anything on it?" he asked the victim. "No," said the carrier, "the dog liked it just as it was."

91. A couple of fellows paid a high price for a "bird dog" and took him out for a field test. After an hour, one said in disgust, "This dog is no good. We might as well sell him." "Let's throw him in the air one more time," said the other. "If he doesn't fly, we'll get rid of him."

92. "They had to shoot poor Fido today," Charlie reported. "Was he mad?" asked Dan. "Well, he wasn't too pleased!"

93. A man takes a small dog to a theatrical agent's office, says to the agent: "This dog can do a sensational act." The agent, humoring him, says: "Let's see what the dog can do." With this the dog goes into singing and dancing to "Tea For Two." Then he goes to the piano and plays "Chopin's Polonaise." The agent goes wild and says: "I'll call Vegas right away. I know we can get $100,000 a week for the act." Suddenly the office door swings open. In walks a big dog, picks the little dog up by the nap of the neck and walks out. The agent says to the man: "What was that?" The man answered: "That's the only drawback. That's the dog's mother. She wants him to be a doctor."

94. "I get no respect from my dog. The other day, the dog went to the door and started to bark. I went over and opened it. The dog didn't want to go out; he wanted me to leave." RODNEY DANGERFIELD

Bachelors

95. A bachelor in Jackson, Mississippi explaining why he'd never married, blamed television. He said he'd learned about women from television ads. He'd learned that most of them suffer indigestion, bad breath, excessive perspiration, rough hands, hairy legs, arthritis, neuritis, and iron-poor blood. They have falling hair, short tempers, chronic fatigue, dull eyes, headaches, bad skin, constipation, and excess fat and, he said, "Who wants to put up with all that?"

96. A bachelor is a guy who gave up waiting for the right girl and is doing his best with the wrong ones.

97. A 40-year old bachelor complained to a friend that no matter what women he brought home as a potential bride, his mother took an immediate dislike to her. The friend advised him: "Find a girl like your mother, then she's bound to like her." Six months later, the bachelor reported to the friend: "I took your advice. I

found a girl who looked like my mother, talked like my mother and even cooked like my mother." "And what happened?" The bachelor replied: "My father hated her."

98. A bachelor described a blind date this way: "She's okay to take out on a credit card, but I wouldn't want to spend cash on her."

99. A bachelor has been described as a man who has both alibis and girls he's never used.

100. Some bachelors have quit chasing girls. They can't find any that will run.

101. Don't be too sure that last minute Christmas shopping male is a married man out to get something just for the wife and kids. It could be just a bachelor with a headache.

102. A bachelor met a gorgeous girl at a party and fell madly in love with her at first sight. "You're the girl of my dreams," he kept telling her all evening. "You're perfect," he told her in the cab on the way to her place. When they got to her apartment, he took the key and opened the door. There in the middle of the living room was a dead horse. The man stared, horrified. "Well, for goodness sake," exclaimed the girl. "I didn't say I was neat, did I?"

103. Bachelor explaining why he always eats out! "The last meal a date cooked for me, I broke a tooth on her jello."

104. Grandpa always had a good piece of advice for the groom at any bachelor's party. He used to say, "An ounce of keep your mouth shut beats a ton of explanation."

105. A young bachelor was trying to impress his dates. He tried every kind of deodorant imaginable, including walking around with an air wick in each pocket. He wore so many deodorants that when he stood still he left a puddle.

106. The unmarried guy in the next department says one advantage he has is he can take a nap on top of a bedspread.

107. My boyfriend likes me just the way I am—single.

Banks

108. Bank president: "Where's the cashier?"
 Assistant: "Gone to the races."

"During working hours?"
"Yes, sir, it was his last chance to make the books balance."

109. Getting a loan from a bank is tough these days because of the tight money situation. A loan officer was standing by the desk of a junior worker when the phone rang and the young man picked it up, "no, no, no, no, . . . yes . . . no . . . no." His boss asked, "What did you say yes to?" "Don't worry, boss," the young man said. "I only said yes when he asked me if I was still listening."

110. It's not easy to be tall and short at the same time, but I know a bank teller who is.

111. Times have gotten hard when you go to the bank to withdraw your life savings and the teller asks if you want it heads or tails.

112. One definition of installment buying from the bank: "By the time you're sick and tired of the thing, you finally own it."

113. A volunteer worker for the United Givers Drive called on the town's leading banker. Thinking he would flatter him into making a sizeable contribution, he said, "I'm honored that your name was on my list because you are rumored to be the most generous man in town." The banker quietly wrote out a check and handed it to the man and said, "Here's a check for $10. Now you can start denying that rumor."

114. "I hear the bank is looking for a cashier."
  "Thought they just hired one a week ago."
  "They did. He's the one they're looking for."

115. There was this fully automated bank in Miami. Seems somebody sent it a card saying THIS IS A HOLDUP, and the computer mailed the fellow $200,000 in unmarked bills!!

116. A woman telephoned her bank. She wanted to arrange for the disposal of a $1,000 bond. The clerk asked her, "Madam, is the bond for redemption or conversion?" There was a very long pause, and then the woman said, "Well, am I talking to the First National Bank or the First Baptist Church?"

117. Times have changed. Banks in the suburbs are now open 'til 7 p.m., but gas stations are closing at 2 p.m.

118. A New York bank is giving away a set of china to anyone who agrees not to rob it.

Born Loser

119. A tall Texas tale involves a loser who switched from cattle to hogs because of a drought. As soon as he had sold the last heifer off of his barren clay pasture, it started to rain. But with feed in the barn, he turned his hogs loose and filled the self-feeders. Then all his hogs died. The veterinarian diagnosed the problem as "Mud Sleeping Sickness," an insidious disease characterized by swine that walk a lot in mud. A mudball starts on their tail and grows with each step. Finally, it gets so heavy, the skin is pulled back so tight, that the hogs can't close their eyes and they all die from a lack of sleep.

120. A born loser is a guy who puts a sea shell to his ear and gets a busy signal.

121. Then there was the somewhat rotund girl who won a beauty prize and was named Miss North and South Carolina, with a little bit of Georgia.

122. Here are a few colorful ways to describe persons of dubious wit besides the commonplace "off his rocker," "lost his marbles," and the like: He doesn't have both oars in the water. She's a cup and a saucer short of a set.

123. Fred attended a meeting the other night and didn't enjoy it a bit. It seems one of the other men was a terrible bore. He says the fellow has quit smoking, his car gets 29 miles to the gallon of gas, and he's been eating tomatoes out of his garden for two weeks.

124. Finkelstein was frantic. For 5 weeks he hadn't been able to do any business because he'd forgotten the combination to the safe. Rifkin, his partner, had gone to the Catskills for a vacation and there was no word from him. Then one day the phone rang. "Thank God you called," Finkelstein shouted into the phone. "I can't do any business. I had to lay off the whole shop, fire the salesmen, refuse orders from our biggest accounts, and just stay here in the office and wait for your call." "What's happened?" asked Rifkin. "It's the safe. I forgot the combination." "But it's so simple. Turn once left and twice right." "But what about the numbers?" "It doesn't matter," answered Rifkin. "The lock's broken."

125. Sam knows a guy, not exactly popular on the job, who retired the other day. Instead of getting a gold watch, he was given a dollar's worth of quarters and a number to call to get the right time.

126. Elevator operator at Belmont Park last week warned visiting

reporters about pickpockets. "When they had sky divers as part of the track's 75th anniversary," he said, "A guy on a parachute felt a hand in his pocket before he landed."

127. Told my apartment manager the apartment had roaches— he raised my rent for keeping pets.

128. During his performance, comedian Shecky Greene revealed what a "loser" he is: "Two nights a week I attend Alocoholics Anonymous, two nights Gamblers Anonymous, and the rest of the week, Weight Watchers."

Boss

129. The boss' job is very secure. It's HIM they can do without.

130. When he got fired from his last place of employment, the boss told him: "You've been like a son to me—insolent, rude, and ungrateful."

131. A telegrapher in the days of the old west was at his key. It was a cold day and a stranger, half frozen, appeared in the company office and complained because a fire had not been started. "I'm too busy sending messages to start a fire," snapped the telegrapher. The stranger wrote out a message to send over the wire. It read: "Send a replacement for the insubordinate operator." It was signed "District Manager." The telegrapher grabbed the bundle of kindling wood and from the wood stove responded, "I'm too busy building a fire to send messages."

132. The store owner wondered how his clerk was living in a penthouse and driving an expensive car on a salary of $150 a week. He asked the clerk, who said, "I sell 1,000 raffle tickets a week at a dollar apiece." The boss asked, "What are you raffling off?" The clerk replied, "My paycheck."

133. The boss is definitely getting old. He hired a new secretary the other day and remarked that he didn't care what she looked like—as long as she knew how to spell.

134. I gave my ex-boss as a reference. He said I worked for him for 20 years and when I left he was perfectly satisfied!

135. The boss is so paranoid about being in charge that someone told him to have a nice time and he snapped, "Don't you tell me what to do!"

136. George was a good chauffeur and an expert mechanic in the

bargain. The dignified society queen who employed him had only one complaint: He was extremely sloppy about his own appearance. One day she decided that the time had come to lecture him on his weakness. "George," she began severely, "How often would you say it is necessary to shave?" George gazed at her intently, "With a weak growth like yours, ma'am," he replied politely, "I should say that every third day would be sufficient."

137.   An executive training seminar was held. The professor was asked what the men actually learned during the six-week course. The professor shook his head and then replied, "The best answer to that came from one man who completed the course. He was asked by his boss, 'Well, what did you learn at the seminar?' The man replied, 'I learned to say incredible instead of ah nuts!' "

138.   A company budget is what we all get along on until the boss needs more money.

139.   And there was the advertising boss who's wife made him give up his three martini lunch because he got to seeing double and feeling single.

140.   My boss is suffering from an identity crisis and an energy crisis at the same time. He doesn't know who he is and doesn't have the energy to find out.

141.   Inexcuseable errors are made by employees. What the boss commits are "justifiable mistakes."

142.   For 25 years, Morris, a cutter in a garment factory had never been late for work. One morning, however, instead of checking in at 9:00 he arrived at 10:00. His face was criss-crossed with adhesive plaster, and his right arm was in a sling. Mr. Schlepman, his boss, demanded to know why he was late. Morris explained, "I leaned out a window after breakfast and fell three stories." His boss shrugged, "That takes an hour?"

143.   A fellow is worried about his job. His boss gave him two cartons of cigarettes, a sack of saccharin, and an asbestos hair dryer before sending him on a three-week vacation to Three-Mile Island aboard a DC-10.

144.   A local factory's bulletin board has this suggestion: "In case of Injury, Notify Your Supervisor Immediately." (Underneath someone had scribbled, "He'll kiss it and make it well.")

145.   A district sales manager, when asked why he wanted to be

vice president of the company said, "Well, it's inside work and there's no heavy lifting."

146.   Boss: "Why aren't you busy?"
   Joe: "I didn't see you coming."

147.   An irritated boss asked his secretary if she had a good reason to be late. "Certainly I have," she said, "It makes the day seem shorter."

148.   Our boss has the competition right where he wants them. Worn out from calling his bluffs.

149.   Sayings from the Bible are very often proved out in business. For example, tell the boss what you think of him—and the truth will set you free.

150.   The company president told his sales manager. "To quiet consumer criticism, I've decided to offer a ten-year guarantee on our product." "But, chief," the manager protested, "our product falls apart in three years." "I know," said the president, "but we'll print the guarantee on paper that falls apart in two years."

151.   Two secretaries sat discussing their bosses during the coffee break. "He's in a bad mood again," one moaned. "All I asked him was whether he wanted the carbon copies double-spaced too."

152.   Two foremen were comparing notes. "Do all the boys in your plant drop their tools the moment the whistle blows?" asked one.
   "No, not at all," replied the other forlornly. "The more orderly ones have their tools put away before that time."

153.   "Why did the foreman fire you?"
   "Well, you know the foreman is the guy who stands around and watches the others work."
   "Yes, anyone knows that. But why did he fire you?"
   "He was jealous of me. A lot of the fellows thought I was the foreman."

154.   The boss invited George to use his pool again this summer. What the boss really said was: "It'll be a cold day in July when you're asked back."

155.   A husband wanted to show his wife who was boss. So he got her a mirror. CLAUDE MCDONALD

156.   An office clerk was telling some friends that her boss had what she called "real executive ability." "What is that?" a friend

asked. "It is the ability to decide something in a hurry and then get somebody else to do it," she replied.

157.   The boss spoke to the office jerk about making advances at the new secretaries. He said he didn't do it—and he would never do it again.

Brides and Grooms

158.   The newlywed couple went to Washington and checked in at the Watergate Hotel. The bride was upset. "Why did we come here?" she wanted to know. "You know the stories about this place. Why, I'll bet there are hidden microphones and tapes and bugs all over the place." "Don't worry," the groom told her. He was an expert in these matters and he'd check it out. So he went over the whole room, looking behind the pictures and the drapes, inspecting the lamps, and the light fixtures. Then he moved the bed and looked under the carpet where he discovered a round metal plate held down by four screws. "Here it is," he said. "I'll just take these screws out and remove this and we'll be all right." So he did. And they got on with their honeymoon. The next day when he went down to check out, the clerk was quite solicitous. "Had everything been all right," the clerk wanted to know. "Had the champagne been properly chilled, the Tournedos Rossini correctly cooked, the flowers fresh, the maid service prompt and efficient?" "Everything was fine, just fine," the groom replied. "Oh good," said the clerk. "Then you weren't disturbed by the noise?" "What noise?" asked the groom. "It was very strange," said the clerk, "and a most regrettable accident, but the couple in the room right below yours were injured about 4 o'clock this morning when the chandelier in their room fell off the ceiling."

159.   The new bride down the street says the glamour has gone from her marriage. She makes the bed, washes the dishes, and three weeks later she has to do it all over again.

160.   A newly-married man said to an old timer, "I really communicate with my wife. I tell her everything I'm doing or thinking." "I don't need to," said the old timer, "she knows what I'm thinking and the neighbors tell her what I'm doing."

161.   When a newlywed served baked ham to her husband, he noticed she had cut the ends off and asked why. "That's the way mother always did it," she replied with a shrug. When his mother-in-law came for a visit, she asked her the same question, "That's

the way my mother did it," she replied. Finally, he asked the wife's grandmother, who answered, "That's the only way I could get it into the pan."

162. A bride-to-be was reviewing her guest list for the wedding when her friend commented that only married people were on the list. "Isn't that rather strange?" was her friend's question. "Not at all," was the reply. "That was Jim's idea, and a clever one! He says that if we invite only married people, the presents will all be clear profit."

163. Sandy McTavish to bride: "Instead of a Niagara Falls honeymoon, we'll drive slowly through a carwash."

164. A wealthy executive honeymooning with his beautiful secretary was discussing her replacement. "I've been thinking of that too," said the ex-secretary and new wife. "My cousin would be just right for the job." "What's her name?" "Joseph David Smith," replied the bride.

Businessmen

165. A businessman wanted to make a killing in the market. His broker knew this, called him and said: "I have a wonderful new issue for you." The man said: "Okay, how much?" "Five dollars a share." So he bought 10,000 shares. Later in the month the broker called him again and said it looked like the stock might hit $10 a share. So he bought 10,000 more shares. In a couple of months, the broker called to say chances looked good for the stock to reach $20 a share and was told: "Get me 10,000 more shares." Six weeks later the man had to raise some money and he called his broker and told him to sell half his holdings. The broker said: "You can't sell." "Why not?" asked the man. "You are the only stockholder," said the broker.

166. Overheard between two business partners. "I think it's about time we taught that new secretary what's right and what's wrong." "Okay," replied the other. "You teach her what's right."

167. Omaha businessman Bob Scone recalls a time years ago when he was in New York and complained about the price of a steak to the late restaurateur, Toots Shor. "Your steak is okay," said Scone, "but I could get the same thing in Omaha for half the price." "Yeah," said Toots, "but you'd still be in Omaha."

168. A man applying for work was asked what his former work

was. "From time-to-time, I was a door-to-door salesman selling wall-to-wall carpeting and back-to-back tape on a day-to-day basis and fifty-fifty commission in Walla Walla, Washington." "How was business." "So-so."

169. Some businessmen have inferiority complexes these days. Their firms aren't being sought by conglomerates.

Cars

170. We got a new foreign car with the motor in the back. Pulled up in front of the Sherman Hotel and the bellboy opened up the back of the car. Before I knew it, the motor was up in the room. HENNY YOUNGMAN

171. A used car dealer explaining how he bids at automobile auctions: "If the seller asks $1,000, he means $800 and he really wants $600—so it's worth $400 and you offer him $200."

172. Motorist: "How much will it cost to fix my car?"
Mechanic: "What is the matter with it?"
Motorist: "I don't know."
Mechanic: "I'd say $139.75."

173. People used to want a car that would stop on a dime. Now they want one that will run on a two-bit fuel.

174. Today most highway robbers are kept in a two-car garage.

175. Every time I buy a new car, I get the feeling it's the one that just rolled off the assembly line. Actually, fell off is more descriptive.

176. Country Music has made it possible for a man to sing "Gonna Catch a Freight Train—Don't Care Which Way It Goes" and then go out and get in his Cadillac and head for the Waldorf Astoria.

177. Drive carefully—the other guy's car may not be insured . . . either.

178. "You seem to have had a serious accident."
"Yes," said the bandaged person. "I tried to climb a tree in my car."
"What did you do that for?"
"Just to oblige a lady who was driving another car. She wanted to use the road."

179. A fellow says his new car has a buzzer that tells him his seat belt isn't on, another that warns him when the car's speed is

over 60, and a light to tell his gas is low. "My wife isn't bad enough," he complains, "now even my dashboard nags me."

180. An alarmed motorist stopped hurriedly beside a small over-turned sports car. "Anyone hurt in the accident?" he inquired. "There wasn't any accident," replied the young man calmly, "I'm changing a tire."

181. A lady rammed her car into a house and it finally stopped inside the den. When her husband asked, "How did you drive the car into the den?" She replied, "I turned left at the bedroom."

182. Recalling his days in the service, Joe told about the free Sunday he and three GI buddies ambled over to the orderly room and saw an old car stuck in a snow-filled ditch. Beside it was their drill sergeant, hopping mad. "Let's push him out," Joe suggested. "No, sir," interjected Joe's pal, a private, "If the Old Sarge wants his car out, let him order it out."

183. A class was asked to write a 150-word essay on the subject of cars. One small boy handed in the following: "Once, my uncle bought a car and took us for a ride in the country. After about 15 miles, it broke down and wouldn't start again. This is only 26 words. The rest aren't fit to write."

184. The mini-car has some advantages. If you flood the engine, you can put it over your shoulder and burp it. (ARNOLD GLASOW in Chicago Tribune)

185. The two biggest features on the new cars are airbrakes and unbreakable windshields. You can speed up to one hundred miles an hour and stop on a dime. Then you press a special button and a putty knife scrapes you off the windshield. HENNY YOUNGMAN

186. A friend of ours who is a nut on classic automobiles bought a car that runs entirely on electricity. He paid $10,000 for it— $5,000 for the car and $5,000 for the extension cord. HENNY YOUNGMAN

187. Happiness is when the slip of paper under the windshield turns out to be an advertisement.

188. A fellow wrote a letter to Ralph Nader complaining about his car. He said his wife told him she was going home to mother. But when she got in the car, it wouldn't start.

189. If your teenager wants to learn to drive, don't stand in his way.

190. "How many miles per gallon do you get on your new car?" "I get seven. My teenager gets the other twelve."

191. I have been reading about this fellow who has made his automobile run on fuel extracted from chicken manure. Whatever its advantages or disadvantages, I'll bet he doesn't have any trouble with siphoners. (JAMES DENT in Charleston, WV Gazette)

192. What the world needs right now is a compact car which, in heavy traffic, will run on the fumes from other cars.

193. He heard it was going to be a hard winter so he bought a heavier muffler for his car.

194. Buy a luxury car and you'll see a big difference. Right away the mechanics start smearing a more expensive type of grease on your upholstery.

195. My neighbor said he stopped driving those economy sized cars when he stopped at a light, and some kid ran up and yelled, "My turn."

196. My car is a modern "runabout." It'll "run about" as far as the nearest mechanic.

197. What this country really needs is a car that eats oats.

198. It's easy to buy a $5,000 car. Just buy a $3,000 one on time.

199. His car was running terrible. Ralph barely made it in a two-bit garage in a fleabitten town. The mechanic peered into the dark recesses of this mechanical monster and gave his diagnosis, "Mister, you got a case of the corrodes." "Can you be a little more specific?" "I guess if I got down to specifics, I'd say what you got is a case of the general corrodes."

200. A state trooper spotted a speeder on an expressway and radioed a patrol car on the ground. The patrolman stopped the speeding automobile and the driver was a bit uncertain how his speeding had been discovered. "How did you know I was speeding?" the offender asked. As he wrote out the ticket, the patrolman pointed skyward. The driver at the wheel looked astonished and exclaimed, "You mean He's turned against me, too?"

201. Overheard at a garage: "When buying a used car, check the radio push buttons. If they are all set on rock stations, chances are the transmission is shot."

202. Motorists seem to be chronically afflicted by two kinds of

car trouble: either the engine won't start or the payments won't stop.

203. The automobile did away with horses. Now it's got a good start on people.

Children

204. During a recent thunderstorm, a mother told her child, "Be quiet while God is doing his work," and he said, "If God can make all that noise, why can't I?"

205. "You say you wish you had six children?"
"Yeah. The reason is I've got twelve."

206. Exactly what went on in the Garden of Eden depends on what Sunday School pupil you talk to. One boy told the story in his own way. "God said, 'Don't eat the apple,' but then the Devil came along and kinda hypnotized them and Eve took a bite and gave it to Adam." Asked how God punished the pair, he said, "He made Adam sit down and write the Bible and made Eve a housewife."

207. First grader to his mother: "I sure wish you'd let me take my bath in the morning instead of at night. Our teacher always asks us whether or not we've had a bath today—and I haven't been able to say yes all year."

208. Once it was thought that children should be seen and not heard. But the way they look and sound today, more interest is developing in a new far out theory—retroactive birth control.

209. The teacher asked the little boy in kindergarten, "Why do you sit in the corner scratching yourself?" And he said, "I don't know where anybody else itches."

210. Mom: "Don't play with boys. They're too rough."
Daughter: "What if I find a smooth one?"

211. Two long-haired boys. "My Dad can lick your Dad," said one.
"Don't be silly. My Dad is your Dad," replied the other.

212. This maid, who was unmarried, announced one day that she was going to have a baby. The husband and wife hadn't been able to have children, so they offered to adopt the child. The maid snapped up the offer. About a year later, the maid was going to have another baby. The husband and wife thought the matter over and said that they'd adopt that child, too. A year later, the inevitable

happened and the maid announced that she was going to have still another baby. The husband and wife again talked it over, and then told the maid, "Our two children would like another sister or brother, so we'll adopt that third baby, too." "Oh, no you won't!" said the maid. "I'll quit if you do!" "Why is that?" "I'm not going to work for any family that has three children."

213. Small boy to mother: "Can I help Dad put on the snow chains? I know all the words."

214. When I was a child, I was so ugly my dad had to hang pork chops on my ears so the dog would play with me.

215. Nothing's apt to make you wonder about heredity more than having children.

216. The teacher explaining to her third graders the importance of penmanship: "If you can't write your name, when you grow up, you'll have to pay cash for everything."

217. When a Sunday School teacher requested each of her pupils to give one verse of Scripture, one small boy recited: "Go ye into all the world and spread the gossip."

218. The five-year-old returning from his first day at school told his mother: "I'm not going back. I can't read and I can't write and they won't let me talk."

219. Amelia (whose sunburn was in the peeling off stage) said to her mother: "I'm only four years old and already I'm wearing out."

220. Children have become so expensive that only people on welfare can afford to have them.

221. How can a society that exists on instant mashed potatoes, packaged cake mixes, frozen dinners, and instant cameras teach patience to the children?

222. A little city girl was visiting Grandma in the country and was asked to break eggs in a bowl. She said. "I'd love to but where's the pull tab?"

223. Small boy: "Dad, how do they catch lunatics?"
Dad: "With face powder, beautiful dresses, pretty smiles. . . ."

224. Statistics show that ex-YMCA members have 1.3 children, while YWCA exes have 1.7 which merely goes to show that women have more children than men.

225. During recess, a first grade boy ran up to the playground monitor and said: "Teacher, did you see a little girl with a short skirt and makeup on? She's been chasing me and bothering me and won't leave me alone . . . and I can't find her anywhere."

226. A young family was discussing the imminent arrival of the second child. The parents decided they would have to move to a bigger house. Their first-born listened gravely, then shook his head. "That wouldn't work," he said, "He'd follow us!"

227. Little Betsy's grandmother told her they didn't have television when she was a little girl. "Then what did they turn off when you were bad?" asked the four-year old.

228. A man was telling his grandson the story of Cinderella. When he finished, the wide-eyed lad looked at him and asked, "When the pumpkin turns into a beautiful coach, is that figured as straight income or capital gain?"

229. A little girl's brother set a trap to catch birds. She thought it was wrong and cruel. She cried at first, but then her mother noticed she became happy again and asked why. "I prayed for my brother to be a better boy." "What else?" asked her mother. "I prayed that the trap would not catch birds." "And what else?" "Well, then I went out and kicked the trap to pieces."

230. Lady called a record store, "Do you have Eyes of Blue and Love that's Real?"
    "No, but I have a wife and 11 kids."
    "Is that a record?"
    "I don't think so, but it's as close to it as we want to get."

231. A boy took his pet rabbit to a veterinarian to discover why the rabbit was ailing. "What you been feeding it?" the doctor asked. "Goat's milk," the boy replied. "Don't you know better," the doctor said, "than to use that greasy kid stuff on your hare?"

232. "It's extraordinary that Mrs. Jenkins can never see the mischief her children are always getting into," said one mother to a friend. "Well, they say a mother never sees faults in her children," replied the other. "Nonsense. I'm sure I could recognize my own children's faults . . . if they had any."

233. "Father, what's the difference between a gun and a machine gun?" young Eddie asked. Dad replied: "There is a big difference. It is just as if I spoke, and then your mother spoke."

234. A little boy caught in mischief was asked by his mother, "How do you expect to get into Heaven?" He thought for a moment and then said, "Well, I'll just run in and out and in and out and keep slamming the door until they say, "For goodness sake, come in or stay out. Then I'll go in."

235. "Tabby is in Heaven now," consoled the mother of the little girl whose cat had died. "What would God want with a dead cat?" asked the little girl.

236. A lady was visiting a friend the other day while a 7-year old boy was showing a playmate through the house. When they came to the bar, he heard the youngster announce proudly, "And this is my father's chemistry set."

237. The kindergarten teacher asked a new arrival what her father's name was. "Daddy," replied the little girl. "No, I mean his first name—what does your mother call him?" "She doesn't call him anything," said the little one. "She likes him."

238. The 1st-grader asked his mother why his father brought home a briefcase of material each night. When the mother replied, "Daddy has so much to do that he can't finish it all at the office, so he has to work at night," the boy asked, "Well, why don't they just put him in a slower group?"

239. A teacher in the county routinely discussed stories in literature class and then asked, "Now what was the moral to that?" When she was absent one day, the substitute simply read the stories and held no discussions. One little boy raised his hand and declared, "I'm sure glad you're teaching us today 'cause you don't have any morals."

240. An 8-year old boy objected to going to Sunday School. "Shucks," he griped. "I bet dad never went to Sunday School when he was a kid." His mother assured him that dad went regularly. "OK," the boy agreed reluctantly. "But I bet it won't do me no good either."

241. The problems of her future had been weighing heavily on 5-year-old Julie. She decided to consult her mother. "If I get married someday," she asked, "will I have a husband like papa?" "Yes, dear," answered her mother. "And if I don't get married will I be an old maid like Aunt Susan?" "Yes." "Well," Julie murmured to herself, "I am in a fix."

242. A five-year-old girl had just received two gifts for her birthday

and couldn't stop telling about them. Finally her mother couldn't stand to hear about them one more time and said, "Now, listen, we're having company for dinner, and it isn't nice to boast about your belongings in front of people. Please don't mention your watch or cologne at the table." The little girl sat squirming but quiet, during the meal. But when her mother stepped out to the kitchen, the child said quietly, "If anybody hears or smells anything, it's me."

243.   Try this on the little nippers: What would you get if you crossed an elephant with a rooster? When they say they don't know, tell them you don't either. But when it wakes you up in the morning, you'd better get up.

244.   Two 5-year-olds. Pretty girl passes. (5 year old) "When I stop hating girls she's the first one I'm gonna stop hating."

245.   A first-grader was impressing his classmates by telling them, "When I grow up, I'm going to be a lion tamer. I'll have lots of fierce lions, and I'll walk in the cage, and they'll roar. . . ." He paused a moment, looking into the faces of his properly awed classmates, and then added meekly: "Of course I'll have my mother along with me!"

246.   An 8-year-old boy came home with two ice cream cones in his hands. When his mother asked him how much he had spent, he told her he hadn't spent anything.
   "Did someone treat you?" she asked.
   "No."
   "Did you steal them?"
   "No."
   "How did you get them without spending your money?"
   "I told the girl at the ice cream place to give me a chocolate cone in one hand and peach in the other. Then I told her to reach into my pocket, but to be careful and not to disturb my pet snake."

247.   After the mother had given birth to triplets, the father asked his 4-year-old son what he thought about the blessed events. "Well," the boy said as he looked his father in the eye, "you better start finding a place for them. They won't be as easy to get rid of as them kittens was."

248.   After crawling into Grandfather's lap, little Freddie asked, "Were you in the ark, Grandpa?" The grandfather replied, "Why, no, son." The youngster persisted, "Then why weren't you drowned?"

249. After a five-year-old girl showed a kindergarten classmate the new weight scale in the bathroom, the visitor asked, "What's it for?" The other girl replied, "I don't know. All I know is that when you stand on it, it makes you very mad."

250. "Now children," smiled the Sunday School teacher sweetly, "I want you to be so still that you can hear a pin drop." After a silence that seemed quite long to the children, a small boy over in the corner shouted, "Okay, let 'er drop!"

251. "See that mother pig over there—she's a big one, isn't she?" the farmer's wife told a little visitor from the city. The little boy answered: "She ought to be. I saw her yesterday and she had ten little ones blowing her up!"

252. A Czech teacher asks little Jan to define socialism. "It's five feet tall," she says. "How do you know that?" her teacher asks. "Well, my father is six feet tall," says Jan, "and he says he's got it up to here."

253. The little boy punched his mother in church and asked, "What's the lady next to me singing?" "Alto," whispered the mother. "No wonder she sounds so funny," blurted out the lad. "We're singing 'Joy to the World.' "

254. "Jimmy, there were two slices of cake on the table last night when we went to bed, and this morning there is only one. How do you explain that?" "I don't know, Mom. I guess it was so dark I just didn't see the other piece."

255. A six-year-old was telling her friends how to behave at her birthday party, which her father planned to host and chaperone. "He's okay if you do what he tells you," she said, "and when he hollers at you to sit down, you'd better not wait 'till you can find a chair."

256. By way of Steve Mitchell of the Palm Beach Post, a collection of school-kid malapropisms published in the journal of the National Retired Teachers Association. A selection of them: When asked what her father did for a living, one little girl replied, "He's a civil serpent."

257. A mother was preparing for dinner guests one evening, so she reminded her little girl to say her prayers before she went to bed. Next morning the mother asked, "Did you say your prayers last night?" "Well," the little one explained, "I got down on my knees and started to say them and all of a sudden I thought: I

bet God gets awfully tired hearing the same old prayer over and over. So I crawled into bed and told Him the story of the three bears."

258.   The sweet little girl had an awful fight with her friend. Her mother scolded her, saying: "It was the devil who made you pull Barbara's hair." "That may be," answered the child, "but kicking her shin was all my idea."

College

259.   If college costs get much higher, anyone who can afford to go won't need to.

260.   Dr. Ralph Phelps, Howard Payne University's new president, told HPU board members about two rabbits that were chased by a pack of beagles. The rabbits ducked into some bushes and crouched there, panting. One said to the other: "Do you want to try to out run 'em? Or just stay here until we outnumber 'em?" That got a laugh—but it wasn't the end of the story. Dr. Phelps said the other rabbit replied: "What are you talking about, you fool? We're brothers!" That got another laugh and enabled Dr. Phelps to make his point: "I want you all to keep in mind, we're brothers."

261.   A college boy said to his roommate, "The drought back home is really bad this time." "How can you tell?" asked his roommate. "I got a letter from Dad," he said, "and the stamp was fastened on with a paper clip."

262.   A Minneapolis area college newspaper bears the unusual name of "None of the Above." Seems the students were asked to vote on a name for the paper. Several proposed names were listed in a multiple-choice arrangement and students were called upon to vote for one. Students who disliked all the suggested names could register their feelings by marking a box indicating "none of the above." None of the Above won overwhelmingly.

263.   A college professor appeared before his class one day with his face badly cut and patched here and there with adhesive tape. "What on earth happened to you?" inquired a student. "I was shaved today," explained the professor, "by a man who was graduated summa cum laude from Harvard, speaks several languages, and is an outstanding authority on French history." "Good grief!" the student exclaimed. "If he's so highly educated, how come he's a barber?" "He isn't," sighed the professor. "I shaved myself."

264.   A college student left the library late one evening and when he got to his car in the parking lot, its battery was dead. The nearest lighted building was a sorority house. He explained his situation to the young woman who answered the door and she permitted him to go inside and use the phone. A voice called from upstairs: "Susan, you know you are not supposed to have any visitors on week days after 10 o'clock!" "It's okay," Susan replied, "His battery is dead."

265.   A bit of graffiti, discovered on the wall of a men's room in the Engineering Building at the University of Nebraska at Omaha: "You should realize these four walls are the last refuge of male privacy." A rejoinder, however, was scrawled below: "Think again." (Signed) The Cleaning Lady.

266.   There's a story, sworn to as true by an alumnus who got it from his college football coach, about the swivel hipped, glue fingered, fast as lightening running back the coach recruited and who, he was certain, would break all sorts of scoring records and be All American by his sophomore year—if he could manage to remain in school that long.

The release of mid-semester grades confirmed the coach's worst fears. The only thing his prize athlete was passing was the bread at the training table. The coach was down, but far from out. He was a man who prided himself on his powers of verbal persuasion and a past master at the inspirational half time locker room speech. So he called the boy into his office, sat him down in a chair in front of his desk and lifted the dam on a massive overflow of oratory.

"It's time," he told the player, "that you started to think seriously about your future. Nobody from your family ever graduated from college. Imagine the joy in the hearts and the pride on the faces of your old mother and daddy when they see you walk up there four years from now and get your diploma. They'll know you're an educated man, ready to go out and make a good living for yourself. You can't play football forever, you know. Suppose, God forbid, you get hurt. You've got to have a profession, something you can do to make a living with the opportunities open to a doctor or an engineer or anything you make up your mind to be. But you've got to make the grades to stay in school."

The coach continued talking in that vein, growing more impassioned as he went along. He waved his arms, he shouted, he whispered, he wept. He painted a glowing word picture of the rich, full life which lay open for the educated man. And as he talked, he noticed that he seemed to be making an impression on the lad.

The boy's face was flushed, his fists were clenched and his jaw was determinedly outthrust.

The coach was thundering into his closing. "Now," he shouted, the perspiration pouring down his face, "I want you to tell me. What is it you want more than you want anything else in this world?"

The boy leaped to his feet, his face shining. "Coach," he gasped, "I want a motorcycle."

267. A professor of physics from UCLA was crossing the border into Tijuana on a Sunday afternoon. The Mexican border guard singled out his car and asked a few questions. "What business are you in, Senor?" The professor replied, "Physics." The Mexican guard pondered this for a moment, then went over and discussed it with another guard and returned, "Wholesale or retail?" he asked.

268. A local college professor couldn't get a new mechanical gadget assembled. He gave it to his yard man and within five minutes, it was operating. "How did you do that so quickly when I couldn't even figure where to start?" The yard man shrugged his shoulders and said, "I can't read. Instructions were useless. When you can't read, you have to think."

269. Soon after his arrival in Dallas, Dr. James H. Zumberge, the new president of Southern Methodist University, learned that there is hope even for college presidents.

Zumberge told a group of businessmen about his encounter in downtown Dallas with an elderly woman who was ringing a bell at a Salvation Army collection station.

After Zumberge put some money in the Army's kettle, the woman asked him if he was "saved."

When he said he supposed so, she pursued, "I mean, have you given your full life to the Lord?"

Zumberge decided he had better enlighten the lady by telling her who he was.

"I am the President of Perkins School of Theology."

The lady thought about that for a moment, and then insisted, "It doesn't matter where you've been, or whatever you are, you can still be saved."

270. A boy was attending college. His roommate told him: "I hear they have a new case of malaria in the dorm." "Good," replied this cousin, "I'm getting awfully tired of that Fresca."

Congress

271.   When JFK was Senator, he sent a quotation to the Library of Congress and requested the author's name. Researchers checked through book after book. They culled ancient manuscripts, poured over Sanskrit, translated things from Egyptian but could find no source of the quote. Timidly, they called the Senator's office and reported their inability to track down the quote. "Oh, that's okay," said an assistant. "Senator Kennedy wrote that himself. He just wanted to make sure nobody else had said it."

272.   A group of congressmen were conferring. Said one: "We've got a one hundred and twenty million dollar appropriation to spend. What are we going to do with it?" "I've got an idea on how to spend it!" said a Democrat. "How about building a bridge over the Mississippi River, lengthwise!"

273.   A candidate for Congress called upon a minister for his support in the upcoming election. "Before I give you my decision," said the man of the cloth, "let me ask a question. Do you partake of intoxicating beverages?" "Before I reply" said the candidate, "tell me, is this an inquiry or an invitation?"

274.   The interesting thing about Congress is not that it does so many things that are questionable, but that it goes about its business of doing them with such grave, considered and pompous indifference to good morals; like opening its sessions with a chaplain's prayer and then spending the rest of the day cutting throats.

275.   Texas Representative Jim Wright said throughout his long career in Congress he has never felt he's had the direct power that he had as mayor of Weatherford, Texas. He offered an example: One day, while he was Weatherford's mayor, a woman called him and said some small boys were shooting song birds in her yard with a BB rifle. She thought the mayor should do something about it. After she'd hung up, another woman called and said some sparrows were nesting in the eaves of her house and making nuisances of themselves. She thought the mayor should do something about it. And what sort of direct power, you wonder, did he exercise? "I just transferred the boys," he said.

276.   The return of congressmen from those mighty important overseas junkets where they studied the better hotels, sampled the native restaurants, and studied mass transit from the soft seats of chauffeured limousines, makes us think of a flight of ducks—whirring of wings, fast travel, short stops for food and rest, and an awful lot of quacking.

277. A foreigner visiting America decided to witness a joint session of Congress. After sitting in the visitors' gallery for over an hour, he left and met a Washington friend. "Well," asked the Washingtonian, "what did you think of it?" "The American Congress is strange. A man gets up and speaks and says nothing. Nobody listens—then everybody disagrees with him!"

278. Our best hope for remedial action, perhaps our only hope, is Gold's Final Solution Law. It would force Congress to pass no law the legislators themselves don't understand. And baby, they ain't too bright. (Bill Gold in Washington, DC Post)

Cooking

279. I ain't saying my wife's cooking is greasy—but our kitchen disposal developed an oil slick.

280. The advance proofs of a cookbook for gringos recently came our way. Wildest recipe is for a salad. You cut up lettuce, tomatoes, cucumbers, and green peppers. Then you add a dash of tequila and the salad tosses itself. HENNY YOUNGMAN

281. "They say a woman's work is never done—and my wife's cooking proves it."

282. Hear about the cannibal who wrote a cookbook? It's titled: "How Best To Serve Your Fellow Men."

283. A fairly newlywed husband whose eyebrows and hair were somewhat singed was overheard explaining his appearance: "I helped my wife fix breakfast this morning—I put out the fire."

284. There are 49 different kinds of food mentioned in the Bible. It will probably come as a shock to some teenagers that the pizza isn't one of them.

285. Eating Kentucky Fried Chicken by the pool is IN. What you don't eat, you rub on as a suntan lotion substitute.

286. A woman returned to her table at a Las Vegas restaurant after having visited the ladies' room. She said to the waitress, "Tell the owner that the graffiti here is in very bad taste." The waitress replied, "Well, next time try our chili."

Cowboys

287. A young cowboy was raised in a proper home and his mother had taught him the art of courtesy. Whenever he occasionally forgot

his courtesy, he was able to develop a line of flattery that got him out of trouble. The cowboy happened to step on an elevator in which he and a middle-aged fussy socialite were the only occupants. He forgot to take off his hat. When the snobbish woman asked, "Don't you take your hat off to ladies?," he quickly replied, "Only to old ones, ma'am."

288.   A Catholic bronc rider on his first ride was asked how long he hung on. "Exactly 14 Hail Mary's."

289.   Dude asks cowboy "how come that cow doesn't have horns?" He explains, "Well, some cows have horns and some don't have horns. Some are born with horns and we dehorn them. Some breeds aren't supposed to have horns. There are lots of reasons why cows don't have horns but the main reason why cows don't have horns is cause it ain't a cow, it's a horse."

290.   "Gee, Pop, there's a man in the circus who jumped on a horse's back, slips underneath, catches hold of its tail, and finishes up on the horse's neck." The cowboy responded: "That's nothing. I did all that, and more, the first time I ever rode a horse."

291.   A cowboy fell off his horse and broke his leg. That smart horse grabbed his master's belt in his teeth and dragged the cowboy home to safety, then the horse even went to fetch the doctor. An admiring friend praised the horse's intelligence to his owner. "Aw, he ain't so smart," said the cowboy. "He came back with the veterinarian."

292.   Walt Garrison, former Dallas Cowboys running back, asked if coach Tom Landry ever smiles: "I don't know. I only played nine years."

Dancing

293.   Some of the dance steps are so wild at our favorite discoteque, they won't permit premarital dancing.

294.   How about the belly dancer who got a stomach cold and couldn't shake it. Boy was she upset!

295.   All this disco dancing makes you wonder what happened to country swing? Come to think of it, there are a lot of old boys from the country who remember the only swinging done in town was on a front porch hammock.

296.   You probably know that belly dancing is the only profession where the beginner starts in the middle.

297. Fellow walking on a dirt road past a country beer joint. A barefoot woman was sweeping off the porch. "See, you've had a big fish fry," he commented. "Why do you say that, we ain't had fish for years." "Well, I see all them fish scales you're sweeping out." "Naw, we had a square dance here last night. Them's toenails."

298. What's considered congestion is successful atmosphere on the dance floor.

Daughters

299. The minister's wife was visiting a member of the congregation, and mentioned, with particular pride, that her daughter had won first prize in a music recital. "I know just how you must feel," said her hostess understandingly. "I remember how pleased we were when our pig got the blue ribbon at the fair last year."

300. The clergyman's small daughter watched him preparing next Sunday's sermon. "Daddy," she asked, "does God tell you what to say?" "Yes, he does, dear," he replied. "Why?" "I was wondering why you cross so much of it out," she said.

301. He was worried about his little daughter getting up ill in the middle of the night. So he consulted one of his know-it-all friends. "Does she drink milk before she goes to sleep?" "Yes." "That's the trouble," said the wise guy. "If you feed a child milk before bedtime, she goes to sleep and tosses from side to side, milk turns to cheese, cheese turns to butter, butter turns to fat, fat turns to sugar, sugar turns to alcohol and, the first thing you know, the kid wakes up with a hangover."

302. "How is your daughter getting along in her bookkeeping class at school?" a lady asked her next door neighbor. "Terrific," the girl's mother said. "Now, instead of asking for her allowance, she just bills us for it."

303. My daughter doesn't think it's time to clean up her room until her phone rings and she can't find it.

304. A reader says his daughter is attending West Virginia University and she has been dating two students—one a Dairy Farming major and the other an English major with ambitions of becoming a poet. Both have asked her to be their bride and the poor girl is in a quandry. She can't decide whether to marry for butter or for verse. JAMES DENT

305. "Maybe you don't like my boyfriend," said the daughter to

her father, but you notice he calls for me in a $10,000 sports car!" "That's nothing," replied the father, "I used to take your mother out in a $25,000 bus!"

306. "I just walked into Mabel's house last night and her mother demanded to know my intentions." "Boy, that must have been embarrassing." "Not as embarrassing as when Mabel yelled from upstairs, 'Mother, that's not the one.'"

307. The banker's daughter returned home at three o'clock in the morning from a dance. Her father greeted her sternly. "Good morning, child of the devil," said he. Her reply: "Good morning, father."

308. "My teenage daughter gave us a time last night," a weary office worker said. "She started to run away from home. Luckily she never got beyond the front door." A concerned colleague asked, "What happened?" "The telephone rang," the father replied.

309. "You're going to have to be more economical. Do you know what being economical means?" said the father to his preschool daughter. "Yes," she said sullenly, "That means spending money without getting any fun out of it."

310. Dr. R. L. Warren and a colleague were reminiscing about the cute sayings and doings of their kids. The colleague told about the experience of his wife when she decided it was time to tell their two daughters, ages 5 and 7, about the birds and the bees. She sent off for the booklet recommended by the PTA and, having read it, called the girls in for a long chat. When she had finished she said, with her heart in her throat, "You may ask me any question you want to." The oldest said, "Anything?" She said "yes, anything," and took a deep breath, thinking, "Here it comes." The little girl asked: "Can we have a new baseball bat?"

Doctors

311. "What's the matter with you, Jack? Never saw you scowl so much." "Got rheumatism. Doctor told me to avoid all dampness. You have no idea how uncomfortable it is to sit in an empty tub and go over yourself with a vacuum cleaner."

312. One good place to study ancient history is in the doctor's waiting room.

313. The guy down the hall who was in an accident, got differing professional opinions. His doctor told him the neck brace can come off, but the lawyer told him to wear it another month.

314. Doctors tell you that if you eat slowly, you will eat less. This is particularly true if you're a member of a large family.

315. The office hypochondriac asked to be buried next to a doctor.

316. "I don't drink, don't smoke, don't chase women," I said. "Just as I thought, no initiative," replied the doctor.

317. He tried to get revenge on his doctor by paying him with a check signed illegibly. The pharmacist cashed it.

318. "You may not be able to read a doctor's handwriting and a prescription, but you'll notice his bills are neatly typewritten." EARL WILSON

319. His doctor told him what he needed was an exciting hobby and suggested Russian Roulette.

320. During recent surgery, all I could think of was that only the day before, the same hands cutting into my body missed a three-inch putt.

321. "What would you do if a doctor told you you had one hour to live?" "See another Doctor, quick."

322. Man went to doctor. "I don't brush my teeth, I eat garlic and onions and I don't have bad breath. What's wrong?" "You need an operation." "Yeh?" "Yeh, on your nose."

323. "Above all," the doctor said, "you must eat more fruit, and particularly the skin of the fruit. The skin contains all the vitamins. What is your favorite fruit?" The patient looked gloomy. "Coconuts," he said.

324. Patient to Doctor: "I feel so rotten I think I'll kill myself."
   Doctor: "Now, now. Leave that to us."

325. Patient: "I'm so nervous. This is my first operation."
   Doctor: "I know how you feel. It's my first one, too."

326. Doctor: "I'm afraid your husband will never be able to work on the farm again."
   Wife: "I'll go right in and tell him. It'll cheer him up."

327. A man was advised by his doctor to run ten miles a day to improve his home life. Two weeks later his doctor called to ask, "How's your home life?"
   He replied, "I don't know, I'm 140 miles from home."

328. A physician reports a patient came into his office for an examination the other day and, after it was over, the fellow said: "All

right, Doc. Now I don't want you to give me a bunch of tongue twisting scientific talk. Just tell me straight out in plain English what my problem is." "All right," said the doctor. "You're fat and you're lazy." "Fine," said the patient. "Now give me the scientific terms so I can tell my friends."

329. A doctor, rushing an expectant mother to a Houston hospital, didn't quite make it. The baby was born on the lawn in front of the maternity ward. When the bill was received by the new father, he objected to one item: "Delivery room, $50." He returned the bill for correction. The revised statement came back three days later. It read: "Green fees, $50."

330. A doctor friend tells us of a patient who had a glass eye. One of his favorite diversions is strolling into a restaurant and ordering a meal. While the waiter stands by, he studies the menu and casually uses the fork to scratch his eyeball.

331. A patient came into the office without an appointment and at a time when the office nurse was out to lunch. The doctor recognized the patient as an old customer, but drew a mental blank when he tried to identify him. The doctor ushered the patient into an examining room, held a stethoscope to his chest and ordered, "Say, 'Ah.' "
"Ah."
"A-ha!" said the doctor. "Now then, I want you to spell your full name very slowly."

332. A doctor, who always insisted on seeing a woman patient with a nurse, or her husband, called in a couple as his day began to fade. He had had a busy 10 hours of it. The woman had a mole on her stomach that was worrying her. It was below her navel. The doctor had her remove her clothing, while the man stood. "That's just a little mole you've had all your life," he told her. The woman, who was strikingly attractive, threw on her clothes and rushed from the office. "What's the matter with your wife?" asked the doctor of the man. "Wife? Never saw her before in my life," he said. "I just came for a flu shot."

333. More and more doctors are running their practices like an assembly line. One fella walked into a doctor's office and the receptionist asked him what he had. He said, "Shingles." So she took down his name, address, medical insurance number and told him to have a seat. Fifteen minutes later a nurse's aide came out and asked him what he had. He said, "Shingles." So she took down

his height, weight, a complete medical history and told him to wait in an examining room. A half-hour later a nurse came in and asked him what he had. He said, "Shingles." So she gave him a blood test, a blood pressure test, an electrocardiagram, told him to take off all his clothes, and wait for the doctor. An hour later the doctor came in and asked him what he had. He said, "Shingles." The doctor said, "Where?" He said, "Outside in the truck. Where do you want 'em?"

334.   A doctor's phone rang at 3:00 a.m. The women at the other end asked, "What do you charge for a house call?" Sleepily, the doctor mumbled, "Ten dollars." "And how much for an office visit?" "Five," muttered the doctor. "All right," the lady said briskly, "I'll meet you at your office in twenty minutes."

335.   A fellow went to his doctor for his annual physical checkup. The doctor told him he was in perfect shape. As the man left, he suddenly fell to the floor. The nurse rushed over to him and could find no pulse. He was obviously dead. "What shall we do?" said the nurse. "First thing," said the doctor, "we turn him around so any other patients coming to see me will think he was on his way in rather than just leaving."

Drinking

336.   Products now have built-in obsolescense. My neighbor says he has worn out his third shot glass in the last ten years.

337.   He got so drunk he had a snake in his hand trying to kill a stick.

338.   He got so drunk he tried to take his pants off over his head—and made it.

339.   The office bore found that glasses change his personality. Especially when he emptied one after another.

340.   The car dealer's teetotaling wife says if the Lord meant us to drink whiskey, he would have made it a lot cheaper.

341.   Five-cents-a-glass whiskey is still available, a recent autopsy reveals.

342.   With all the warnings we're getting about eating and drinking, it's obvious that the best way to remain healthy is to eat what you don't want, drink what you don't like, and be sure to do what you'd rather not.

343.   Remember when Eli Whitney yelled: "I've just invented the cotton gin!" "Big deal," his brother-in-law snorted. "Who needs a fluffy martini?"

344.   By the end of the month, we're down to drinking plain ice water—now known as Economy on the Rocks.

345.   Judge to drunk: "You've been coming to me for ten years."
   Drunk: "Can I help it you don't get promoted."

346.   Sir Charles Chaplin, after being knighted by Queen Elizabeth II: "I feel wonderful. I was most impressed with the ceremony. And now, I am going to get drunk."

347.   He's got a brother who owns a flower shop and he spends so much time at a nearby bar they call him, "The Petrified Florist."

348.   The rum dandy's not bad. It's got sugar in it for energy, milk for pep, and the rum gives you dandy ideas of what to do with energy and pep.

349.   "I find drinking is very beneficial. It certainly removed warts and pimples. Not from me, but from those I have to look at." JACKIE GLEASON

350.   Folks who say we spend more for alcohol than for education just don't realize the things you can learn at a drinking party.

351.   It's the first time I ever saw anybody drink Parcel Post Style. That's where you go in half-bagged and come out completely smashed!

352.   People keep asking me how I always manage to be in such good spirits. I owe it all to health food. Every morning I get up and drink the juice from three martinis.

353.   I wonder why it's so much easier to sit down after drinking standing up than it is to stand up after drinking sitting down?

354.   He has saloon arthritis—every night he is still in another joint. Unfortunately, he can't join AA because he's never sober long enough to memorize the pledge.

355.   A speeding car went out of control, hit a telephone pole and then rolled down a hill and overturned. A few seconds later the driver crawled out with only a few cuts and bruises. A bystander, who had seen the accident rushed down to the man and said: "Are you drunk?" "Of course," the other replied. "What do you think I am, a stunt driver?"

356. A man bought a grandfather's clock at an auction sale and since it was only a short distance to his home, was transporting it on his back. But on the way a drunk staggered out of a tavern, bumped into the man and they went down in a pile. Infuriated, the man with the clock shouted, "Why don't you look where you're going?" To which the drunk replied, "Well, why don't you wear a wrist watch like other men do?"

357. Drunk to stranger on street, "What time is it?"
Stranger, "It's 11 o'clock."
Drunk, "I must be going crazy. All day long I keep getting different answers."

358. A car owner reported to the police that thieves had victimized his automobile. "They've stolen the steering wheel, the brake pedal, the accelerator, the clutch pedal, and the dashboard," he stated. Before a police sergeant could investigate, the owner telephoned again. "Don't bother," the man said, with a hiccup. "I got into the back seat by mistake."

359. A bus passed by a big feedlot where the odor was so strong an elderly lady was forced to go for her smelling salts. A drunk in the next seat woke up and yelled, "Lady, put the stopper back in that bottle. It's smellin' up the whole bus."

360. "The drinking neighbor doesn't like to hear Georgie's drum but he's subtle about it," said a young mother. "Why?" asked Georgie's father. "He gave Georgie a knife and asked him if he knew what was in the drum."

361. A sign on a wall at a tavern in Victoria, Minnesota proclaims, "We don't have a town drunk—we take turns." Understand there was a mixup last Saturday night and six guys thought it was their turn.

362. George Gobel says you know you've had too much to drink the night before by the questions your host asks the next morning . . . like . . . "did you know you ate our cat last night?"

363. A drunk staggered up to a hotel desk late one night and demanded another room. "But you have the best room in the house, sir," answered the desk clerk. "I don't care," was the stubborn reply. "I want another room and I want it quick." Realizing that it would do no good to argue or reason with him any further, the desk clerk turned to the pageboy and said, "Move this gentleman out of 505 and put him in 508, right away." Completely satisfied, the inebriated

guest moved toward the lift. "Would you mind telling me, sir, why you don't like 505?" said the clerk. "Well, for one thing it's on fire!"

364. Friend to persistent imbiber, "You ought to set a limit to the amount of booze you can drink and stop when you reach your limit." "That's the trouble," countered the other fellow. "I always get drunk before I get to it."

365. A drunk went into a bar and immediately announced, "The drinks are on me for everybody." After everyone had bellied up to the bar and drank their fill, the drunk found out he didn't even have his wallet. He apologized but the bartender threw him out on his ear. Two weeks later the same drunk came into the same bar and announced, "Set 'em up. Drinks for everybody. But not you bartender. You get mean when you drink."

Farmers

366. The Secretary of Agriculture asked a farmer for the loan of a dime to call a friend. A weathered old hand thrust a hand deep into his worn out overalls and delivered this line: "Here's two dimes. Call all your friends."

367. A little thank-you gift was sent from Russia's communist party to our Secretary of Agriculture for selling such cheap wheat. It was a Russian recording of "I Love You a Bushel and a Peck."

368. A city slicker out for a drive in the country ran over a pig. He stopped, jumped out and apologized to the farmer standing nearby. "Don't worry," said the driver, "I'll replace your pig." "You can't," replied the farmer. "You're too dang ugly."

369. On his knees, a farmer was close to the road with his ear to the ground in a corn field. Tourist stops to ask directions. He looks up, says, "Shhhhh," then puts his ear to the ground listening with even greater intensity. Curiosity got the best of the tourist so he dropped in position and listened for a full five minutes. Finally he says to the hayseed, "I don't hear anything." The farmer replied, "I know. It's been that way all day long."

370. A farmer said he was pinning future hopes on his three close friends—God Almighty, Montgomery Ward, and Governor Brown. His neighbor said he was banking on Jim Beam, Jack Daniel, and Sweet Gypsy Rose.

371. One farmer I know gave up the whole business, quit worrying

and retired. Says his retirement has worked so well his self-winding watch stops every night.

372.   A lady at a Supermarket checkout counter unloaded a quart of milk, a dozen eggs, a TV dinner, six cartons of cigarettes, hand lotion, suntan lotion, face cream, work gloves, flashlight batteries, two magazines, and the latest hit record. She paid her bill and went out grumbling: "Food costs so much these days. No wonder the farmers are getting rich."

373.   Two Tuscan farmers were talking about last summer's drought. "It could have been worse," said one. "I remember when the grape crop was practically nothing. My grandmother drank six acres of vino at one meal."

374.   Joe, the farmer, had accumulated $350,000 and was going to retire. As was customary, neighbors gave a farewell dinner, and Joe was asked to say a few words. "I owe my retirement in part to my thrifty habits," Joe said. "Even more, I owe it to the good judgment of my wife. But still more, I owe it to my aunt who died and left me $349,500."

375.   A young man had just returned from agricultural college and was visiting a neighboring farmer to show off. "Your methods are so old-fashioned," the visitor declared. "Why, I'll bet you don't get ten pounds of apples from that tree." "I dare say you're right," said the farmer. "That's a pear tree."

376.   A logging foreman sold a farmer a power saw that he guaranteed would cut down 15 trees a day. A week later, the farmer returned to report that the saw must be faulty—it averaged only three trees a day. The foreman picked up the saw and pulled the starter cord on the engine. The saw promptly revved up into its loud whine. "Hey!" demanded the startled farmer. "What's that noise?"

377.   Socialite, "My entire dining room goes back to Louis the 14th." Farm wife, "That's nothing, my whole living room goes back to Sears the 15th."

378.   Cloyd Grump and his wife, Bessie came to town on Saturday and decided they would eat at the town's new landmark, the drive-in restaurant. One look at the menu, though, and Cloyd hopped up from the table, dragged Bessie out of the restaurant, shoved her into the truck, and drove off fullspeed toward the farm. "Cloyd, what'n blazes are you up to?" Bessie gasped as soon as she could speak. "Did you see the price of the hamburger sandwich?" he asked,

gritting his teeth and standing on the accelerator. "Sure. A dollar eighty-nine. But what. . . ." "That means we got a $48,000 cow standin' out in the south pasture without us there to guard 'er!"

379. A farmer offered his daughter a pet rock. She said, "Cool Daddy. Make it Rock and Roll."

380. A farmer was asked how he harvested apples in his orchard. He explained that he was trying out a new method—feeding apples to hogs since apples were down and hogs were up. Said he held the hogs up and let 'em eat, movin' from tree to tree til they got full. The newspaper reporter asked if that wasn't awfully time-consuming. Farmer says, "Yeh, but shoot, what's time to a hog?"

381. A farmer sent his nephew a crate of chickens but the crate burst open just as he started to take them out. He wrote his uncle, "I chased 'em through my neighbor's yard but I only got back eleven." "You did alright," wrote back the uncle, "I only sent you six."

382. A traveling salesman, caught in a torrential storm, stopped overnight at a farmhouse. In the morning, he looked out on a flood tearing through the frontyard. He watched pieces of fence, chicken coops, branches, and an old straw hat floating past with the rushing current. Then he saw the straw hat come back, this time moving upstream past the house! Then he saw it go down again. Pretty soon it came back upstream and by now the salesman wondered if he had gone crazy. Finally, he called the farmer's daughter. "Oh," said the rural miss, after a glance out the window. "That must be Granddad. He said yesterday that in spite of hell or high water, he was going to mow the lawn today."

383. A farm hand came to work quite late one morning. "Sorry," he apologized. "I had car trouble." "What happened to your car?" inquired the boss. "I was late getting into it."

384. A farmer took his first trip to the zoo. He saw a baboon. His grandson asked what it was. "I think it's a cowman, the seat of his pants is worn out."

385. "I'm taking a shortcut through your field to catch the 4:45," said a tresspasser. "If my bull sees you, you'll catch the 4:15," replied the farmer.

386. "I have to report that you're in the habit of turning your poultry into that field and then trying to deliberately run over them with your auto. What's the idea?" "The idea is," replied the farmer, "that I've lost more'n a dozen hens this past summer by sudden death on the highway, so I'm training them to dodge."

387. Farmer carrying pig under arm. An acquaintance says, "Hey, did you win that at the fair?" The little pig says, "I certainly did."

388. A city dude asks a farmer standing on the bank if he can cross this country creek in his new convertible. "Sure, no problem." The guy tries it and promptly sinks out of sight. He comes up sputtering, cussing, and swimming for his life. When he confronts the country traffic director, he replies, "I don't understand that." Holding his hand edgewise across his breastbone, he continues, "It's usually only up to here on my ducks."

389. A neighboring farmer was heard talking, across the fence, to himself, "Hey, why are you talkin' to yourself?" his friend asked. He replies, "First, I like to hear a smart man talk. And next, I like to talk to a smart man."

390. A Quaker farmer was milking a cow that showed a mean temperament. After much frustration, he addressed the cow, "Thou knowest that I am a Quaker and can't strike thee and cannot curse thee, but what thou does not knowest is that tomorrow I am going to sell thee to a Baptist and he's gonna knock the hell out of thee."

391. Sign in a watermelon patch: "One melon has been poisoned, beware. . . ." When the farmer checked his field he found someone had stopped and put up a sign of their own. It read: "Now there are two. You beware."

392. A large crowd gathered for the funeral of the farmer's mother-in-law, who had been kicked to death by the farmer's mule. But the predominance of men among the mourners was a cause of comment, even by the minister who asked why there were so many men present. "Oh," said the farmer, "they all want to buy that mule."

393. A farmer can't win nowadays. If he does something wrong, he's fined, and if he does something right, he's taxed.

394. One farmer finally got real fed up with speeding cars which constantly scared his livestock and children. He erected a sign which

immediately began to slow down the motorists who were passing his place. The sign read: "Nudist Camp Crossing."

Fathers

395. My father thought nothing of getting up at 6 o'clock in the morning—and I don't think much of it either.

396. Two fathers were talking and one said, "I finally taught my son the value of a dollar. So now he wants his allowance in Swiss francs."

397. "Daddy," asked the little boy, "what was your greatest ambition when you were a kid?" "To wear long pants, son. And I got my wish. I don't know anybody who wears his pants longer than I do."

398. My father grew up during the depression when nothing went to waste. The people in the neighborhood were so hard up that anybody who had garbage to throw out was considered well to do.

399. My father's tip for the day: "Keep your nose to the grindstone and your two feet on the ground—and you'll not only wear off your nose, but you'll have a heckuva time getting your pants on."

400. After waiting a long time for a man to get through with the phone directory, a frustrated waiter offered to help him find the number he wanted. "No, thanks," he replied, "I'm just looking for a nice name for my baby."

401. The father of new identical twins grew so disgusted with people making goo-goo eyes at the babies that he developed a perfect answer to the question, "Are they twins?" He would reply: "No, they're not twins. I have two wives."

402. A Miami Beach oral surgeon who has eight kids does all the mechanical work on the family cars. A neighbor asked him if he really enjoyed tinkering with the engine. He said, "No, but with eight kids and a wife, the only place I can be alone is under the car."

403. The family heir was ecology minded, loved Ralph Nader and EPA. He told his father, "I can't stand all this dirt, trash, and pollution." His understanding Dad replied, "Alright, let's get out of your room and go talk someplace else."

404. A former basketball coach says that he went through some

lean years with a few of his teams. "I was at one school and we just couldn't seem to win at all," he says. "I came home once after the team had taken an awful shellacking and my kid—he was about 6 years old at the time—said to me, 'You ain't a very good coach, are you Daddy?' The only thing I could think to say to him was Don't say ain't!"

405.   Oscar Arnold has a problem at his house. "I find it very difficult," reports Oscar, "for a 5-foot 10-inch father to get through to a 6-foot 4-inch teenage son about the nutritional deficiencies of junk food."

406.   Triumphant father to mother watching teenage son mow the lawn: "I told him I lost the car keys in the grass."

407.   A man received a note from one of his children that said: "After watching you take care of the rest of the family all these years, doing without things for yourself, spending time with us when you could have been doing something else, I've finally decided what I want to be when I grow up. "Single."

408.   From the Kiwanis Club of South Orlando bulletin: The man who supports two wives is not necessarily a bigamist . . . he may have a married son.

409.   A fellow says he was lecturing his teenage son the other day and he told him. "You've got to learn to take criticism. After all, you're going to be a husband and father some day."

410.   Pat Ternal's youngsters haven't been allowed to have jelly since he went to work one morning with a doorknob in his hand.

411.   Tim: "Dad, can we paint the car green?"
   Dad: "Certainly not!"
   Tim to Peter: "See, I told you we should have asked."

412.   "We have learned to space our children. Ten feet apart is just about right." SAM LEVENSON

413.   "What a boy you are for asking questions," the father declared. "I'd like to know what would have happened if I'd asked as many questions when I was a boy." The son answered: "Perhaps you'd been able to answer some of mine."

414.   Stanley's father was distressed to find out that his son was planning to take up sky diving. "Are you sure you want to do it, son?" he reasoned with the lad. "Why go into any sport where you have to do it right the first time?"

Fishing

415.   A fisherman returned from Texas with a report on this year's mosquito crop: "The mosquitoes are so big," he said, "I slapped one that had three woodticks on it."

416.   It's that time of year when fishermen get that faraway lake in their eyes.

417.   Junior planned to go fishing until his mother insisted he take his little sister along. "No," Junior told her. "The last time she tagged along, I didn't catch any fish." "I'm sure she'll keep quiet this time," mother said. "It wasn't the noise," said Junior. "She ate all the bait."

418.   People living together without getting married is particularly disturbing to the guy who has just been arrested for fishing without a license.

419.   Recently, when Harry Rogers, Happy Britt, Harry Easler, and Harry Floyd went fishing, they took along a cooler full of beer. They proceeded to take a blood oath among themselves that they would not pop a top until they caught a fish. Thirty minutes later, they hadn't even had a nibble. And there were nine IOU's in the cooler.

420.   There were two Sunday fishermen who heard bells ringing in the distance. One said, "You know, Al, we really ought to be in church." Al rebaited his hook and answered, "Well, I couldn't go anyway; my wife is sick."

421.   "Wait'll you see the big bass I caught!" exulted the happy angler. "It's a beauty! But honey, although the fishing trip was fun, I really missed you. I'm so glad to be back. I'm just not happy when I'm away from you, sweetheart." The wife replied: "I'm not cleaning that fish."

422.   A fisherman lost his wedding ring in a lake. Three years later while fishing in the exact spot where he lost his treasured memento he was absent-mindedly thinking of the loss when a huge bass struck his line. His intuition told him to open the fish on the spot. Hurriedly his knife probed the innards. Then suddenly his blade struck something hard and solid. It was his finger.

423.   Sunday School teacher: "Do you suppose Noah did a lot of fishing?" Six-year-old: "What? With only two worms?"

424.   A man spent two weeks fishing at an expensive resort and didn't get a bite. But on the last day of his vacation he caught

one fish. "See that fish," he said to a bystander, "it cost me $1,000." "Ain't you lucky," said the bystander, "that you didn't catch two."

425.   Two solemn-faced men went fishing in an old boat. For three hours neither moved a muscle. Then the one up forward became a bit restless. "Darn it, Sam," grumbled his companion, "that's the second time you've shifted your feet in the last half hour. Did you come out here to fish or dance?"

426.   During noon recess of a case in Rock Island, Lincoln walked out to the railroad bridge and came to a boy sitting on the end of a tie, with a fishing pole out over the water. And Lincoln, fresh from the squabbles and challenges of the courtroom, said to the boy, "Well, I suppose you know all about this river." And the boy said, "Sure, mister, it was here before I was born and it's been here ever since." Lincoln smiled, "Well, it's good to be out here where there is so much fact and so little opinion."

427.   Since the earth's surface is one quarter land and three quarters water, it seems obvious that we are intended to spend three times longer fishing than mowing the lawn. GENE BROWN

428.   Mrs. Lowell was reminded of a tooth story involving Herb Maurice and Jim Holmes, who work for the same West Texas company. Each called the office one Monday to say he wouldn't be in to work that day. Each gave the same reason: That he had to have some dental work done. Later, one of the men in the office asked Jim for an explanation. "Herb and I went fishing," he replied. "When we were out in the middle of the lake, Herb took out his dentures and put them on the boat seat. I decided I'd play a prank on him. When he wasn't looking, I put his teeth in my pocket. Then later, when I got the chance, I took my dentures out and put them where his had been. We fished awhile, then decided to go to another spot. Herb picked up the teeth and tried several times to get them in his mouth. He got fiery mad and threw them as far as he could and said, 'Those dang things have never fit me right!' Well, I froze, because mine fit perfectly and cost me a bundle, besides. I sat stunned a few seconds, then reached in my pocket, got his teeth, threw them as far as I could and said, 'Mine don't fit, either.'"

Friends

429.   I have a friend who is such a perfectionist, if he were married to Raquel Welch, he'd expect her to cook.

430.   I have been advised by my Bulgarian friend that they have

just introduced a new million dollar lottery. The winner gets $1 a year for a million years.

431. I had a friend, a three-fingered pickpocket, who stole nothing but bowling balls.

432. A friend of mine, a rodeo cowboy, eventually gave up the circuit out of fear. He was afraid of the road hazards. His pickup was so old it was paid for.

433. A friend says he would have bought life insurance sooner if he'd known it would make his wife a better housekeeper. Now she's even waxing the bathtub.

434. An elevator operator complained that he was getting tired of people asking him for the time. A friend suggested that he hang a clock in his elevator. A few weeks later, the friend inquired as to how things were going. "Just awful," declared the elevator operator. "Now, all day long, people ask me, 'Is that clock right?' "

435. Wilbur Smith returned from a long anticipated trip to Paris and was greeted by a friend. "And how did you like Paris?" inquired the friend. "Wonderful," replied Jim. "I wish though I could have made the trip 20 years ago." "When Paris was really Paris, eh?" inquired the friend. "No, when Wilbur Smith was really Wilbur Smith."

436. A portly office worker and his skinny friend were discussing yoga, a method of achieving mental and physical body control through exercise. The picture they were viewing showed a young woman with legs pointed toward the ceiling. She was supported on the back of her neck and braced by her two arms. "It doesn't look very comfortable," said the skinny friend. "Oh, I don't know," replied the portly one for sake of argument. "Could you do it?" the skinny one asked. After some more consideration of the picture, the portly one admitted he couldn't. "For one thing my tummy would fall in my face and I'd smother," he said.

437. "What sign were you born under?" I asked my friend. "Emergency Entrance," he replied.

438. My friend says the only way to vaccinate a girl so it won't show these days is to have her inhale it.

439. I've got a Texan friend who is so wealthy he has a walk-in wallet.

440. A friend of mine went to a class reunion. That is where your

classmates have changed so much not many of them recognize you.

441. A friend spent years trying to get it all together—only to discover he didn't have the strength to carry it.

442. A friend told me the other day he is so poor his hearing aid is on a party line.

443. I have a friend who is so sneaky. He's the type who'll sneak into your bedroom, pull out the string on your pajama pants and then yell fire.

444. It's fine to love your enemies, but while you're at it, treat your friends a little better, too.

445. Quoting speaker Joe Griffith: "A friend believes that determination is the key to success. He makes it a point to finish something every day of his life. Yesterday it was a six-pack."

446. A man asked if a mutual friend told the truth or exaggerated a little. "I'll let you judge," said the man. "Last week he was describing a fish he caught and dislocated both shoulders."

447. A friend in the Bronx told me: "If Diogenes ever came through our neighborhood with his lamp—they'd steal it."

Government

448. Hear about the government official who took an I.Q. test and couldn't spell I.Q.?

449. Why bother to climb the ladder of success? Wait a while and the government will probably build an escalator.

450. A camper tourist insists that a sign atop Hoover Dam, which weighs 12 million tons, reads: "U.S. Government Property. Do Not Remove."

451. Findings by the surgeon general of the U.S. Government opened the door for development of a tasteless cigarette for people who know they shouldn't smoke and don't want to know about it when they do.

452. The Government can't understand how this country could have been formed in 1776 without Federal matching funds.

453. The government is finally getting closer to the people. It's going broke right along with them.

454. A stranger walked up to a farmer and showed him his card.

"I am a government inspector," he said, "and this card entitles me to inspect your farm and grants immunity from any interference." A few minutes later, the farmer heard screams from his pasture, where the inspector was being chased by a bull. Leaning over the gate, the farmer yelled at the top of his voice, "Show him your card, mister. Show him your card."

455. At a meeting of savings and loan officials, a speaker was complaining, in front of the proper government officials, of their constant meddling through endless regulations when a loud buzzer went off, a warning device on a machine. The speaker quipped, "That buzzer is kind of like the government. It's just so much noise and we ought not to pay that much attention to it."

456. Two government employees were surveyed by a third government agency. "What do you do here?" #1 answered, "I don't do a thing." #2 wrote, "I help him." The agent reported that although there was some duplication these two employees provided a base for the survival of a critically needed job—his own.

457. "The government is spending money like a bunch of drunken sailors," complained one taxpayer to another. "No, they're not," replied his buddy. "Drunk sailors spend their own money."

458. A local sage predicts the President will appoint an old foe, our state senator, "Ambassador to the Bermuda Triangle!"

459. Sign in a Chicago bankruptcy court: "You finally caught up with the Joneses, so did the government."

460. The government says the cigarette industry has developed a huge new box that is seven feet in length and is filled with a years supply of cigarettes. When you are finished with a pack, the box can be used as a septic tank—or you can get buried in it.

461. Income tax time is when the government asks three questions: How much do you make? How much do you have left? How come?

462. "My attitude toward my chosen profession is: If I have caused just one person to wipe a tear of laughter, that's my reward. The rest goes to the government." VICTOR BORGE

463. An anecdote relayed by a visitor to Russia has a Russian telling his companion, "There is a rumor the government will soon allow anybody to leave the country who wants to. If this is true, what will you do?" The companion replied, "Climb a tree." "Why?" "So as not to be trampled in the rush."

464. Show me a happy man and I'll show you a busy man. Therefore, we owe our happiness to the government.

465. One reason the unemployment figures keep dropping is that the government keeps hiring more and more people to report them.

466. We understand there's a new bumper sticker out that reads, "If the government ran it, crime wouldn't pay."

467. "In Washington they use the Seven Dwarfs approach to government. You go to any government agency, and one out of every seven you meet is dopey." JOEY ADAMS

468. Ben Willis liked Mark Russell's pithy analysis—"Washington is where they do badly that which doesn't need doing at all."

469. The Russians are getting paranoid about defections. A kid in school raises his hand to go to the bathroom and a government agent follows him to make sure he stays in the country.

470. Government spending gives you an idea why all new laws are called bills.

471. Three inmates in a Peking prison asked each other how they had gotten into such a fix. "I am here because I supported Deng Xiaoping." said one, referring to China's controversial vice premier. "I am here because I opposed Deng Xiaoping," said the second inmate. The two looked at the third man, who said: "I *AM* Deng Xiaoping."

Hunters

472. A wealthy world traveler was showing his guests the trophies he had brought back from a hunting expedition in India. Indicating a tiger-skin rug, he boasted, "When I shot this tiger, it was a case of him or me!" "Well," said one of the unimpressed guests, "he sure makes a better rug."

473. A young Englishman felt blue after a day's shooting in India. "I did not do so well today," he told his Indian attendant. "Oh; the young sahib shot very well, very well indeed," the diplomatic Hindu said, "but God was very merciful to the birds."

474. The newsletter published by the Texas Tourist Council reports: "One of our Texas deer hunters found himself in a heavy shooting area so he climbed up a tree to avoid being mistaken for a deer. It worked. The fellow who shot him thought he was a bear."

475. Wife: "Where are you going?"
Hubby: "Skeet shooting."
Wife: "Well, don't expect me to clean 'em!"

476. Stationed in Australia, an American executive decided to go on a kangaroo hunt. He climbed into his jeep and instructed his driver to proceed to the plains in quest of a kangaroo. No sooner had they reached the wide-open spaces when they spotted one, and the driver drove the jeep in hot pursuit. For some time they went at breakneck speed without gaining on the animal. Finally, the driver shouted, "There's no use chasing that thing, sir." "Why not?" asked the executive. "Cause we're now doin' 65, and that critter ain't even put his front feet down yet!"

477. The members of the hunting party had been asked to bring only male hounds. One near indigent member, however, was down to his last hound, a female, and out of courtesy was permitted to include her. The pack was off in a flash. In seconds they were completely out of sight. The confused hunters stopped to question a farmer in a nearby field. "Did you see some hounds go by here?" "Yes," he said, "and it was the first time I ever saw a fox runnin' fifth."

478. A man says he recently saw three unsuccessful deer hunters driving home. He could tell they were unsuccessful, he said, because they had tied a squirrel on the top of their car.

479. A woman persuaded her husband to take her deer hunting. He found a good stand for her, told her not to move and left her alone. Soon he heard the sound of gunshots and raced back, fearing that she had shot herself. When he reached the scene, his wife was holding her gun on a man and shouting, "You leave that deer alone! I shot it, and it's mine!" Replied the man, "If you say so, lady, it's a deer and it's yours, but just let me get my saddle off of it!"

480. Many people who are uninformed about outdoor sports are under the impression that all hunting and fishing consists of is hunting and fishing. The truth is that only three percent of hunting and fishing involves actual hunting and fishing. The other 97 percent is devoted to getting ready for hunting and fishing.

481. A good example of futility and frustration is a bird hunting for worms on Astroturf.

Husbands

482. One suburbanite wife to another: "You say your husband is as good as gold? Well, all I can say is that night before last, at the Smith's party, he cornered me and went off the gold standard."

483. A husband came home completely out of breath. His wife asked what was wrong. "Nothing, honey. I just ran all the way home behind the bus and saved 50 cents." "Well, if you must continue this running craze," she said, "Why don't you run home behind a taxi and save three dollars?"

484. "What I mean is," exclaimed the insurance salesman to a bewildered rural prospect, "How would your wife carry on if you should die?" "Well," answered the farmer reasonably, "I don't reckon that's any concern of mine—as long as she behaves herself while I'm alive."

485. "I'll say this for television," the husband announced to his wife. "What's that?" she asked. "The more unsuitable the program, the quieter it keeps the children," the husband observed.

486. "I expect my husband to be just what he is now twenty years from today," bragged Alice. "But that's unreasonable," replied Mary. "Yes, that's what he is now," said Alice's mother.

487. "Who you working for now?" I asked a husband. "Same people. Wife and six kids," replied the husband.

488. Overheard: "You say your husband owns property in Las Vegas?" "Yes, the Riviera Hotel is holding his luggage!"

489. Some people run to get their blood circulating. My husband gets that same effect by watching cheerleaders.

490. A lady claims that her husband is a do-it-yourself man. "Every time I ask him to do something, he says, 'Do it yourself.' "

491. A fellow was talking to a friend on the phone. "I am master in my own home and I can play golf any time I want to . . . just hold the phone a minute while I find out if I want to."

492. Some ladies were discussing husbands. "Husbands are like photographers," said one. "All they want you to do is keep still and look pleasant."

493. My husband's so cheap that when I suggested we eat out, we ate in the garage.

494. George was always being dragged along on shopping trips by his domineering wife, but now, no more! On the last trip his wife held up a frilly nightgown in a crowded department store and asked him if he liked it. Gentle George's moment had come, and he replied loudly, "I sure do! But will your husband?"

495. A husband groaned as he got out of bed one morning. "I feel very schizophrenic today," and his wife replied, "that makes four of us."

496. A real estate agent was showing an old farmhouse to a woman prospect who made a few sketches on a pad and admitted, "I could do a lot with that house." But then she added wistfully, "On the other hand, I believe I said the same thing the first time I saw my husband."

497. The housewife next door complains her husband is dull and unimaginative: "Some topless dancers went on strike—and he was the only one who read their picket signs."

498. Golfer Lee Trevino was getting dressed to go out with his wife Claudia when he noticed her fussing over her hair. "Honey, don't bother," he said. "You're going out with me tonight. Nobody is going to notice you."

499. "The modern husband believes that a woman's place is in the home, and he wants her to go there immediately after work."
BONNIE FRANKLIN

500. At a reception a young, attractive woman was talking to a friendly stranger who had arrived late. "I don't know what's the matter with that tall man over there," said the young woman. "He was so attentive awhile ago but he won't look at me now." "Perhaps he saw me come in," said the stranger. "He's my husband."

501. An angry husband shouted at his wife, "You talk too much." "I knew that," shouted the wife, "when I said 'I do.' "

502. Knowing her husband's habit of sampling everything she baked, a woman left a note on a dozen fresh tarts: "Counted—one dozen." On her return she found only 10 tarts and a note: "Think metric!"

503. The husband was bad about drinking, but his wife was a kindly, Christian lady. One Saturday afternoon the radio announced the coming of a tornado. Their home would be in its path. The lady caught the inebriated husband by the hand and led him to a

ravine about 150 yards from the house. The storm came and limbs began to blow over the ravine. The lady became frightened and said aloud, "Lord, take care of me and my drunken husband." The husband said, "Honey, don't tell him I'm drunk, tell him I'm sick."

504. Her husband was not the type to compliment her at all, so Mrs. Richards was surprised when he called her an angel. "Why did you call me an angel, dear?" she asked coyly. "Because," replied Mr. Richards irately, "you are always up in the air, you are continually harping on one thing or another, and you never have a damned thing to wear."

505. "I'm not myself today," I remarked to my wife. "Yes," she replied, "I noticed the improvement."

506. The woman was telling her troubles to the judge in domestic-relations court. "The only time my husband ever brought a ray of sunshine into my life," she said, "was when he came home at dawn, slammed the door and the Venetian blind fell off the window."

507. Harry's wife dreamed she was in the arms of another man and then she dreamed she saw Harry coming and yelled: "My husband!" Harry woke up and jumped out the window.

508. The thing that keeps a lot of husbands broke is not the wolf at the door, but the mink in the shop window.

509. Overheard: "When my husband came home from that cocktail party, he ran over the lawn, flattened some shrubbery, rammed into the garage, and tore off the overhanging door. Imagine the damage he might have done if he had been driving the car."

510. Joggers make dependable husbands. In those outfits they wear, home is the only place they can go.

511. A husband is a person who is under the impression that he bosses the house, when actually he only houses the boss.

512. George was having a "night out" with the guys from the office and before he realized it the morning of the next day had dawned. Dreading his wife's reaction to his late homecoming, he suddenly hit upon an idea. He rang his house and, when his wife answered, he shouted excitedly, "Don't pay the ransom dear. I escaped!"

513. A woman spends half of her life looking for a husband. After she finds one, she spends the other half looking for her husband.

Jobs

514. At a coffee break, a fellow was saying that his brother-in-law was a "customer service representative" for one of the utility companies. What was that, someone wanted to know? And a voice from the lower end of the table broke in to explain: "That's a very pleasant person who tells you that they have absolutely no record of your previous complaints."

515. Poor Jim. In order to get the job they made him shave off his mustache, sideburns, and beard. And when they saw his face, they wouldn't hire him.

516. A retired carpenter reports that he never hired men who smoked cigarettes or didn't wear belts. Smokers, he said, are always stopping work to light up and men who don't wear belts are always stopping to pull up their pants.

517. A new employee reported to his wife, "You get five days sick pay the first year and ten days a year after that. They must figure the longer you work here, the sicker you get."

518. Pat Murphy was employed at the local brewery. One day while stirring a large vat of beer he lost his balance and fell in. Pat's wife was called to the brewery and given the awful news of his drowning. After regaining her composure she allowed that she assumed his death was "at least merciful and quick." The foreman shook his head saying, "I don't know about that Mrs. Murphy. He got out twice to go to the bathroom."

519. A young worker who had been loafing for most of the past year approached an older man just before he was to be reviewed for a raise. "Do you think," he asked anxiously, "that if I really work hard for the next two weeks, I'll get a raise?" "Son," the older worker replied, "you make me think of a thermometer in a cold room. You can make it register higher by holding your hand over it, but you won't be warming the room."

520. Golfer Sam Snead of retirement: "I once thought of becoming a political cartoonist because they only have to come up with one idea a day. Then I thought I'd be a sportswriter. They don't have to come up with any ideas."

521. Businessman Mike Ford used to have a barber who was a real character. Very independent. Just how independent? "Well," says Mike, "there was the time the barber slapped a steaming-hot towel on a customer's face. The customer howled in pain, threw

off the towel and demanded: Why did you do that?" "Had to," said the barber. "It was burning my hands."

522.   In Jerusalem two elderly men were sitting on a park bench discussing the war. "How long do you think it will last?"
   "Two months, the most!"
   "So quick?"
   "My son joined the Army and he never yet held a job for longer than two months in his life!"

523.   The personnel manager of a large firm was interviewing an applicant for a job. "How long did you work for your last employer?" he asked the man. "45 years," the man replied. "How old are you?" "37." "How could you work on a job for 45 years and you are only 37 years old?" "Overtime."

524.   The plumbers were discussing their respective jobs. One young plumber began complaining loudly about how hard he had to work. "Ah, pipe down," said one of the older men. "When I first started in this business, they let us lay two lengths of pipe and then turned the water on—and we had to keep ahead of it!"

525.   If everybody knew the world was going to end tomorrow, you'd have one heck of a job getting an estimate for a new roof. FRANKLIN P. JONES

526.   A clever young fellow applied for a job in answer to an ad but was told by the manager, "You're much too late. I already have more than 1,000 applications here on my desk." "Well, then," said the young man, "why not employ me to go through them and classify them for you?"

Judges

527.   "What's the charge against this man, officer?" the southern country judge asked. "Bigotry, your honor," the officer answered. "He's got three wives." The judge said: "I'm surprised at yo' ignorance, suh. That's trigonometry, not bigotry."

528.   Judge: "So you're a locksmith? What were you doing in that bookie joint when the police raided it?"
   Prisoner: "I was making a bolt for the door."

529.   Judge told the defendant: "It's alcohol and alcohol alone that's responsible for your condition."
   The Defendant replied: "You've made me very happy, Judge. Everyone else tells me it's all my fault."

530. Judge, "It seems to me you've been coming up before me in this court for the past 20 years."

Prisoner, "Yes, Judge, you've been a big disappointment to me. I thought by now you'd be governor."

531. The prosecuting attorney said the defendant hit his wife over the head with an oak leaf. "An oak leaf!" snorted the judge. "An oak leaf never hurt anybody." "Your Honor," pursued the prosecutor, "It was an oak leaf out of a dining room table."

532. An Indian petitioned a judge in a New Mexico court for permission to change his name to a shorter one. "What is your name now?" asked the judge. "Chief Screeching Train Whistle." "And what do you wish to change it to?" The Indian folded his arms and grunted, "Toots."

533. The judge eyed the man at the bar sternly. "Your wife charges you with not having spoken to her in five years," he said. "What is your explanation?" "Well, your honor," replied the man, "I didn't think it was polite to interrupt her."

534. A cross-eyed judge was trying three cross-eyed prisoners. He turned to the first cross-eyed prisoner, and said, "What's your name?" And the second cross-eyed prisoner said, "John Brown," and the cross-eyed judge said, "I wasn't talking to you," and the third cross-eyed prisoner said, "I didn't say anything." HENNY YOUNGMAN

535. An industrialist was fighting a case in tax court. He looked at the bench and told his Honor, "As God is my judge, I do not owe this tax." The judge said, "He's not. I am. You do."

536. The judge asked the defendant whether he knew the difference between right and wrong. "Sure I do, your Honor. It's simply that I hate to make decisions."

537. A Judge recalled the best alibi he ever heard during his term on the bench: "A man involved in an auto accident and charged with reckless driving testified: 'It was my wife's fault—she fell asleep on the back seat.'"

Kids

538. "Well, Mary, how do you like your little brother?" the visitor asked. Mary responded: "Oh, he's all right, I guess, but there are a lot of things we needed worse."

539. Sometimes kids get very confused about Christmas. Like one little kid asked his mother, "Is it true that Santa Claus brings us presents?" She said, "Yes, that's true." He said, "And the stork brings us babies?" She said, "Yes, that's true." He said, "And the Police Department protects us?" She said, "That's right," He looked up at her and said, "Then what do we need Daddy for?"

540. A local boy played the part of Judas in the pageant play "King of Kings." His part (Judas) was not even mentioned in newspaper reviews so the next issue the local paper gave him special mention on page one. Headlines read, "Local Boy Betrays Christ."

541. A 10-year old boy was a chronic cusser, so the school psychiatrist sent him to one of those ultra modern do-what-you-like type schools. Later, the boy told the doctor that he had really been helped. "You don't cuss anymore?" asked the doctor. "I still do," replied the boy, "But now I'm proud of it!"

542. Woman: "Son, can you direct me to the bank?"
  Boy: "Yessum, for a quarter."
  Woman: "Isn't that mighty high?"
  Boy: "Not for a bank director."

543. I felt unwanted as a kid. Mama would wrap my lunch in roadmaps.

544. First boy: "I have my father's eyes and my mother's nose."
  Second boy: "I have my grandfather's forehead and my uncle's ears."
  Third boy: "I have my sister's socks and my brother's pants!"

545. A World War II veteran, telling the story of Pearl Harbor to his son, asked the four-year old if he could use the word "infamy" in a sentence. The boy thought about it, then said, "Billy always beats me up 'cause he's got it infamy."

546. The teacher was explaining the habits of dolphins to her class. She concluded her lecture, "A single dolphin will have as many as 2,000 babies." A pupil raised his hand, "And how many" he inquired, "do the married ones have?"

547. What's so special about pet rocks? I gave one to a six year old kid. He had it apart in an hour.

548. Names go in cycles. It's hard to believe they enrolled a kid in kindergarten the other day named "Presidential Tape Thompson."

549. My kid won a Farrah Fawcett-Majors Look-Alike Contest. Lord, how I wish that boy would get a haircut!

550. A first grader said he was asked one question on his quiz for the day and almost made 100. He was only three seats away from the right answer.

551. The garden was at its peak of production, and Mother was busily putting some of its fruits away for next season. As she opened the freezer to deposit a batch, she noticed a row of plastic freezer containers, each containing a fly that was frozen stiff. She was removing the containers and puzzling over them when her 8-year-old son bounded in. Seeing what Mother was doing, he said, "Oh, Mama, don't take those out of the freezer! Those are TV dinners for my turtle!"

552. "You say your Dad never liked you?" "No. He used to encourage me to practice my electric guitar while I was in the bathtub."

553. The principal was delivering a lecture to the little ones on hall safety procedures. "Now what would you do if you saw one of your classmates fall down a flight of stairs?" was the question. "I'd run to the office quickly for help?" a little boy replied. "Good, now what would you do if you saw a teacher fall down the stairs?" The same kid thought for a minutes, then asked, "Which one?"

554. One day, instead of serving the usual hot meal, the school cafeteria handed out peanut butter and jelly sandwiches as the entree. After lunch, a satisfied first grader marching out the door complimented the cafeteria manager: "Finally you gave us a home-cooked meal."

555. The 3rd grade teacher was trying to break her class of the "I seen" habit. "You should never say 'I seen him do it,' " she sternly admonished. "Yeah," piped up a voice from the rear. "Specially if you ain't sure he done it."

556. "When I was a kid, I was so poor—in my neighborhood the rainbow was in black and white." RODNEY DANGERFIELD

557. A teacher was telling her class about the discovery of the law of gravity. "Sir Isaac Newton was sitting on the ground looking at a tree," she explained. "An apple fell on his head, and from that, he discovered gravitation. Wasn't that wonderful?" "It sure was," piped a small lad in the back of the room, "and if he had been sittin' in a school lookin' at his books, he wouldn't have discovered nothin'!"

558. Two year old Jamey was having trouble getting to sleep one

night, so his mother offered to stay with him until he dozed off. "Mom" was six months pregnant, and Jamey noticing a movement asked her what she had inside her. She explained to him that a baby was in there and that it would soon be a brother or sister. Jamey pondered that for a few moments, and then asked, "Do you have a door in your back?"

559. Teacher—"If I lay two eggs on this side of the table and I lay two eggs on the other side, how many eggs will I have laid all together?"
Kid—"I don't think you can do it."

560. His kids are having to learn good manners the hard way—without seeing any.

561. "I remember a time when I was a kid and had a fever. They put a thermometer in my mouth. I remember the words of my old man, 'All right kid, bite hard.'" RODNEY DANGERFIELD

562. Quoting comic Pat Cooper: "My kids ask to go on vacation in Hawaii. I don't understand that. When I asked my father to send me on a vacation, he told me to go out and sit on the fire escape and I did. When it started to rain I knocked on the window to come in, and he said, 'I can't hear you. You're on vacation.'"

563. Kids are tricky. This morning an eight year old asked if they have a Fourth of July in England. I said, "Of course not." He said, "Then what comes after their third of July?"

564. A father had given his son a dollar for his birthday. All afternoon, the lad trotted around his neighborhood, getting his bill changed to silver at the grocer's, back to a bill again at the baker's and so on. Observing all this hustle and bustle, the father asked him the reason for his strange behavior."Well you see, it's like this," replied the young entrepenuer, "Sooner or later somebody is going to make a mistake and it's not going to be me."

565. They say no man knows his true character until he has run out of gas, declared bankruptcy, and raised a teenager.

566. The lad had come home from school and dashed right back out of the house. His mother called to him, "Where are you going?" The son yelled back, "Out to play." "With those holes in your shoes?" "No, with the kids across the street."

567. The 7-year-old girl had taken her 4-year-old brother to a birthday party. After awhile, her hostess said, "Your brother surely is

a quiet child. He hasn't moved for 30 minutes." "It's the first time he's worn a necktie," the sister explained. "He thinks he's tied to something."

568.   The minister came upon a marble game in progress and was shocked by the language he heard. He asked reprovingly, "Do you know what happens to little boys who talk like that?" "Yeah," said one of the little boys, "they grow up to be golfers."

569.   A small boy returned home from school and told his father that he was second in his class. Top place, he explained, was held by a girl. "Surely, John," said the father, "You're not going to be beaten by a mere girl!" "Well, you see, Father," explained John, "girls are not nearly as mere as they used to be."

570.   The father said, "Junior, one more bite like that and you'll leave the table." The lad responded, "One more bite like that and I'll be through."

571.   A kid from a forced racially balanced high school was discovered who couldn't read or write. He commented, "Why of course I can't read or write. I've spent all my life on a dang bus."

572.   Two hitchhiking soldiers in Nebraska noticed a small boy leading a mule along a country road. "Hey, son," one of the soldiers said, "how come you're holding onto your brother so tight?" The youngster responded, "To keep him from joining the Army."

573.   "Is your mother home?" the salesman asked a small boy sitting on the steps in front of a house. "Yea, she's home," the boy said, scooting over to let him past. The salesman plied the doorbell, got no response, knocked once, then again. Still no one came to the door. Turning to the boy, the fellow said, "I thought you said your mother was home." The kid replied, "She is, but this isn't where I live."

Lawyers

574.   On his 80th birthday, criminal lawyer Clarence Darrow confided to an equally aged friend that his memory was beginning to fail him. "Mine is as good as ever," boasted the friend. "Why, I can remember the first girl I ever kissed." "I envy you," sighed Darrow. "I can't even remember the last."

575.   A no-nonsense elderly lady was on the witness stand. The prosecuting attorney, testing her mental capacity and eyesight, pointed to the defense and asked, "Can you identify that man?" "Yes, he's one of the biggest crooks in the county." Obviously pleased, he lowered his voice sweetly and asked, "Can you identify

me?" "Yes, you're a crook, too." With that the judge banged his gavel and ordered the two attorneys to approach the bench. In hushed tones he whispered, "If either one of you birds ask if she knows me, I'll hold you in contempt of court."

576. A lawyer who finally settled a very involved estate case was telling some of his fellow barristers all the gory details. "It was a tough fight all the way," he concluded. "The heirs got almost as much as I did."

577. A lady wrote her lawyer that her husband got thrown out of a bumper car at the county fair and "bumped" unmercifully by a zealous crowd. "He wasn't hurt," she wrote, "but if you'll take the lawsuit case, I'll hit him two or three times with a hammer."

578. A lawyer appearing in a case asked the witness: "Now, Mr. James, did you or did you not, on the date in question or at any other time, previously or subsequently, say or even intimate to the defendant or anyone else, whether friend or acquaintance or in fact a stranger, that the statement imputed to you, whether just or unjust, and denied by the plaintiff, was a matter of no consequence or otherwise? Answer!Did you or did you not?" The witness pondered for a little while and then said: "Did I or did I not what?"

579. An office boy with a brokerage firm, Chester by name, was charged with stealing well over $500 in postage stamps. The eager young lawyer he retained made a brilliant plea in which Chester's integrity was especially illuminated. Chester was swiftly exonerated. "Gee," he gushed. "How can I every repay you?" "The price of justice is my fee," said the lawyer. "It's $500. There's no rush though, if you're a little pressed." "Oh, I can pay you right away," said Chester, "if you accept stamps."

580. A lawyer and a preacher were taking an ocean cruise. The ship hit a storm and the lawyer fell overboard. Almost immediately eight sharks formed a two-lane escort for the guy and helped him all the way back to the ship. "It was an act of God," the lawyer told the clergy. "No, the minister said, "just professional courtesy."

581. The young lawyer told his associate, "I feel like telling that judge where to get off again." "What do you mean, again?" "Well," the lawyer replied, "I felt like it last week, too."

582. "Sir, I would like your opinion about a very important matter," said the youth, as he stood, haltingly, in the presence of the great lawyer. "Do you think, sir, that your daughter would make

a good wife?" "I do not," was the answer. "That will be ten dollars."

583. 1st lawyer: "Soon as I realized it was a crooked deal, I got out of it!"
2nd lawyer: "How much?"

584. Mark Russell on bar association conventions: "All the members come together to mourn their dear, departed brothers—who are serving in minimum-security prisons doing three years at hard tennis."

585. A lawyer's kid was doing his English homework. He asked Dad what comes after a sentence and he told him "an appeal."

586. "Your Honor," the lawyer told the court in Nairobi, Kenya, "I submit that my client did not break into the house at all. He found the parlor window open, inserted his right arm and removed a few trifling articles. Now, my client's arm is not himself, and I fail to see how you can punish him for an offense committed by only one of his limbs." "Your argument," answered the Judge, "is very well put. Following it logically, I sentence the prisoner's arm to one year's imprisonment. He can accompany it or not, just as he chooses." Whereupon the defendant calmly removed his artificial arm and walked out.

587. Apprehension is what a surgeon feels when he's operating on a lawyer who specializes in malpractice cases.

588. Returning to his birthplace, Clarence Darrow met a doctor friend. "If you had listened to me," said the doctor to Darrow, "you, too, would now be a doctor." "What's wrong with being a lawyer?" "Well, I don't say all lawyers are crooks, but even you will have to admit that your profession doesn't exactly make angels of men." "No," said Darrow, "you doctors have the better of us there."

Marriage

589. "I gave my wife two gifts for her birthday."
Neighbor: "That was generous. Why did you do that?"
"Well, she said she wanted something to protect her and something to drive. So I gave her a hammer and a nail."

590. Husband: "In our six years of marriage we haven't been able to agree on anything."
Wife: "It's been seven years, dear."

591. Mr. and Mrs. Ralph Birdsong, Decatur, Georgia, after each lost their first marriage partner, married and put their two children

each into one family and one home. A new acquaintance asked Ralph the ages of his children. Ralph replied, "15, 14, 13 and 11." The stranger quipped, "What happened—were you in the Navy one year?"

592. KEEPING THE PEACE
To keep your marriage brimming
With love in the loving cup,
Whenever you're wrong admit it,
Whenever you're right shut up.

593. HE: "I dreamed I was married to the most beautiful girl in the world."
SHE: "Were we happy?"

594. "My wife has this terrible irritating habit of staying up till 2 to 3 a.m." "Good gosh. Why on earth does she do that?" "She's waiting for me to come home."

595. Phyllis Diller: "Fang (her husband) is so cheap he didn't want to spend $2 for a marriage license until I convinced him it worked out to only two cents a pound."

596. The husband was going over the monthly accounts. He looked over the check stubs and chided his wife, "Water bill, gas bill, grocery bill, gasoline bill . . . honestly, Ethel, you just have to stop this wild, riotous, carefree spending!"

597. Annually, on the average, someone has to: Wash an acre of dirty dishes, scrub five miles of floor, and shave 35,000 square inches of face. That could explain why so many henpecked fellows are wearing aprons and beards.

598. Eve asked Adam if he had been running around behind her back and he asked, "with who?"

599. Most women could be cured of jealousy if they'd just take one good, impartial look at their husbands.

600. A couple named Brown wanted a child but, concluding they couldn't have children, they adopted one. As so often happens, almost immediately afterwards, Mrs. Brown became pregnant. When the child was born, the parents were ecstatic. They agonized over the choice of a name. The child was so special, they felt, that Bill or George or Bart or Herman would be too plain. They settled on Fantastic. Fantastic Brown had a wonderful childhood, except for all the kidding he took over his first name. He hated it. He enjoyed

a successful professional life and, in his old age, finally became critically ill. On his deathbed, he begged his wife: "Please leave the "Fantastic" off my tombstone. Just put 'Brown.'" He died and, as he had asked, she left the "Fantastic" off the tombstone. But just to have "Brown" and the birth and death dates would be too plain, she felt. She wanted something about how wonderful a husband he had been. So, under the "Brown," she had these words engraved: "During his marriage, he never looked at another woman." And now everyone who passes the tombstone murmurs: "Fantastic!"

601. "Married life in the old days was simpler. If a man had a fight with his wife, he just went out and got drunk. Today, if he has a fight, he checks with his lawyer, sees a psychiatrist, spends an hour with his marriage counselor—and then goes out and gets drunk." Comedian SLAPPY WHITE

602. "If it weren't for my wife," he complained, "we'd be one of the nicest couples in town."

603. A Midwest preacher received this thank-you note from a bridegroom he had married: "Dear Reverend, I want to thank you for the beautiful way you brought my happiness to a conclusion."

604. A boy was too timid to ask a father for his daughter's hand. So, he called the father. "Do you care if Jane and I get married?" he asked. "No," the father said, "who is this?"

605. His wife says he leads a dog's life: "He comes in with muddy feet, makes himself comfortable by the fire, and waits to be fed."

606. If the Lord didn't mean for us to gamble, he would never have invented matrimony.

607. She: "You vowed to love, honor and obey me. You don't love me."
    He: "Two out of three ain't bad."

608. He's a do-it-yourself man with a when-are-you-gonna-do-it wife.

609. Every man needs a wife. Many things go wrong that can't be blamed on the government.

610. A wife said, "I have an enduring marriage. You'll never know what I have endured."

611. "Were there powder marks on the man's face when his wife shot him?" "Yeah, that's why she shot him!"

612. George Bernard Shaw said: "Marriage is popular because it combines the maximum of temptation with the maximum of opportunity."

613. We've had adult education for thousands of years. It's called marriage.

Men

614. An executive is trained to know when to delegate responsibility and authority. That training came in handy for one executive when lightning struck his house. It cracked the ceiling, knocked the medicine cabinet door open, spilling medicine and breaking bottles, shattered a light bulb, and blew out the electric wiring in the room air-conditioner. The man and his wife were standing in the room, looking at the smoke coming from the air-conditioner, wondering what to do next. Then his background as an administrator came to the fore. He told his wife: "Touch it and see if it shocks you."

615. "Fortune knocks at every man's door once in a life, but in a good many cases, the man is in a neighboring saloon and does not hear her." MARK TWAIN

616. A man is never so weak as when a pretty girl is telling him how strong he is.

617. His hair's so thin you can see when he has a dirty thought.

618. The office tightwad says he's sorry he bought a cheap toupee. Now he's losing hair that isn't even his.

619. Men spend thousands on hair transplants and toupees when what is really needed is more women who like bald men.

620. An opportunist is a man who listens carefully to what you say you'd like to do and does it himself.

621. "Do you know a man with one eye named Ed?" "I don't know, What's the name of his other eye?"

622. Irish Proverb: Courtin' a girl is like dying—a man has to do it for himself.

623. Clothes don't make the man. Particularly walking shorts.

624. A consultant is a man who borrows your watch to answer your question of what time it is.

625. History has so many unsung heroes—like the man who first

ate a tomato to prove they weren't poisonous. Then to build his confidence, he ate a toadstool!

626.   If Avon sponsored Lawrence Welk, he could say, "Avon and a two!"

627.   Circus manager to the Human Cannonball: "You can't quit. Where will I find another man of your caliber?"

628.   A south Florida citrus grower says his orange crop and hairdo are being thinned all too regular. He knows that the Bible says even the hairs on his head are numbered but each year it gets a little easier for the Lord to take inventory.

629.   A communist is a man who likes what he doesn't have so well that he wants you not to have it either.

630.   There are two kinds of cattlemen: Those who go broke and those who stay broke.

631.   The only war I ever approved of was the Trojan war; it was fought over a woman, and the men appreciated what they were fighting for.

632.   Sportscaster Lindsey Nelson says his long career has taught him three things:
   1. Never play poker with a man named Ace.
   2. Never eat at a place called Mom's.
   3. Never invest in anything that eats or needs painting.

633.   When we see men of worth we should think of equaling them; when we see men of contrary character, we should turn inwards and examine ourselves.

634.   Two men standing in the unemployment line. One man says: "It frightens me sometimes when I realize that this administration, with its fiscal irresponsibility, is my sole means of support."

635.   You may not know that the greatest cause for heart attacks in men over 60 is women under 30.

636.   It was Collie Small who got off one of World War II's great ad libs under fire. During the Battle of the Bulge, he was riding in a jeep that spun so violently out of control that he was thrown out, sailing through the air to land headfirst in a snowbank. "Gee, Mr. Small," said his anxious driver, digging him out, "That was some swan dive." "T-t-tell me," sputtered Collie, spitting snow, "D-did I keep my f-f-feet together?"

637. A leading wit once said, "Man is the only animal that laughs. But then he is the only animal that has a legislature."

638. When the good guy is threatening the bad guy because the bad guy threatened the good girl, the good guy declares: "If you touch one hair on her pretty little head, I'll fill you so full of lead you'll leave pencil marks when you sit down."

639. One of the nicest things about being bald is that when company comes all you have to do is straighten your tie.

640. A young man walked into a swanky jewelry store and informed the clerk that he was in the market for an engagement ring for his girl. The jeweler placed a tray of rings on the counter and stood back to allow the buyer to make his selection. The youth picked up a sparkling diamond and asked the price. "That's exactly $1,000," replied the jeweler gently. The young man looked startled, and then whistled. He pointed to another stone. "And this one?" "That, sir," said the jeweler even more gently, "is two whistles."

641. The gambling boom in Las Vegas is incredible. One day a man went to the drugstore because he had a headache and wanted to buy some aspirin. The clerk said, "Why not make it double or nothing?" The gambler agreed, made the bet and lost. He left with two headaches.

642. Ed Story says the only thing he can lick any more is a postage stamp—and that has to have its back turned.

643. While waiting at a bus stop, a man stepped on a pay scale and dropped in a penny. He received a card: "Your name is John Jones, you weigh 165 pounds, and you are waiting for a bus." This brought him up short. He felt it couldn't happen again, so he dropped in another penny. The second card read: "Your name is John Jones, you weigh 165 pounds, and you are waiting for a bus." Completely shaken, he went in a nearby novelty store, purchased some dark glasses and a mustache, rolled up his coat collar, took off his hat and pushed his hair down over his forehead. He crept back to the scale, put in another penny, and received another card. It read: "Your name is John Jones, you weigh 165 pounds, and while you were messing around, you missed the bus."

Money

644. "What would you have if you had $100 in one pocket and $20 in the other?"
  "Somebody else's pants."

645. A vaseline company was taking a survey and was told by one man that vaseline was used in his home for cuts, bruises and to save money. The surveyor asked, "How do you use it to save money?" "We put it on the refrigerator handle," said the man. "It keeps the kids out."

646. The $2 bill has been brought back and may well become known as the honest dollar.

647. Money says on it "In God We Trust." That's because we exclusively lend it to people we can foreclose on.

648. The government reports that 20 percent of the population is trying to live within their means. What are they trying to do—mess up our economic recovery?

649. Money isn't everything. Usually, it isn't even yours.

650. A group came into Las Vegas from Chicago. One of the men on that trip won $100,000. Now he didn't want anyone to know about this so he decided not to return with the others, but took a late plane. He got home at 3 a.m., went into the backyard of his house, dug a hole and planted the money in it. The following morning he walked outside and saw—there was nothing but an empty hole. Then he noticed there were footprints leading to the house next door, which was owned by a deaf-mute. On the same street lived a professor who knew sign language and was a friend of the deaf man's. So this fellow got a pistol from his house, rousted out the professor and the deaf-mute, and said to the professor, "You tell this guy that if he doesn't give me my $100,000 back, I'm going to kill him." The professor conveyed the message to his friend, and his friend replied in sign language: "I hid it in your backyard under your cherry tree." The professor then turned to the enraged fellow, and said: "He's not going to tell you. He said he would rather die first."

651. McTavish was the proud owner of a new cash register. One day when an old friend came into the shop and bought several items, the customer noted that McTavish pocketed the money instead of putting it into the drawer. "Why not ring it up?" he asked. "You'll be forgetting it." "Oh, I'll not forget," replied the Scot. "I keep track in my head until I get five dollars an' then I ring it up. It saves wear-r and tear-r on the machine."

652. "My wife is always asking for money," complained a friend of ours. "Last week she wanted $200. The day before yesterday she asked me for $125. This morning she wanted $150." "That's

crazy," I said, "What does she do with it all?" "I don't know," said our friend, "I never give her any." HENNY YOUNGMAN

653. Making money is getting to be like bees making honey. You can make it, but they won't let you keep it.

654. What good is happiness? It can't buy you money. HENNY YOUNGMAN

655. A fellow had some bad luck at Las Vegas. Lost $1,000. Said he got even though. He stole 400 sweet and lows.

656. My wife went into a gas station the other day and asked for $5 worth. "Where you want it?" the attendant asked, "behind the ear or on your wrists?"

657. Sidewalk cafes are popular. A guy went to one of them, ordered a drink and couldn't pay. The proprietor threw him inside.

658. The other day I went down to the Internal Revenue Department. Thank heavens! I'm all paid up until 1947. HENNY YOUNGMAN

659. Three fellows went to church. When it came time to take the offering, they discovered they didn't have any money. So, to keep from being embarrassed, one fainted and the other two carried him out.

660. A reader says he was a patient recently in a hospital and they were so money-hungry that they had pay bedpans.

661. The occasion was a testimonial dinner for the town's leading citizen. "Friends," he said, "when I came to your city, I had one suit, one pair of shoes, and all my earthly possessions wrapped up in a handkerchief. This city has been good to me—and I worked hard. Now I'm president of the bank, own 10 buildings and five companies. Yes, my friends, your town has been good to me." After the banquet, an awed youngster approached the great man, hoping to find out his secret of success. "Please sir," he asked, "what did you have in that handkerchief?" "Well, young man," the millionaire reported, "had about $30,000 in cash and $850,000 in securities."

662. Money can be lost in more ways than won, yet most of us have two chances of becoming wealthy—slim and none. (EUGENE P. BERTIN, Pennsylvania School Jnl, 9–71)

663. A couple of panhandlers met on the street after an especially tiring day. "To look at me now," one said, "you'd never believe that I once lived the life of Riley: Winters in the sun, deep sea fishing, fine cars, beautiful women, the best cuisine." "Well, what

happened?" the other asked. "Riley reported his credit cards missing," the first one replied.

664. Milton Berle says Pete Rose got $800,000 a season to play for the Phillies, "$100,000 to play baseball, and $700,000 to live in Philadelphia."

665. A neighbor says he didn't realize it was less than three months 'til Christmas until he made the final payment for last year's gifts.

666. Money—Taking it with you isn't important. The real problem is just making it last until you are ready to go.

667. A neighbor says he's now making enough money to live like he wanted to. Back in 1969.

668. The kids tell me that, more than anything else, they would like to have something from me that I made myself. I asked them what it was and they said . . . "money!"

669. A financial genius is a man who can earn money faster than his family can spend it.

Mothers

670. My mother used to grab my ear and lead me on the desired path of action. She called it "child guidance." She called my father's contribution an "uplifting experience."

671. There's nothing like a letter from home. This one reportedly came from a Kentucky mother to her son:
Dear Stanley:
I write to let you know I am still alive. I am writing slowly as I know you don't read fast. You won't know the house when you come home—we moved. We had trouble moving, especially the bed—the man wouldn't let us take it in the taxi and we were afraid we might wake your father.
Your father has a nice new job and very responsible. He has about 500 people under him—he cuts the grass at the cemetery. Our neighbors, the Browns, started keeping pigs. We got wind of it yesterday.
I got my appendix out and a dishwasher in. There is a washing machine in the new house here, but it don't work too good. Last week I put 14 shirts in the washer and pulled that chain. They whirled around real good but then disappeared. I think something is wrong with the machine.
Your uncle Dick drowned last week in a whiskey vat at the distil-

lery. Four of his work mates dived in to save him, but he fought them off bravely. We cremated his body the next day and just got the fire out this morning.

I went to the doctor with your father last week. The doctor put a small glass tube in my mouth and told me not to open it for ten minutes. Your father wanted to buy it from him.

It rained only twice last week—once for three days and once for four days. Monday was so windy that our chicken laid the same egg four times . . .

Your loving mother,

672.   First mother: "My three boys stick together. When one gets into trouble, neither of the others will tell on him."

Second mother: "Then how do you find out which one to punish?"

First mother: "That's simple. I send all three to bed without supper. The next morning I spank the one with the black eye."

673.   A lady vowed that all her children would have what she never was able to get—an education. If it had not been for a local college, she could not have kept her word. She had 12 kids. Said she had so many she ran out of names to call her husband.

674.   A mother described to her small son the happy times of her girlhood, as riding ponies, sliding down haystacks, and wading in a brook at the farm. When the woman finished, the boy sighed and said, "Gee, mom, I wish I'd met you earlier."

675.   A wife had just had an operation. The three kids were left home with the husband who took off from work to manage the household in her absence. When she returned, he commented to a neighbor, "If I am ever reincarnated, I do not want to come back as a mother."

676.   Two cannibals, a mother and son, were stalking through the jungle. Suddenly, there was a roar in the sky, and the child ran to his mother to receive her protection. "It's all right," said the mother. "It's an airplane." "What's that?" asked the boy. "Well, it's a little like a lobster. There's an awful lot you have to throw away, but the insides are delicious."

677.   Alan King says that he has three brothers who are doctors. "But when I'm sick the only one who makes a house call is my mother."

678.   "My mother had morning sickness AFTER I was born."

679.   The man who remembers what he learned at his mother's knee, was probably bent over it.

680. You can always tell when spring is near by the first screech of a Little League mother.

681. Jack Stroube once asked the mother of a large family why she dressed all her children alike. "When we had just four children, I dressed them alike so we wouldn't lose any of them," she said. "Now that we have nine, I dress them alike so we won't pick up any that don't belong to us."

682. First woman: "How are your children doing in school?"

Second woman: "Better," said the weary mother, "but I still go to PTA meetings under an assumed name."

Mountaineers

683. Mountain climbers tie themselves together to keep the sensible ones from going back home.

684. A mountaineer and his son came for their first visit in a fair-sized town. The man just hadn't ever seen anything like those asphalt streets. Rubbing his bare feet on the hard surface, he remarked to the boy. "Wal, y' cain't blame 'em fer buildin' a town here. Th' ground's too dern hard to' plow."

685. Jed was a nice mountain boy and he was on his first train when Phillip met him. "We were all draftees on our way to Army camp. Jed was from 'way back in the hills—I mean 'way back, but he was one of those guys you like right away and we became friends," explained Phil. "The third day we were at camp he came over to me all flustered and I said, 'What's the matter, Jed?' He said, 'They're giving out uniforms today and I don't know any of my sizes. My mother bought all my clothes for me when she went to the city.' I said, 'No sweat, Jed. You're just a little bigger than I am, so when I give my size, you just give one size bigger.' He said 'OK' and we got in line. The sarge yelled, 'Shoes,' and I said '9.' Jed said, '10.' The sarge yelled 'Pants,' and I said, '30.' Jed said '31.' The sarge yelled 'Shirt,' and I said '16.' Jed said, '17.' The sarge helled, 'Hat' and I said, '6 & $\frac{7}{8}$.' Jed said, '9 & $10\frac{9}{11}$.' "

686. An old mountaineer had lived a full and not exactly saintly life and now was on his deathbed. He summoned his weeping wife to him. "Sairy," he said, "go to the fireplace and take out the third stone from the top." She did as instructed and found a hole. "Retch" down in there," said the dying patriarch "and bring up what you find." Again she obeyed. Reaching down, her fingers touched a large

Mason jar. With some effort she pulled it up. The jar was stuffed full of cash. "Sairy," said the old man, "there's a heap of money in there. And when I go, Sairy, I'm agoin' to take it with me. I want you to take that there jar up to the attic, Sairy, and set it by the winder. I'll get it as I go by on my way up to heaven." His wife followed his instructions. That night, the old mountaineer died. Several days after the funeral, his wife remembered the Mason jar. She climbed up to the attic. There was the jar, still full of money, sitting by the window. "Oh," the widow sighed, "I knowed it. I knowed I should have put it in the basement."

687.   A mountaineer saw his first motorcycle on the road. He raised his rifle and shot it. "Did you kill the varmint?" asked his wife. "Hit it, but didn't kill it," he said. "I can hear it growlin'—but I shore made it turn that poor man loose."

688.   When someone told the old mountaineer, "Your neighbors are honest, I hope," he said, "Yep, they is." "But you keep a loaded shotgun near your chicken coop," the other man declared. The mountaineer replied, "Yep, that keeps 'em honest."

689.   And then there was the mountain man who put a silencer on his shotgun because his daughter wanted a quiet wedding.

Newspapers

690.   This item appeared in a box on the front of page one of the Prestonburg Kentucky Times: "The Times is late this week and we want to apologize. The trouble started in a cornfield several years ago. From there it grew, fermented, aged in wood, was bottled in bond, and last Tuesday it finally reached our linotype operator."

691.   "Why do people in your town keep on buying your newspaper when they already know what everybody in town has done that week?" a big-city reporter asked a small-town editor. The rural editor pointed out: "They buy the paper because they want to see which ones got caught."

692.   The young reporter ran into the newsroom of the Washington newspaper, shouting, "Stop the presses! I've got the story of the year!" "What happened," yawned the seasoned editor, "did a man bite a dog?" "No," replied the reporter. "A bull threw a senator."

693.   An ad in a paper by an editor, looking to create a little curiosity in the want ad section to see if people were reading it, read: "For sale, one Gittzensnorker, green, with power flaker, two match-

ing flamilists including automatic bleem, recently overhauled from side to side. Sacrifice for quick sale, $77.75."

Two readers with a sense of humor quickly answered the ad. One said he was interested, "Your ad sounds just like what we need." He described himself as a purchasing swapskeller.

Another wrote, "We will trade two antiques, but one has broken fanning mill, pingpong manipulator is broken and shake-a-ling straw moving parts is broken on the second prize model. Does your bleem have a long stroke on the gitchenmakisit?"

But, the prize answer was this one: "In regard to your ad in Sunday's paper regarding a gittzensnorker, I'm interested, but I think your price is way too high for a used one."

694. When San Francisco reporters get around to talking about malapropisms and scrambled language in general, the name of Supervisor James B. McSheehy inevitably comes up. The late columnist Arthur Caylor favored, "This has all the earmarks of an eyesore." My own favorite is "I deny the allogation and defy the alligator." Here are some more McSheehyisms:

"Let's grab the bull by the tail and look the facts squarely in the face."

"The roosters have come home to hatch."

"You can't straddle the fence and still keep your ear to the ground."

695. A recent correction in Community Life magazine: "Mai Thai Finn is one of the students in the program and was in the center of the photo. We incorrectly listed her as one of the items on the menu."

696. From the Rangeman's Journal:

"Livestock are animals that are bred and raised in the western states to keep the producer broke and the buyer crazy. Livestock are born in the spring, mortgaged in the summer, pastured in the fall, and given away in the winter. They vary in size, color, and weight.

697. A woman called a newspaper to complain of a story about her wedding. Editor: "Why, did we mention age?"

"No, but you said my husband was a well-known collector of antiques."

698. The following headline in a local paper threw City Hall into an uproar:

HALF THE CITY COUNCIL ARE CROOKS

A retraction in full was demanded of the editor under threat of a libel suit. Next afternoon the headline read:

HALF THE CITY COUNCIL AREN'T CROOKS

699. If you don't think there's a divine plan, just read the paper and explain to me how come everybody dies in alphabetical order?

700. I read in our local newspaper an interesting ad: "Anyone found near my chicken house at night will be found there the next morning."

701. A fellow downtown just passed 40 and went into bifocals. Now he can't keep up with what's going on in the world. He can only read the bottom half of the newspaper.

702. Ginny DeRuelle, just back from the Sun Belt, says she saw this note in a New Mexico weekly: "Due to a shortage of space, a number of births will be delayed till next week."

People

703. An Englishman was talking with a clerk in the Mandarin Hotel. "Here's a riddle," said the clerk. "My mother gave birth to a child. It was neither my brother nor my sister. Who was it?" "I can't guess," said the Englishman. "It was I," laughed the clerk. "Haw! Haw! Very clever. I must remember that," chortled the Englishman. The Englishman then asked the riddle at his club: "Here's a riddle, old chap. My mother gave birth to a child who was neither my brother nor my sister. Who was it? What? You can't guess? Do you give up?" "Yes." "Haw! It was the clerk at the Mandarin Hotel!"

704. A man who was very much interested in old books ran into an unbookish acquaintance of his who'd just thrown away an old Bible which had been packed away in the attic of his ancestral home for generations. He happened to mention it. "Who printed it, do you know?" asked the book lover. "Somebody named Guten-something," recalled the man with an effort. "Not Gutenberg?" gasped the book lover. "You idiot, you've thrown away one of the first books ever printed. A copy sold at auction recently for over $400,000!" The other man was unmoved. "My copy wouldn't have brought a dime." he announced firmly. "Some fellow named Martin Luther had scribbled all over it."

705. Henry Ward is said to have gone into a short-order restaurant where he was amused by the way the waiters gave orders to the cook—such as, "sinkers and a cow" (doughnuts and milk) and "one on the city" (a glass of water). "I'll give the waiter an order that he cannot translate into his jargon," said Ward to a friend. "Waiter, let me have two poached eggs on toast, with the yolks broken." "Adam and Eve on a raft; wreck 'em," screamed the waiter.

706. "London has to be the foggiest place on earth," one traveler told another. "Yes," the other person said, "London is certainly foggy. But I've been in a place that was much foggier." The first traveler asked, "Foggier than London? Where was that?" "I don't know," came the answer. "It was so foggy I couldn't tell."

707. One of the Sweetwater, Texas' big annual promotions is a rattlesnake hunt. At the banquet, one of the local boosters was talking about a fellow who comes from Honolulu every year to take part in the rattlesnake hunt. Another fellow said he'd participated in the hunt several times. "How many rattlesnakes have you gotten?" someone asked him. "None," he said. "Then what do you have to brag about?" "When you're looking for rattlesnakes," he explained, "none is plenty."

708. If you kick the person who caused most of your troubles, you couldn't sit down for a month.

709. Someone once observed that a person with six children is better satisfied than a person with six million dollars. The reason: the individual with six million dollars always wants more.

710. Why does a woman say she's been shopping when she bought nothing? The same reason a man says he's been fishing when he hasn't caught anything.

711. A recession is the period where a person starts living on his income until he gets his confidence back.

712. Uncle Fred has taken so many vitamins and iron pills, his heirs will be squabbling over mineral rights to his body.

713. Never underestimate your ability. Others will do it for you.

714. I never take tranquilizers. If I do, I become so nice, I forget I dislike some people.

715. The closest to perfection a person ever comes is when he is filling out a job application.

716.   What were Alexander Graham Bell's famous first words? "Da-Da."

717.   When folks look you in the eye and boast what they'll do tomorrow, stand your ground and look right in their yesterday.

718.   There are only two classes of people who complain about having to pay taxes—men and women.

719.   A Yankee in the Florida everglades admired a native's necklace. "Alligator teeth," the native explained. "More valuable than pearls." "Why?" asked the tourist. "Anyone can open an oyster," the native shrugged.

720.   Things are rough. People are worried. I saw a man lying in the gutter, I walked up and said, "Are you sick? Can I help you?" He said, "No, I found a parking space, I sent my wife out to buy a car." HENNY YOUNGMAN

721.   A fellow stammered. He was asked if that presented a problem. "N-n-no. We all have pecularities." "I wasn't aware that I had any," said the inquirer. "D-d-do you stir tea with your right hand?" "Well sure." "T-that's your pecularity, m-m-most people use a teaspoon."

722.   A tribe in Borneo was having a terrible time with its crops and finally the chief got an idea. "We'll send a telegram to the Soviets telling them we are having agricultural problems and need their assistance. They will send us seeds and tractors and 100 young technicians to help us. Then, we'll send a cable to the U.S. telling them the Russians sent us seeds and tractors, and they'll send twice as much seed and 500 technicians. And when all the technicians arrive—we'll eat them."

723.   When you see how some people work, you wonder what they'll do when they retire.

724.   Civilization is a family driving a $10,000 car pulling a $20,000 trailer looking for a free place to park.

725.   Bruce Bliven, editor of the New Republic for 30 years, noted that he had learned something valuable from his New York experience: "When you are being mugged, yell 'Fire,' not 'Help.' Everybody wants to go to a fire but nobody wants to go to a mugging."

726.   Hiring people smarter than you proves you are smarter than they are.

727. Some people who claim to have a sixth sense seem to be lacking the other five.

Philosophy

728. The best way to convince a fool that he is wrong is to let him have his own way.

729. A hunch is a feeling that makes you certain about something you know nothing about.

730. If some guys ate their heart out, they would break a tooth.

731. This is the age of tension. Almost everyone lives in fear of bending an IBM card.

732. The difference between a wool sweater and the federal budget is that sometimes a wool sweater will shrink.

733. While most people are fundamentally decent, there are some who insist on forgiving you.

734. Know what you're doin'. Don't be like the near-sighted guy who mistook the Prell for the Scope and gargled to death.

735. Here's to the iron curtain—may it rust in peace.

736. The nice thing about a laugh is that so much of you has a good time.

737. The wonderful things they can do for neurotics these days makes most of us feel we're missing something by being well adjusted.

738. Go on painting the town and you're apt to kick the bucket.

739. Most of us are quick to recognize a good thing the moment the other fellow sees it.

740. Try to be nice to everyone until you have made your first million. After that, they'll be nice to you.

741. Ours may well be known in history as the "Out Generation"— out of pocket, out of mind, out of patience, out of oil, out of money, out of line, and out on strike when we should have been working.

742. If you think nobody cares if you are alive—miss a couple of car payments.

743. Poise is often a matter of being too stupid to know you should be embarrassed.

744. Don't ignore the panhandler who asks you for a dime for a cup of coffee. Follow him and find out where you can still get a cup of coffee for a dime.

745. The easiest way to refold a road map is later.

746. By the time you're somebody's sugar, you have to go on saccharine.

747. A dedicated scholar is a man who has discovered something more interesting than women.

748. It's hard to be fit as a fiddle when you're shaped like a cello.

749. There are still opportunities to get rich. Just think of the guy who got the Drano concession for the Alaska pipeline.

750. Early to bed, early to rise, enables you to save enough to do otherwise.

751. Researchers should be good in geometry. They know all the angles and talk in circles.

752. Hiding your head in the sand is a mighty poor way of holding your end up.

753. The worst thing about retirement is having to drink coffee on your own time.

754. About the only thing you can do on a shoestring these days is trip.

755. To get maximum attention, it's hard to beat a good, big mistake.

756. If you want to write something that has a chance of living on forever, sign a mortgage.

757. Few things in life are more satisfying than parking on what's left of the other fellow's dime.

758. I'm glad the mood rings are gone. It was such a strain to get in a mood that matches your outfit.

759. There's a motorbike that runs on laughing gas—it's a Yamaha-ha-ha.

760. The dream of the older generation was to pay off the mortgage. The hope of today's young families is to get one.

761. Nervousness is when you feel in a hurry all over and can't get started.

762. The trouble with having a place for everything is how often it gets filled up with everything else.

763. A computer performs complex calculations in one ten-thousandth of a second—and mails out statements ten days late.

764. Some of the streets downtown need repairing. They've got less tar in them than the new cigarettes.

765. An old philosopher reminisced about his old grandpappy "who lived to be 94 and had a walking rocker, which moved a couple of inches every time he swayed. After eating, he would light his pipe, sit down on the ground level porch and start rocking and daydreaming. Trouble was the rocker had no sense of direction and was liable to take off any which way, including backwards. Generally, wound up in a fence corner, or the blackberry patch, and once against a beehive. Got out on the road a couple of times and scared the daylights out of some skittish horses. Narrowest escape was when he rocked into the creek, making history as the first amphibious rocking chair pilot. Took a full pint to revive him. We finally chained the chair to a tree in the yard and grandpappy wore a circular ditch two feet deep. Had to half-sole the rocker several times. The ditch is still there. A young archeologist who discovered it pronounced it an outstanding ceremonial Indian mound."

766. The eyes of other people are the eyes that ruin us. If all but myself were blind, I should want neither for clothes, fine houses, nor fine furniture.

767. Alice Longfellow, "I have a simple philosophy for life . . . Fill what's empty. Empty what's full and scratch where it itches. Instead of just biting the bullet maybe we ought to try getting the lead out."

768. The creative mind is the playful mind. Philosophy is the play and dance of ideas.

769. When you've got the world by the tail, don't let go to reach for the moon.

Politicians

770. If George Washington never told a lie, how can he sit there on a dollar bill that is worth 43¢ and not at least grin?

771. They say George Washington never told a lie, but he never had to fill out an income tax form, either.

772. Most politicians, by the way, are very forthright people—which means they are right about a fourth of the time.

773. Only one man in a million understands politics in the U.S. Isn't it odd how we keep running into him?

774. The mayor lost face the other day, trying to put his foot down while he had it in his mouth.

775. Mark Twain once described a perfect political audience as "intelligent, witty, capable, inquisitive . . . and drunk."

776. Paraphrasing an article by Rep. Hinshaw of California in the Congressional Record:

In the beginning, God created heaven and earth. Quickly He was faced with a class action suit for failure to file an environmental impact statement. He was granted a temporary permit for the heavenly part of the project, but was stymied with a cease and desist order for the earthly part. Appearing at the hearing, God was asked why He began the earthly project in the first place. He replied that He just liked to be creative. Then God said, "Let there be light," and immediately the officials demanded to know how the light would be made. Would there be strip mining? What about thermal pollution? God explained, light would come from a huge ball of fire. God was granted provisional permission to make light, assuming that no smoke would result from the ball of fire, that He would obtain a building permit and, to conserve energy, would have the light out half the time. God agreed and said He would call the light day and the darkness night. Officials replied they weren't interested in semantics. God said, "Let the earth bring forth green herb and any such as may seed." The EPA agreed so long as native seed was used. Then God said, "Let the waters bring forth the creeping creatures having life, and the fowl that may fly over the earth." Officials pointed out that this would require approval of the Game and Fish Commission coordinated with the Heavenly Wildlife Federation and Audubongelic Society. So everything was okay until God said He wanted to complete the project in 6 days. Officials said it would take at least 180 days to review the application and the impact statement. After that there would be public hearings. Then there would be 10 to 12 months before . . . God said, "Forget it."

777. Old politican on stump, "Them's my views and if you don't like 'em, why I'll change 'em."

778. Politician: "What we need is a working majority!"
Voice in back: "No, what we need is a majority working!"

779. Card found in politician's wallet: I am a candidate. In case of accident, call a press conference.

780. "I've heard a lot about you, Senator."
"Maybe," replied the politician, "but you can't prove a thing!"

781. Did you hear about the political speech writer who cleaned his own turkey? It was a case of a gobbledegooker degooking de gobbler.

782. "Do you like conceited politicians as much as the other kind?"
"What other kind?"

783. Next time I'm going to vote a straight ticket—as soon as I can find out which party is going straight.

784. A politician in Washington said it's no disgrace to be poor—and it attracts a lot less attention.

785. Sir Winston Churchill was once asked what qualifications he thought most essential for a politician. Without hesitation he answered: "It's the ability to foretell what will happen tomorrow, next month, and next year—and to explain afterward why it did not happen."

786. A contractor wanted to give a government official a sports car. The official objected, saying, "Sir, common decency and my basic sense of honor would never permit me to accept a gift like that." The contractor said, "I quite understand. Suppose we do this. I'll sell you the sports car for $10." The official thought a moment. "In that case, I'll take two."

787. A politician who had changed his views rather radically was congratulated by a colleague. "I'm glad you've seen the light," he was told. "I didn't see the light," came the terse reply. "I felt the heat."

788. At a press conference years ago, reporters were trying to pin down then Vice-President Alben Barkley to a yes or no answer on a controversial issue. Barkley, not ready to commit himself, was deliberately evasive. "I can only say at this time," he told them, "that some of my friends are for it and some against." "How about you, Mr. Vice-President?" persisted one reporter. "I am for my friends," said Barkley.

789. Citizen boasting of the greatness of the new President, "He's

bigger than Washington, bigger than Lincoln, . . . Roosevelt, Eisenhower." Newsman, "Is he bigger than God?" "Well, I wouldn't say that . . . but he's young yet."

790. A small-time politician sent out thousands of fund requests to voters living in his district. Not having a mailing list, he addressed the letters to "Box Holder." A few weeks later he received a $5,000 check in his mail. Overjoyed, he looked at the signature to see who had been so generous. The check was signed, "Box Holder."

791. Three men were arguing over which profession was the oldest. Said the surgeon: "The Bible says Eve was made by carving a rib out of Adam. I guess that makes mine the oldest profession." "Not at all," said the engineer. "In six days the earth was created out of chaos—and that was an engineer's job." Said the politician: "Yes, but who created chaos?"

792. "Well, then," said the first Senator, "if you can't give me your word of honor, will you at least give me your promise?"

793. After giving a typical stirring, double-talking promise-making speech, the politician looked out at the audience and confidently asked if there were any questions. "Just one," came a voice from the rear, "Who else is running?"

794. A local politician was given a great testimonial dinner which ended in wild applause. "Blah," shouted one dissenting voice as the senator was introduced. "Sir, I agree," remarked the old veteran as he smiled down on his adversary, "But what can the two of us do against so many?"

795. The candidate flashed a toothy smile at the audience in the packed hall. "I'm truly delighted to see this dense crowd gathered here tonight to support my candidacy," he announced. "Don't be too delighted," shouted a voice from the crowd, "We ain't that dense!"

796. Senator Hornblower's son was about to follow his famous father's footsteps into the political arena, and the veteran statesman was giving him a few pointers. "M'boy," he said, "two qualities will take you far in government and save your hide from the vicissitudes of political reality. M'boy, those two qualities are integrity and astuteness." "Thanks Daddy," said the youth. "But how about boiling some of that eloquence down to what I can handle? I mean, tell me what you mean by 'integrity.' " "Integrity, son, means that when you give your word, keep it." "And what is 'astuteness'?" "That means don't be dumb enough to give it."

797.   A local politician just home from Washington D.C. complained from a soapbox, "Why I just discovered that the CIA has been making an intelligence survey on me. I think it's an outrage." A voice from the crowd yelled, "Senator, if they discovered anything intelligent about you, it ain't an outrage . . . it's a miracle."

798.   A politician whose father had been hanged described it: "He died serving the public. He was participating in a public function when the platform gave way."

799.   Our neighbor is very upset. His doctor told him to give up wine, women, and song—and he wants to go into politics.

800.   We took the country away from the Indians who scalped some of us and turned it over to the politicians who skinned the rest of us.

801.   Some politicians shake your hand before an election and your confidence after.

802.   In Russia, so the story goes, Joseph Stalin was looking for an assistant. He asked a dozen applicants the same question, "How much is two plus two?" Eleven job seekers gave the same answer. The twelfth fellow got the job because he replied, "Comrade, how much would you like it to be?"

803.   The bar association has given us a new definition for death: "A human body with irreversible, total cessation of brain function." We should be grateful for such enlightenment as a new and startling approach to politics that tells us what is really wrong with our country—so many bodies voting and holding office, though legally dead.

804.   At a testimonial banquet for an attorney in San Francisco, the M.C. announced, "We invited both the President and the Secretary of State to be here tonight, but both declined—the President because he doesn't know Marvin—and the Secretary because he does."

805.   Political polls are very expensive. First you hire somebody to deny one is being taken. Then you hire another guy to leak the results.

806.   There's one thing the Democrats and Republicans have in common—our money.

807.   One lesson we could all learn from politicians is that when you say someone is ignorant, dishonest, and incompetent, it doesn't

mean you won't laugh and joke together the next time you meet at a party.

808. Immortal words of a politician: "Let them who don't want none have memories of not getting any."

809. Our most famous politician was once described as a revolving jerk. That is, no matter which way you look at him he's still a jerk.

810. They are just like everyone else; only politicians are always in the scrutiny of the spotlight. Many of them are so crooked, they have to screw their socks on.

811. Trying to emphasize a lesson on charity and kindness, the politician said, "If I saw a man beating a donkey and stopped him, what virtue would I be showing?" "Brotherly love," said a voice from the back of the room.

Psychiatrists

812. On his first visit to the psychiatrist, the nervous young man explained that his family made him seek help because he preferred cotton socks to woolen ones. "That's no reason for you to see me," retorted the physician. "In fact, I myself prefer cotton socks." "Really?" the happy patient exclaimed. "Do you like yours with oil and vinegar or just a squeeze of lemon?"

813. "After six years and $20,000 worth of analysis, I've finally realized what my trouble was," the psychiatric patient said. "What was it?" a friend asked. "If I'd had the $20,000 in the first place," the patient responded, "I wouldn't have needed the analysis."

814. "I wish you'd examine my husband," said the woman to the psychiatrist. "He blows smoke rings from his nose and I'm simply terrified." "That is odd," admitted the psychiatrist, "but it's nothing to be worried about. Many smokers blow rings." "Very true, doctor," said the woman, "But my husband doesn't smoke."

815. Psychiatrist to sad-eyed patient: "My dear man, you have no inferiority complex, you are inferior."

816. Patient lying on psychiatrist's couch: "Doctor, nobody takes me seriously anymore."
    Doctor: "You're kidding."

817. Psychiatrist: "I'm not aware of your problem, so perhaps you could start me at the beginning."

Patient: "All right. In the beginning I created the heavens and the earth. . . ."

818. Hear about the fellow who studied psychiatry and got a B.S., M.S., and Ph.D? He went nuts by degrees.

819. A fellow paid a psychiatrist $50 to treat him for his inferiority complex and then was fined $25 for talking back to a traffic officer on the way home.

820. Psychiatrists tell us that one out of every four Americans is mentally ill. Check your three closest friends. If they seem all right, you're the one.

821. Worried wife as she watched her husband fishing in a bucket of water in the living room, to a friend: "I'd take him to a psychiatrist, but we need the fish."

822. A famous psychiatrist was conducting a course in psychopathology for medical students. One day a student asked: "Professor, you've told us so much about the abnormal person and his behavior; could you tell us something about the normal person?"
"If we ever find him," answered the lecturer, "we'll cure him."

823. Two executives ran into each other at the door of their psychiatrist's office. "Hello," said one. "Are you coming or going?" "If I knew that," said the other, "I wouldn't be here."

824. The difference between a psychologist and a psychiatrist is simple. One of them drives you crazy and the other examines you to find out how far.

825. Helen Mills tells of a monkey that was used in tests out at Salt Flat to gauge reaction to G-forces. First they put the monkey in a high-speed sled. Then they handed the monkey a banana. Then they released the sled. The sled would take the monkey through five G's before hitting a braking system of water. After a few rides, the monkey started pushing the banana away.

826. Human Psychology is a funny thing. Everybody wants to be normal, but nobody wants to be average.

827. Hear about the patient who visited his psychiatrist and was told, "You're insane."
"I want a second opinion."
"OK, you're ugly, too!"

828. A psychiatrist asked a patient what the complaint was.

"Well, it seems that people won't talk to me."

"OK," he says. "Next."

829. A psychiatrist was examining a friend and asked, "Do you ever hear voices without being able to tell who is speaking or where the voices are coming from?"

"Sure."

"When does this occur?"

"When I answer the telephone."

Race Horses

830. A horse-racing enthusiast reported his latest venture with the nags to a friend. "I went to the track on the eleventh day of the eleventh month," he said, arriving at 11:00. My son was 11 that day, and the 11th race showed 11 horses. So I bet all my money on the 11th horse on the card." "And he won?" asked the friend. "No," the sportsman replied sadly. "He came in eleventh."

831. The racehorse owner asked his jockey why he hadn't ridden through a hole that had opened up on the final turn. "Sir," the jockey replied wearily, "did you every try to go through a hole that was going faster than your horse?"

832. Two men were talking about a friend. "I can't understand why he loses so much money at the racetrack and yet he is so lucky when he plays poker." "That's easy to understand," his friend said. "They don't let him shuffle the horses at the track."

833. Al Coffman may want to talk with Flossie the Waitress about how she picked a long shot winner. "How did you manage that?" asked the neighborhood bookie. "I just stuck a pin in the paper, and there it was," she replied. "But yesterday," said the bookie, "how did you get four winners?" "Oh, I cheated a little," confessed the lady, "I used a fork."

834. "The last time I played a horse," Danny Klayman says, "it took him so long to finish, the jockey kept a diary."

Relatives

835. A husband and wife had been arguing for hours, and the little woman finally reached the breaking point. "I'm going home to mother," she wailed. "I should have listened to her ten years ago!" "Go ahead," he answered, "She's still talking!"

836. "My mother-in-law has been living with us for years and is driving me crazy," a man told his neighbor.

"Why don't you ask her to move?" the neighbor asked?

"I'd love to, but I can't," was the reply. "It's her house."

837. "You say your mother-in-law has a cold heart?" asked the bartender. "I'll put it this way," replied the bar fly, "She had heart surgery and instead of rubber gloves the surgeon wore mittens."

838. "He can't drink and he can't play cards," a man declared about his new son-in-law. A friend responded, "That's the kind of a son-in-law to have!" "Naw," the man declared. "He can't play cards—and he plays. He can't drink—and he drinks."

839. Father: "So, you want to become my son-in-law?"

Daughter's steady: "No, sir, not really. But, if I marry your daughter, I don't see how I can avoid it."

840. A local heart surgeon reported an interesting side effect in his business, "My 72-year-old uncle has an electronic pacemaker for his heart. It's great except that every time he sneezes, the garage door opens."

841. A poverty stricken uncle of mine waxed philosophical when he said, "If I pray for a chicken, sometimes I get it and sometimes I don't. If I pray for the Lord to send me after a chicken, I always get it."

842. My grandmother wondered "if medicine has advanced so much in twenty years, how come I felt so much better twenty years ago?"

843. My grandfather said: "I survived WWII, three auto accidents, two bad marriages, two depressions, 13 company strikes, three mortgages, government audits—and a fresh teenager tells me I don't know what life is all about."

844. "Don't you ever do anything quickly?" I asked my mother-in-law.

"Yeh. I get tired." she snapped.

845. They gave my grandfather a watch when he retired and in a week it quit working, too.

846. My uncle says "Baloney is flattery laid on so thick that it cannot be true, and blarney is flattery laid on so thin we like it."

847. My uncle had so many freckles he looked like he had swallowed a $5 bill and broke out in pennies.

848. For that sister-in-law who "has everything," give the gift that keeps on giving: a pregnant guinea pig.

849. My mother-in-law thinks the way to get it all together is to let it pile up.

850. My Scottish grandfather never gave up. He refused to make a will. On his deathbed, he held an auction.

851. I had a Scottish uncle who had a garbage disposal and let it die of malnutrition.

852. My uncle just donated his body to science. He's preserving it in alcohol till they need it.

853. A hotel is where you stay when you ain't got no relatives.

854. My grandfather's jokes are so old, even the young people he used to tell them to are dead.

855. My mother-in-law who is a hypochondriac, joined the Disease of the Month Club and already feels much worse.

856. Overheard: "Only one thing that keeps my brother-in-law from being a barefaced liar is his moustache."

857. The bookstore doesn't mind when my cousin drops in and reads a book for a half hour or so during lunch hour. What does bug them is he turns down the corner of a page so he can find his place the next day.

858. My mother-in-law is cheap! Who else would spend two weeks in the soaring beauty and towering grandeur of the Rocky Mountains—and send you a picture postcard of the motel pool?

859. My brother-in-law's idea of year-end celebration is to have a Christmas they'll never forget and New Year's they can't remember.

860. The smog is really bad in Los Angeles. I have an uncle there who is one of those painters who paints only what he sees. He hasn't painted anything in three years.

861. "What kind of soldier was my grandfather?" "Well, on Veterans day he hangs out a white flag," replied my grandmother.

862. My aunt quit smoking cold turkey. It was too hard to keep it lit.

863. For awhile, my mother-in-law had the first apartment in space. Her water heater blew up.

864. My brother-in-law is so dumb, he just bought a motorcycle with an air-conditioner.

865. I couldn't warm up to him if we were CREMATED together!

866. I don't know what makes you tick, but I hope it's a TIME BOMB!

867. My brother-in-law was told he looks like a movie star. King Kong.

868. The price of bigamy is two mother-in-laws.

869. Maybe my brother-in-law isn't stupid, but he thinks Polident is a talking parrot.

870. This is the Chinese year of the snake . . . which means your brother-in-law ought to have a good year.

871. My brother-in-law is so dumb, he recently burned his face bobbing for french fries.

872. Since they have started giving men's names to hurricanes, the fellow across the hall would like to suggest Herbert. He says that's the name of his brother-in-law, who's the biggest blow-hard in the country.

873. I never forget a face, but in your case I'm willing to make an exception!

874. My uncle explained what's meant by "a waste of natural resources": "For example, putting Raquel Welch on a radio show."

875. Trouble with my uncle is he runs out of ideas long before he runs out of words.

876. Someday my brother-in-law is going to go too far, and when he does, I hope he'll stay there.

877. My brother-in-law is one of the few men who gets obscene phone calls. He finally put an end to it though. He paid his bookie.

878. My grandfather's pacemaker must be on a well-used electronic frequency. Every time he sees a pretty girl walk by, his garage door flies open.

879. I told my brother-in-law if you ever get a penny for your thoughts—give change.

880. My grandfather says the valley he lives in is so polluted you get obscene echoes.

881. My sister-in-law is so skinny she needs suspenders to hold up her girdle.

882. My aunt feels it would be a disaster to get rid of her hostilities since she simply doesn't have time to be nice to everybody.

883. I don't know what makes my brother-in-law so obnoxious, but whatever it is, it works.

884. My brother-in-law found a box on the side of the road marked "Water skis." He opened it and sure enough there they were—a beautiful pair of water skis. He spent the rest of the day looking for water with a hill.

885. A political candidate I know indignantly rejects Secret Service protection. He regards it as a direct insult to the quality of the surveillance his mother-in-law has provided all these years.

886. Beautiful spring weather makes you feel so lackadaisical you wouldn't even help your mother-in-law . . . move out of your house.

887. "My mother-in-law is so nearsighted she nagged a coat hanger for an hour." HENNY YOUNGMAN

888. I just got back from a pleasure trip. I took my mother-in-law to the airport.

889. Now I know why my mother-in-law always smiles. Her teeth is the only part of her face that isn't wrinkled.

890. My mother-in-law is so cold-hearted, she has to add antifreeze to her Pacemaker.

891. During the depression, Doyle Smith was a boy living in Walter, Oklahoma. "Each night," he says, "either I or one of my brothers would go out in the woods and put a flashlight on a cottontail. The rabbit's eyes glowed in the beam of light. We shot them right between the eyes; it was our meal for the next day.

892. My brother-in-law is missing a screw somewhere. I asked him what he thought of censorship.
"Greatest boat afloat," he said.
I asked how he felt about marijuana.
He replied, "It's terrible. The food's cold, beer's hot. I ain't never going there again."
I said, "No, I'm talking about dope you dummy. What do you think of LSD?"
"Greatest President we ever had," he replied.

893. "Is that your mother-in-law's portrait hanging on the wall?"
"Yes. I call it The Framing of the Shrew."

894. My uncle is a moonlighter who holds two jobs so that he can drive from one to another in a better car.

895. Early settler wrote, "The rain is all wind, the wind is all sand, I'm 4000 miles from nowhere and one-half from Hell. The only way things could be worse is if I had to go home to live with my mother-in-law."

896. My uncle says his wife has the face of a saint. A Saint Bernard.

897. My Aunt Ida is so fat she has more chins than a Chinese phone book.

898. My sister-in-law says that she was able to rent a 40th floor apartment for only $75 a month. Then she found out why it was so cheap. There are 40 floors but only 39 roofs.

899. My brother-in-law is not really two-faced—if he had two, why would he be wearing that one?

900. My Uncle Bill tells about a friend who had lost a lot of weight due to illness. "Why," the fellow said, "I ain't nothin' but breath and breeches!"

901. My uncle believed in reincarnations. His will left everything to himself.

902. Grandmother says her husband never chases women: "He's too fine, too decent—too slow."

903. My uncle, who is a wood carver made a work of art out of a tree infected with Dutch Elm disease. He placed it with some others and a week later the whole bunch died.

904. My Uncle Wilbur brags he has 50,000 shares of Xerox. He really only has one share; he xeroxed the rest.

905. My uncle just back from Las Vegas reports, "What a place! You can't beat the sunshine, the climate or the slot machines."

906. My aunt tells the story about the usher who was walking up the aisle of a movie theater when he noticed a fellow in the center section who was sprawled over three or four seats. He approached the patron and whispered: "I'm sorry, sir, but you're taking up too much room. Your ticket just entitles you to one seat, you know." The usher trotted off to the office where he informed

the manager of the situation. The manager accompanied him back down the aisle. "Listen, fellow," said the manager. "You can't sprawl out like this, taking up all these seats. Look at you there—one leg over the arms of one seat, the other leg over the back of the seats in front of you, your arms all spread out. Where did you come from, anyway?" And the fellow groaned and managed to lift one hand to motion upward as he gasped, painfully, "The balcony."

907. A bully hit my grandfather with his fist. "That's karate, got it in Japan," he replied.

My grandfather goes to the truck, returns to crack him on the head. "That's crowbar. Got it at Sears," he quips.

908. When he has money, a distant relative can be very distant.

909. Not everybody was ruined in the 1920 crash. My uncle got lucky, borrowed $20,000 and invested it in the market the day before the crash. When he jumped out the window he landed on the guy that lent him the money.

910. The nicest thing about my brother-in-law (an egotist) is that he never goes around talking about other people.

911. Perhaps no man is more articulate than my uncle who can give directions without taking his hands out of his pockets.

912. They caught my brother-in-law sticking his tongue out at the snakes at the zoo yesterday. He said they started it.

913. Adam had the most beautiful woman in the world and no mother-in-law. No wonder he called it paradise.

914. If it weren't for giving directions, my mother-in-law wouldn't have an exercise program.

915. My uncle commented recently on his condition after his first spring exercise following a long winter: "I felt fine until I started walking around. Then my body tried to kill me."

916. My brother-in-law says he's not a failure. He just started at the bottom and liked it there.

Religion

917. "My first parish was out in the country," the retired preacher said, "and one day one of my parishoners, a teen-age girl, came to me for some counseling. She told me she was keeping company

with a boy and being inexperienced, she wanted some advice from me on how to conduct herself. Well, I wasn't very much more experienced. So I gave it some thought and I finally told her:"

"Daughter," I said, "I'll tell you what to expect. First, the boy will ask you to sit close to him. That's all right. You can do that. Then he will want to put his arm around you. That's all right, too. You can let him do that. Next he will want to hold your hand. Let him hold your hand. There's nothing wrong with holding hands. But then the boy probably will ask you to lay your head on his shoulder. Now, daughter, don't do that. Don't put your head on his shoulder because that would worry your preacher."

"In a few days, she came back to my study. 'You sure do know your stuff,' she told me. 'It happened just like you said. I sat over close to that boy. I let him put his arm around me. And I let him hold my hand. And then he said to put my head on his shoulder. But I didn't.'

"I told her I was proud of her."

"But sir," she went on, 'I told him I wasn't going to put my head on his shoulder. You put your head on my shoulder I told him. Let YOUR preacher worry.' "

918.   A minister stopped by a garage to inquire about a new automobile. His questions were relayed to the shop foreman in the rear of the building.

"How many miles to the gallon?" a salesman called to the foreman.

"Thirty," he shouted back.

"It's the preacher."

"Sixteen!"

919.   Jimmie Dykes, a former Philadelphia A's star, was in the Phillies' press room one day telling stories. . . . "I saw an Irish priest friend of mine last week who asked me: 'Jimmie my boy, are you leading an exemplary life?' " Dykes, who was over 78 years old, said, "I told him, 'Father, at my age it is compulsory!' "

920.   A pastor rode by one Sunday morning to see a farmer-parishioner at work harvesting.

"Brother," the minister lectured him, "Don't you know that the Creator made the world in six days and rested on the seventh?"

"Yes," said the farmer as he looked uneasily at the thunderheads in the sky. "I know all about that, but He got done and I didn't!"

921.   A woman asked a Methodist minister to do a burial ceremony for her dog. The preacher didn't want to do it, and said he had a

previous duty for the time she requested. He suggested she see the Baptist minister, if she had no objection to another denomination. That made no difference to her, she said, and asked what she should offer the other minister. "Whatever you can afford," the Methodist replied. "How much did you have in mind?" The woman said she thought $300 would be about right. The preacher looked at his schedule again, "I see I can squeeze you in tomorrow after all. Why didn't you tell me you had a Methodist dog?"

922.   An older preacher told a new preacher, "If you ever forget the marriage ceremony, start quoting Scripture until you remember it." Sure enough, he forgot and the only Scripture he could remember was, "Father, forgive them, for they know not what they do."

923.   A new parson was about to be hired for a West Texas Nondenominational Church.
   "You aren't Baptist, by chance?"
   "No, why?"
   "Well, I was just going to say, we have to haul our water 12 miles."

924.   An Irish priest is driving and his car breaks down. He lifts the hood, goes under the car, but can't find anything wrong. A horse nearby is watching and says, "Adjust the carburetor, pump twice, and the car will start." He adjusts the carburetor, pumps twice, and, to his amazement, the car starts. He drives down the road and stops at the first tavern he passes. The bartender, Paddy, is one of his parishioners. He tells him what happened, and Paddy asks, "Was it a white horse or a black horse?" The priest says, "It was a white horse." Paddy says, "You're lucky, Father. The black horse doesn't know anything about cars."

925.   Mr. Goldberg was brought into traffic court for speeding. The judge was Jewish.
   "But your Honor," Goldberg pleaded, "I was just trying to get to the synagogue in time to hear the rabbi's sermon."
   "Did you make it?" the judge asked.
   "Yes, your honor, I did."
   "Case dismissed!" the judge said, banging the gavel. "That's punishment enough."

926.   Groucho Marx got into an elevator and there was a young priest in the elevator.
   The priest said, "Mr. Marx, may I shake your hand and thank you on behalf of my mother for your wonderful show? It's given

her so many hours of pleasure. She'll feel so happy that I saw you and thanked you for it."

Groucho looked up at the priest and said, "I didn't know you fellows were allowed to have mothers."

927.   Minister's wife selling tickets to a church benefit approached the congregation tightwad. He said, "I have another engagement that night, but I'll be with you in spirit." She replied, "That's fine. Would your spirit like a $5 seat or the $10 section?"

928.   A hill country minister was preaching when a thunderstorm came up. A bolt of lightning hit the steeple and smashed the windows in the church. The minister looked heavenward and said, "Oh, Lord, you know what you are doing." Then, a tornado-like gust descended and blew the roof off the church. Pained, the minister looked skyward and said, "Lord, you know what you are doing." Then, came a flash of lightning and bent the TV antenna on the minister's quarters. "You know what you're doing, Lord? You're messing around with Barbara Walters!"

929.   A local minister plays golf with two retired school administrators a lot and although he makes some bad shots too he doesn't say much, just turns red in the face and stomps the ground. Then one day the preacher hit some awful shots and, after the round, threw his golf clubs down and said, "After a score like that, I am tempted to use some words like you fellows use sometimes. I think I will just quit!" "Aw, preacher," said one, "you wouldn't quit playing golf just because you make a bad shot once in a while, would you?" "I meant I think I'll quit preaching," explained the minister.

930.   The preacher exhorted: "Look what the good Lord has done for all of you. Each of you ought to give a tenth of all you get." One member of the congregation showed his enthusiasm: "Amen, but a tenth ain't enough. I say, let's raise it to a twentieth."

931.   A husband went home after a long, dull service in his church. His sick wife asked him about the sermon. "Well," he said, "the only reason it wasn't hissed is that the congregation couldn't hiss and yawn at the same time."

932.   A Methodist revivalist exhorted, "Come on and join the army of the Lord."

"I've already joined," called back a recent convert.

"Where did you join?" the preacher responded.

"In a Baptist church."

"Why," said the preacher, "you aren't in the army, you're in the Navy."

933. A church custodian, with a record of long and harmonious service, was asked how he managed to get along with the various women's groups who held frequent meetings in the building. Custodian, philosophically, "Oh, I just git in neutral and let 'em push me about."

934. A headline reads: "Parking is big problem in religion." So the pride in the family pew has been matched by that in an assured space in the parking lot at the church. Following the announcement that a church was being designed on stilts with parking space underneath for the worshippers' cars, a member predicted, "When the roll is called up yonder, I'll be in the basement, trying to find a place to park."

935. Calvin Coolidge, when he was in the White House never talked very much. He was most often referred to as "Silent Cal." As the story goes, Cal attended a church service one morning by himself because Mrs. Coolidge wasn't feeling too well. Upon returning to the White House, Mrs. Coolidge asked "Silent Cal" if he enjoyed the sermon. He replied, "Yep."

"What did the preacher preach about Cal?"

"Sin."

"What did the preacher say about sin Calvin?"

"He was against it."

936. The clergyman was walking through the village when he met one of his parishioners. "How's your cold, Donald?" he asked. "Verra obstinate," replied the parishioner. "And how is your wife?" "About the same."

937. Three young boys were bragging about their dads.

"My dad writes a couple of lines," the first boy said, "calls it a poem and gets $10 for it."

"My dad makes dots on paper, calls it a song," the second said, "and gets $10 for it."

"That's nothing," said the third boy. "My dad writes a sermon on a sheet of paper, gets up in the pulpit and reads it and it takes four men to bring in the money."

938. At a little crossroads general mercantile store in Texas, a kindly old man always had a Bible quote for each sale he made. When an elderly woman came in and took almost an hour holding spools of thread to the light to match a piece of fabric and at last found what she wanted, the storekeeper rang up the 10-cent sale,

thought a moment, then said: "Seek and ye shall find." When a little boy, with 5¢ to spend, stood for a full 15 minutes changing his mind in front of the candy case and finally made his selection, the storekeeper thought a moment, then said: "Suffer the little children. Let them come to me." Then a brand new pickup, pulling a matching horse trailer, pulled up one day. Out stepped a dressed-to-kill western dude who breezed into the store and asked: "You got any horse blankets? Really good horse blankets?" The store-keeper had just one horse blanket. But he said, "Yes, sir." "It's got to be the best you've got," the dude said. "I'm taking my horse to the Quarter Horse Show down the road and I want him to really look his best." The storekeeper went into his back room, took down his only horse blanket and carried it out to the counter. "How much?" asked the dude.

"Twelve-fifty."

"Too cheap." exclaimed the dude. "I need a blanket for the finest Quarter horse this side of the Rio Grand! Show me something better."

The storekeeper took the blanket to the back room, refolded it, then carried it back to the counter. "This one's $22.50" he said.

"You still don't get my message, said the dude, "I want the finest blanket you've got and I don't care what it costs."

The storekeeper took the blanket to the back room, refolded it, wrapped it in tissue and put it in an opentop gift box. He carried it back to the counter and said: "You're in luck—this one just came in. It's $55.50 with tax." "Now you're talking!" the dude exclaimed. "That's what I wanted all along." He carried it out, the storekeeper rang up the sale, thought a moment, then said: "He was a stranger, and I took him in."

939. When Leon Uris, known throughout the world for his novels, arrived in Ireland, he was asked the must question: "Are you Protestant or Catholic?" "I'm a Jew," said Uris, author of "Exodus," "Battle Cry," "Topaz," "The Angry Hills," and "QB VII."

"Ah, yes," said the Irish questioner, "But are you a Protestant Jew or a Catholic Jew?"

940. Houston recently got an ordained woman priest. Her mother now calls her my daughter, the Father.

941. The preacher said, "We will sing #400 in your hymnal. If that page is gone, turn to 200 and sing that one twice."

942. Blessing for our times. "Dear Lord, bless this food and the tender hands that unfroze it."

943. To give you an idea how low he rates, he called Dial-A-Prayer—and they hung up on him.

944. Pupils in a religion class at Omaha's Sacred Heart Grade School were asked to write prayers. One result: "Dear God: Count me in. Lonnie."

945. The rabbi always says: "I speak according to the law of Moses."

The priest says: "I speak according to the Church."

The Protestant says, "It seems to me. . . ."

946. In his novel about a show biz comic, "A Stranger in the Mirror," author Sidney Shelton recounts the time Groucho Marx's 10-year-old daughter Melinda was asked to leave the swimming pool at an exclusive Hollywood club where she was taken by a Gentile friend. Groucho telephone the manager: "Listen, my daughter is only half Jewish; would you let her go into the pool up to her waist?"

947. Jerry Clower, in his book, "Ain't God Good!" tells of a time he went on the Mike Douglas TV show wearing a piece of jewelry that is a combination of the cross and the star of David. He explained that he wears it because he believes what the Bible says about people who wear the cross and people who wear the star of David. After the show, he recalls, a lady from New York approached him and said she understood about the cross and about the star of David. "But what about the carat diamond?" she asked. "Well, lady, that represents the self-centeredness and the hillbilly in me, and I'm trying to overcome it," Clower replied. "Pray for me."

948. We must not get ourselves in the dangerous situation of looking like we are harmless in all situations. We have to be tough, like the Quaker who caught a burglar in his living room at night. He flipped on the light, leveled a double barrel shotgun at him and said, "I mean thee no harm but thou art standing where I am about to shoot."

949. Moses freed the Jews, Lincoln freed the slaves and Billy Carter freed the Baptists.

950. I hate Hilton Hotels because I never can decide which to read—Hilton's biography or Gideon's Bible.

951. A minister has learned how to make the collection. His ushers pass the plate before he delivers the sermon and the larger the collection, the less he speaks.

952. It was a farewell dinner for the minister, who was being transferred to another parish. A little old lady was saying goodbye to

the gentleman and concluded: "I'm sorry you're going. I never knew what sin was until you came here."

953. Sunday School teacher: "Moses wandered forty years."
  Kid: "Couldn't find a place to park, eh?"

954. Did you hear about the fellow that exercises religiously? He does one push-up, shouts, "Amen," and quits.

955. A minister had performed so many shotgun weddings, he renamed his church Winchester Cathedral.

956. Libber to Preacher, "Why do you say Amen instead of Awoman?"
  "Cause we sing hymns and not hers."

957. Two inexperienced yachtsmen were storm-tossed on the Atlantic, headed for New York harbor. One turned from his chart table to the other and said, "I think you ought to take off your hat."
  "Why?" asked his worried shipmate.
  "Because," replied the amateur navigator, "according to my calculations, we're inside St. Patrick's Cathedral."

958. A priest, a protestant minister, and a rabbi formed a clandestine threesome because they loved to play poker. The mayor of the town in which they lived had just made a promise to clean up gambling in the city. The trio met at the rabbi's house, as usual, feeling that this small infraction of the law need not apply to the clergy since all winnings were donated to some charity. But somebody tipped off the sheriff who obtained a search warrant, kicked down the door, pistol drawn. Caught all three of them, red handed, all wearing green eyeshades, cards in hand, money on the table. The sheriff yelled, "Hold it right there. You're all under arrest. You have a right to remain silent. Anything you say may be used against you in a court of law. I'll now take a statement from each of you." With that, he turned his pistol on the protestant and asked, "Brother, were you gambling here tonight?"
  The preacher thought to himself, "Oh, Lord, forgive this little white lie . . . No, sheriff, I was not gambling here tonight."
  The sheriff swung his handgun toward the priest and asked the same question. The priest thought to himself, "Oh, Lord forgive me this slight deviation from the truth . . . No sheriff, I was not gambling here tonight."
  The lawman trained his pistol on the remaining member and asked, "Rabbi, were you gambling here tonight?"

The rabbi shrugged his shoulders, placed his palms up in front of his chest and asked, "With who?"

Romance

959. The glowing embers of the fire cast a warm hue into the room. They sat together on the sofa, cozy and sheltered from the storm outside, alone, romantic. Silently, longingly, they gazed into each other's eyes. A question trembled on his lips. Her eyes were wide and wondering. Two souls with but one single thought—which one was going after more firewood?

960. She: "You remind me of the ocean."
He: "Because I'm deep, romantic and restless?"
She: "No, because looking at you long enough makes me seasick."

961. "Since I met you," the dreamy-eyed young man told his date, "I can't eat, I can't drink, I can't sleep . . ." "Why not?" she asked. "Because I'm broke," he replied.

962. Romance today is a problem. If women fall all over you, you don't know whether it's your appeal or their shoes.

963. "Darling," he whispered ardently, "I love you. I adore you. I need you. I can't live without you."
"Please," she gasped, gently pushing him away.
"Why, what's wrong?"
"I just don't want to get serious," she said quietly.
"Who's serious?" he asked.

964. Several current jokes lampoon the resurgence of materialism in Chinese life. A friend asks pretty Miss Wang, "I hear you are not dating Zhang anymore."
"Yes, my feelings toward him have changed."
"Then you will return his watch to him?"
"No, my feelings toward the watch have not changed."

965. Classified and placed by one Jimmy Hom in Daily, Calif.: "Male member of the proletariat wishes to meet female members of the bourgeoisie. Object: Class struggle."

966. The guy at the next desk says, once, when his wife had a twinkle in her eye it meant she was romantic. Now it means she put her contact lens in backwards.

967. They were leaving the cocktail party. "Did anyone," asked his wife, "ever tell you how fascinating, how romantic, how hand-

some you are?" Pleased, the man looked at his wife. "Why, no, dear I don't think anyone ever did." "Well," she snapped, "then where did you ever get the idea?"

Sailors

968.   The stuttering sailor was so excited he couldn't get the words out. The officer whom he was trying to address grew impatient and shouted, "Sing it, sailor, sing it!" The sailor drew a deep breath and sang:

"Should auld acquaintance be forgot
And never brought to mind?
The Admiral's fallen overboard
An' he's half a mile behind!"

969.   A Navy type was reminiscing and said that sometime during the latter days of WWII, a newly minted junior officer reported for duty on his ship. The new officer had been an accountant in civilian life and he was trying very hard to learn all the proper naval terminology so he could be saltier than Admiral Nimitz. Well, this new officer was strolling through the ship and he came on a bunch of sailors in a work party. He heard one of the sailors say something about scrubbing the floor. "Listen, sailor," said the officer, "you don't scrub it, you swab it. And it's not a floor, it's a deck. And you'd better shape up because if the captain ever heard you call that deck a floor, he'd throw you right through one of those little round window's."

970.   On Midway Island in 1945, a homesick sailor watched a transport being outfitted to leave for the states. Shortly before sailing time, he walked on board, tossed his gear on deck, and shouted defiantly at the officer in charge, "I'm NOT going!!! No matter what you say, I'm not leaving this island!"

The officer called the ship Marines who dragged the sailor off to the brig as he resisted valiantly. The ship was underway before the skipper got around to make an investigation. When the ruse was discovered, there were no grounds on which to court martial him. After all, he had said he wasn't going and he had been forced to do so against his will.

Saint Peter

971.   This fellow ran into St. Peter on the street. "The good news," said St. Peter, "is that a place in heaven has been made for you."

The man was overcome with joy. "That's really most terrific, St. Peter," he said. "With news like that I can take almost anything bad. What is it?" "You leave tomorrow," said St. Peter.

972.   At the gates of heaven stood a few ministers and a weekend pilot. The attendant called in and admitted the pilot first, which upset the preachers, who complained, "We should be admitted first. We've done so much for mankind—warning them of fire and brimstone. Why should he get in first?" "He goes first," explained St. Peter, "Because just by flying one day a week this fellow has scared the devil out of more people than all of you gentlemen put together."

973.   A man stood before the Pearly Gates awaiting admission to Heaven. St. Peter asked him what he had done on earth to deserve entrance. He said, "Once I went to Russia. I succeeded in confronting the head of the communist party and I really told him off for persecuting people and keeping the world in a state of tension. Then I slapped him." St. Peter said, "That was very brave, considering that he is always surrounded by armed guards. When did that happen?" "Oh," said the man, "about five minutes ago."

974.   Position on a program is all important. Take the case of a man who had survived the Johnstown flood but died soon afterwards and never had a chance to tell about it on earth. You've read about that 1889 flood, of course—it almost destroyed Johnstown and wiped out seven other towns in the Conemaugh Valley of Pennsylvania. This man reached Heaven and told St. Peter he'd like more than anything to tell about his Johnstown flood experience. St. Peter told him he'd have to wait his turn. Finally, after a long wait, his turn came. St. Peter informed him that he was on that day's agenda. St. Peter consulted his program and told the Johnstown flood survivor: "You'll be on right after a man by the name of Noah."

975.   The young couple stood before the Pearly Gates. "Are you married?" St. Peter asked them. They confessed that they weren't but they would like to be. After a bit of consultation and a little rule-looking up in the books behind the gates, the couple was allowed to enter. "Will you perform the ceremony?" they asked the saint.

"Oh, no," he said. "We'll have to wait until we get a preacher. Just hold yourself in readiness."

Three years passed. Finally St. Peter came hustling up to the couple. "Okay," he said. "We've got a preacher and he's ready to tie the knot. Come along now and we'll get you married."

The couple hung back a little. "We've been thinking," the man said, somewhat uneasily, "and we have some reservations about this whole thing. If the marriage doesn't work out, can we get a divorce?"

St. Peter threw up his hands. "Oh, my goodness," he said. "I really don't think so. Judging from how long it took us to get a preacher up here, I doubt if we ever could get a lawyer."

976.   The new arrival in Heaven was greeted warmly by St. Peter, who said he had just arrived in time for dinner. While it was being prepared, the newcomer noticed that he was all alone, but there seemed to be a big feast going on down below—steak and wine and much revelry. St. Peter returned to serve himself and the newcomer a tuna loaf on a paper plate. Said the newcomer, "I don't mean to complain, but the folks in Hades seem to have it so much better." Said St. Peter, "Well, you know how hard it is to plan a meal for two."

977.   St. Peter and Satan were having an argument one day about baseball. With a beguiling leer, Satan proposed a game (to be played on neutral grounds) between a select team from the heavenly host and his own hand-picked Hades boys.

"Very well," the gatekeeper of the Celestrial city agreed. "But you realize, I hope, that we have all the good players and the best coaches too."

"I know," said Satan calmly, "but we have all the umpires."

978.   Voter to a candidate: "I wouldn't vote for you if you were St. Peter." "If I were St. Peter," said the candidate, "you couldn't vote for me because you wouldn't be in my district."

979.   A man unexpectedly found himself at the Pearly Gates and asked St. Peter, "How did I get here?" "Don't you remember?" St. Peter replied gently. "Your wife said, 'Be an angel and let me drive.' "

Salespeople

980.   A fatherly type went into an appliance store to buy a new refrigerator. A salesman kept bothering him and Dad kept saying. "Just looking," over and over again. Finally the salesman flung his arms around the biggest, fanciest refrigerator in the place and said, rather dramatically, "Sir, this refrigerator will pay for itself in two years!" "Good," Dad replied, "when it does, send it over to the house."

981.   Although he did all the buying for his company, the executive

absolutely would not see salesmen. If he needed more facts about a product, he often said he should send for a salesman. But he never did. One day, however, a direct attack by an enterprising salesman with a new and undisguised sales weapon penetrated his defense. The salesman had a homing pigeon delivered to the executive by a Western Union messenger. Tied to the pigeon's leg was a tag which read: "If you want to know more about our product, just throw our representative out the window."

982.   Mr. Cheatham had a clothing store and he had a suit he just couldn't get rid of. Finally, he told his number one salesman, "Max, we've had this suit for 12 years. I'm going on vacation. When I come back, I want the suit gone. If the suit ain't gone, you're gone . . . Understand?" He came back after a two-week holiday and the suit was gone. He heard moaning from the basement. He went downstairs and there's Max, lying there all bloody, his clothes ripped, his shirt hanging out. "Max what happened?" he asked. "Boss, I sold the suit." "Congratulations," Cheatham says, "But what happened?" Max, "A blind man came in and I got him to take the suit." "Okay, but what happened to you?" "I never did convince his dog."

983.   A salesman tried to sell a carload of horse shoes to a black-smith. The tough smithie didn't like him so he roughed him up and threw him out. The salesman called his boss and told him what happened.
    The boss said, "You go back and sell him those shoes. He can't intimidate me."

984.   A shopkeeper was trying for extra sales.
    "Would you like to see some shoes to match this suit?"
    "No."
    "Socks?"
    "No."
    "How about a tie?"
    "No."
    "Is there anything else at all I can do for you?"
    "Yeh. Stick out your tongue so I can seal this letter."

985.   Some salesmen are so good they can talk you to debt.

986.   The customer's sales resistance was high, and the salesman had tried nearly every angle he could think of. "But it's a beautiful suit." he said. "Why, even your best friends wouldn't recognize you in that suit. Just take a walk outside and examine it in the light."

The customer went out, and when he returned a few moments later the salesman rushed up to him. "Good morning, stranger," he beamed. "What can I do for you?"

987.   A salesgirl in a candy store always had customers lined up waiting while other salesgirls stood around with nothing to do. The owner of the store noted her popularity and asked for her secret. "It's easy," she said. "The other girls scoop up more than a pound of candy and then start taking away. I always scoop up less than a pound and then add to it." (GENE BROWN in Danbury, Conn. News-Times)

988.   A man called a hotel for information. "How much do you charge for a room?" he asked.

"Our rates start at $50 a day," the clerk announced.

"Do you take children?"

"No, sir," the clerk responded. "Only cash or a major credit card."

989.   A man was being shown a farm that was for sale by the real estate agent. Coming to a strip of bottom land that bordered a stream, the man noticed a tree with dried mud extending some six feet up the trunk, and he said, "Does the stream overflow on this land?"

"No, never," the agent hastily proclaimed.

"Then, how did the mud get on that tree?" the man asked.

The agent hesitated, and then said, "From the hogs rubbing themselves against it. And now," he went on hurriedly, "I'll show you the rest of the farm."

"Right now," the man said, "I'd rather you show me those hogs."

990.   Trying to sell a housewife a home freezer, a salesman pointed out, "You can save enough on your food bills to pay for the freezer." "Yes, I know," the woman agreed, "but you see we're paying for our car on the carfare we save. Then we're paying for our washing machine on the laundry bills we save, and we're paying for the house on the rent we're saving. We just can't afford to save any more right now."

991.   Man at the next desk says he knows a salesman called "The Musket." Why, you ask. "Because he's been loaded and fired five times in three years."

Saloons

992.   Some say the saddest four words man every composed are "The Saloon is closed."

993. Scrawled in a saloon: "If Superman is so smart, how come he wears his underwear outside his trousers?"

994. My uncle was in a saloon the other day and got knocked off a bar stool by a guy he once said he could whip hands down. Trouble was he wouldn't keep his hand down.

995. A rough, rugged looking character entered a Western saloon. He had a sheet of paper in his hand. "This," he announced, "Is a list of all the men I can whip."

"Is my name on there?" demanded a little runt of a guy, fingering the two pistols dangling low on his legs.

"Yep."

"You can't whip me."

"You sure?"

"I know it," said the small guy.

"Okay partner," said the big guy, licking a pencil, "I'll just scratch your name off."

996. "Who has the most money to spend? Who has the big limousine? Whose wife has the finest fur coats? The saloon keeper! And who pays for it? You." A temperance lecturer rammed his point home.

A few days later a couple stopped the lecturer and thanked him for his advice. "Oh, you've stopped drinking?" the lecturer exclaimed.

The husband said, "Oh, no, we've bought a saloon."

997. Joe Browne says a woman barged into a local saloon where her husband was and said: "I'll have a double what he has!" The bartender poured a double-header of whiskey and she gulped it down, then gasped: "Yackk! Ughh! How can you drink that awful stuff?" Her husband said, "See, and you think I sit here all day enjoying myself!"

998. Joe E. Lewis (sitting at Lindy's bar): "One drink always makes me dizzy."

Jack Benny: "Really?"

Joe E. Lewis: "Yes—the twelfth!"

999. Some folks try to get in touch with the spirit world through a medium. Others just use the local bartender.

School

1000. "I'm worried about you being at the bottom of your class," said the father to his son.

"Don't worry about it, dad," assured his son. "They teach the same things at both ends."

1001.   In rebuking Junior for his low grades in school, the parents referred to little Robert, a few doors down the street, as an example: "Robert doesn't get C's and D's, does he?" the father asked.

Junior replied: "No, but he's different. He has very bright parents."

1002.   There was a mother who was having a hard time getting her son to go to school one morning. "Nobody likes me at school," said the son. "The teachers don't and the kids don't. The superintendents hate me, the school board wants me to drop out, and the custodians have it in for me. I don't want go."

"You've got to go," insisted the mother. "You're healthy. You have a lot to learn. You've got something to offer others. You are a leader."

"Give me one good reason why I should care?" he asked.

"I'll give you two," replied his mother, "You're 49 years old and you're the principal."

1003.   When his daughter commented on the fabulous new equipment in her high school home economics classroom, the father asked, "What have you learned to cook so far?" The girl shrugged. "We haven't gotten into cooking yet. We're only up to thawing."

1004.   The Student's Psalm:
The monster is my teacher, I shall not pass.
He maketh me face the blackboard,
He destroyeth my love note,
He maketh me put my gum in the trash can,
He maketh me quiet and taketh away my candy,
He waketh me from my sleep and leadeth me to the office for conduct's sake.
His face hardens on me,
He maketh me write 600 words,
He filleth the blackboard with homework.
My notebook runneth over.
Yea, though I walk through the Valley of the Shadow of discipline, I fear no evil.
For I am the meanest devil in the valley.

1005.   Mother: "What did you learn in school today?"
Son: "How to whisper without moving my lips."

1006.   "When I go to junior high school," 8-year-old Susan announced, "I'm going to take shop." "Girls don't take shop," her older brother snapped. "Why not?" she querried. "Isn't that where you learn to buy things?"

1007. I can't believe some of our school graduates. I asked a kid who couldn't spell if he ever read Webster's dictionary. He said he preferred to wait until they made it into a movie.

1008. One university football team is going to try out the three-squad system this year. One will play offense. The second will play defense. And the third squad will attend class.

1009. Florida State Coach, Bobby Bowden talking about one of his linebackers, Reggie Herring: "He doesn't know the meaning of the word fear. In fact, I just saw his grades, and he doesn't know the meaning of a lot of words."

1010. George Bernard Shaw, who said, "The only time my education was interrupted was when I was in school."

1011. "I quit school in the sixth grade because of pneumonia. Not because I had it—but because I couldn't spell it." ROCKY GRAZIANO

1012. In the first place God made idiots; this was for practice; then he made school boards.

1013. Some high schools are now requiring all teenagers to take two years of English. The theory is that every student should know a second language.

1014. So many students are driving to high school these days they're talking about using the buses to pick up teachers.

Secretaries

1015. Secretary: "Your wife wants to give you a kiss over the phone."
Boss: "Take a message and give it to me later."

1016. There was an inexperienced girl who got a job as a medical secretary. She was having trouble with the boss' notes on an emergency case which read, "Shot in the lumbar region." She brightened up shortly and typed in the record, "Wounded in the woods."

1017. One pretty secretary to another: "I must be leading a dull life. I had money left over at the end of last week."

1018. A patriotic blonde is one hundred percent behind the President's energy proposals. She reduced her speed to 30 words per minute on the electric typewriter.

1019.   There have been many scandals in Washington on keeping secretaries on the government payroll. Jake Miller, 60, gray, bald is secretary to Gulf Compress Association. Introducing officers of the association to the members of the annual meeting, the president, aware of a sex scandal in the morning paper, commented on the quality of the association secretary by saying, "Let me make this clear . . . Jake does type a little."

1020.   A secretary was overheard talking with a steno. The secretary asked, "Wouldn't you like to be liberated?" Steno: "Not yet. First, I'd like to be captured."

1021.   The boss was exasperated with his new secretary. She ignored the telephone when it rang. "Finally," he said irritably, "you must answer the phone when it rings." She said, "All right, but nine times out of ten it's for you."

1022.   My friends' secretary told him the other day: "I've added up this column of figures 10 times, Sir."
   "Good for you."
   "And here are the 10 answers."

1023.   An official passes along a story about a secretary in a municipal water department who asked, "is waterworks all one word or is there a hydrant in the middle?"

1024.   A philosophical New Yorker, who gave up all hope of getting perfect letters from his office typist, now sends the letters out as they come from her mill—spelling errors, erasures, and all. He evens matters with a rubber stamp that he had specially made. It marks in the lower left-hand corner: "She can't type—but she's beautiful."

1025.   Two secretaries were talking about their dates the previous Saturday. Said one: "My date was terrible, really terrible. Not only did he lie about the size of his yacht, but he made me do the rowing, too."

Signs

1026.   Sign on a tow truck: "We only deal in crash and carry."

1027.   The traffic signs in Berkeley, California, have been changed from "Walk" and "Don't Walk" to "Right On" and "No Way."

1028. Sign seen on an office wall: "Time is nature's gimmick to keep it from happening to us all at once."

1029. Sign of the times department: About 11 p.m. last Friday, the police radio dispatched an officer with the following message: "Investigate juveniles drinking, fighting, and having fun."

1030. Golf Course sign: Members will refrain from picking up golf balls until they have stopped rolling.

1031. Sign for state legislators: Legalize bingo, keep grandmas off the street.

1032. Sign in cemetery: "A place for everybody and everybody in it's place."

1033. Sign at a car wash: Grime does not pay.

1034. Sign in Bank: Cheer up, the less you have, the more there is to get.

1035. The owner of a large business bought a lot of signs reading: "Do it Now" and hung them all over the office, hoping to inspire his people to be energetic and prompt in their work. Soon after, a friend asked him how it worked out. "Well, not exactly as I expected," he said. "The cashier skipped town with $30,000, the head bookkeeper eloped with my secretary, and three clerks asked for a raise."

1036. Sign in a struggling new business: CUSTOMERS WANTED —NO EXPERIENCE NECESSARY!

1037. Sign in Los Angeles Bakery: LET'S PLAY STORE......YOU BE THE CUSTOMER.

1038. Sign in a barber shop: COFFEE $12—HAIR CUT FREE.

1039. Sign: DON'T PUT OFF FOR TOMORROW WHAT YOU CAN DO TODAY BECAUSE IF YOU ENJOY IT TODAY, YOU CAN DO IT AGAIN TOMORROW.

1040. Sign on a company bulletin board: TO ERR IS HUMAN, TO FORGIVE IS NOT COMPANY POLICY.

1041. Sign on a university bulletin board read: SHOES ARE REQUIRED TO EAT IN THE CAFETERIA. Underneath, somebody had scribbled, SOCKS MAY EAT WHEREVER THEY WANT TO.

1042. Sign in a park for campers: "Don't take anything but pictures, and don't leave anything but footprints."

1043. The hand dryer machine on the wall of the men's room at a restaurant has the usual instructions—"Push button, rub hands gently in the flow of air, dryer shuts off automatically." But beneath the instructions on this machine, someone who obviously feels as I feel about these silly hand-drying devices, has written, "Then wipe your hands on your pants."

1044. In the restroom of a local high school which had installed hot air hand dryers was a neatly taped message that read "Push the button for a message from your principal."

1045. Sign seen at the Oklahoma University Student Union: "My job gives me what I need—an excuse to drink."

1046. Antique shop on Elk City, Oklahoma has a sign that reads, "If you don't know what you want, we have it." Sounds like the Den of Antiquity.

1047. Sign in antique shop: "Come in and buy what your grandmother threw out." I went in and sure enough there was my grandfather.

1048. Sign in front of a church: "Beware—lest the footprints you leave in the sands of time show only the marks of a heel."

1049. Sign on a small sports car: "When I grow up I'm going to be a Chrysler."

1050. Bumper sticker on a milk truck: "Everything I own, I owe to udders."

1051. A sign on a Las Vegas hotel reads: "Honeymoon Suite for $20 per night; $2 for each additional person!"

1052. In the window of a small town newspaper: "Read the Bible to learn what people ought to do. Read this newspaper to learn what they really do."

1053. Houston bumper sticker: "Support Little League Baseball—Cheer for the Astros."

Sons

1054. A British father, at a Dover picnic, was standing at the edge of the white cliffs admiring the sea below, the sandwiches clutched in his hand. His son approached him and tugged at his coat. "Mother says it isn't safe here." said the boy, "and you're either to come away or else give me the sandwiches."

1055. An elderly lady was bragging about her son. "He's a surgeon," she announced proudly.

"That's fine," answered her patient listener.

"And he's performed over three hundred operations," the proud mom continued, "and he hasn't cut himself even once."

1056. I never will forget his fifth birthday. I gave my son a picture of a cake and he sat there all day trying to blow out the candles.

1057. We sent our son off to college to have his character molded, and he came home the moldiest character you ever saw.

1058. My son may be listed in "Who's Who," but he doesn't know what's what, or where or when.

1059. Never do push-ups in the shower area. My son did that once and got athletes hands. It was so bad, he had to use Absorbine Sr. to cure it.

1060. Once the customer thinks he understands how much he will have to pay, he resents being "bumped" to a higher price, whether through hidden extras, bait-and-switch, or any other technique. That kind of selling is too much like the joke about the elderly optician who was teaching his newly graduated son how much to charge a patient. "After you put their new glasses on them," the old man explained, "you say, 'That will be $20.' If the patient doesn't flinch, you add, 'For the lenses.' And if he still doesn't flinch, you add, 'each.' "

1061. My son had a date the other night. He described her as a topless dancer with a bottomless appetite.

1062. His dad was pleased until he came upon Mike's final paragraph. "I would like to go to school at our state university," Mike had written. "When I graduate, I would like to go on to a truck driver's school."

1063. Tennessee is home of country-western music. Freddie Fender's son is now recording under the name of Herbie Hubcap.

1064. The mother and her 14 year-old son were having a discussion about his first girl friend.

"What does she like about you?" Mom asked.

"That's easy," he said. "She thinks I'm handsome, fun, smart, talented, and a good dancer."

"What do you like about her?"

"That she thinks I'm handsome, fun, smart . . ."

1065. My son is so dumb he got a pair of cuff-links last Christmas and had his wrists pierced.

1066. Justice will prevail. Like my son taking a correspondence course—They wanted to bus him to another post office . . . but the notice got lost in the mail.

1067. "My son had to give up his career because of fallen arches."
"He's an athlete?"
"No, an architect."

1068. My son says he wants to take karate lessons so he'll be able to put his fist through a wooden board. It'll be very handy if he's ever attacked by a lumber yard.

1069. At Caesars Palace, you can get a room with a huge mirror over the bed. Sexy. My son stayed there last month. He woke up in the middle of the night, looked up and screamed, thinking he was about to be crushed by a naked sky diver.

1070. My son is majoring in English. Now his diction is perfect when he talks back.

1071. A son said his dad hated him because he wouldn't let him have the family car. Proverbs 13:24 gave him the reference for the argument: "He that spareth the rod hateth the child."

1072. We recently did our spring cleaning. Vacuumed the living room, waxed the kitchen floor, and raked our son's rug.

1073. My son says he took a speed-reading course and the only benefit is that when he reads a paper, he knows the bad news 10 minutes sooner than everybody else.

1074. One of the most discreet and yet explicit letter of reference ever written was a reply made to a company asking for a reference on my son, a former employee: "We have known Mr. X a long time, and when you come to know him as long as we have, you will think the same of him as we do."

1075. You're not going to get anywhere telling your son that his hair looks like a mop. He probably doesn't know what a mop is.

1076. As my son explains it, you have to get it all together if you want to let it all hang out.

1077. Our son described a girl he met at a party this way: "She's so ugly she would make a train take a dirt road."

1078. Reminds me of the jungle that grows in a teenager's room. A whole herd could be lost in there. A friend said his son left home and he hadn't looked in there for 15 years . . . They had to clean the rug with a lawnmower.

1079. My son went to Great Britain on one of those Getaway Vacations. Both of them got away—him and his money.

Speakers

1080. The subject of women's lib does bring up an occasional amusing incident. For instance: There was a meeting in San Antonio and the speaker, although not scheduled to speak on Women's Lib, said that sometimes they carried this thing a bit too far. He had heard that they were objecting to having "LADIES" on restrooms preferring "WOMEN" instead. "Now," he asked the audience, "How many of you would prefer not to be called a 'Lady'?" Twenty-four hands went up, all of them men!

1081. A speaker broke his upper denture plate. The man next to him pulled out a plate from a pocket and handed it to him. He improvised and spoke eloquently. Afterwards, he said, "Thanks. Are you a dentist?" "No, I'm an undertaker," the man replied.

1082. Once, while delivering a speech on "Honesty," Mark Twain told the following story. "When I was a boy, I was walking along a street one day, when I happened to spy a cart carrying watermelons. I was very fond of watermelon, so I sneaked quietly up to the cart and snitched one. I then ran into a nearby alley and, with mouth watering, sank my teeth into the melon. No sooner had I done so, however, than a strange feeling came over me. Without a moment's hesitation, I made my decision. I walked back to the cart, replaced the melon . . . and took a ripe one."

1083. A world famous anthropologist was lecturing on his great discovery, a matriarchal society where women ruled and men were nothing. "Where was this?" asked a news reporter. "Cincinnati," replied the professor.

1084. During the Indianapolis Press Club's annual Gridiron Dinner, Governor Otis Bowen of Indiana was hailed as "The most popular after-dinner speaker since Harpo Marx."

1085. The missionary was the speaker at a dinner in his honor before he was to embark for a distant land. "I want to thank you for you kindnesses," he concluded, "and I want all of you to know that when I am out there, surrounded by ugly, grinning savages, I shall always think of you people."

1086.   At a banquet in London too much food was served and far too many long speeches were made. When Lord Balfour's turn came, the hour was late and he was profoundly weary. "I have been asked," he said "to give an address and I shall beg the privilege of giving my own. It is No. 40, Carlton Garden, and with your kind permission I will go there at once."

1087.   "You seem to be nervous about being the next speaker on the program," a lady said to an obviously tense man. "Me nervous?" he said. "Not at all!" "Then what are you doing in the ladies' room?" she asked.

1088.   Victor Borge told his listeners that they should have heard him the night before at Madison, Wisconsin—they'd be home by now.

1089.   The program chairman of a small luncheon club was trying to persuade a friend of his to make a speech to the group. He was laying on the words of praise. "Well, if I'm as good as you say I am," the friend said finally, "I should charge you a fee." How much do you pay?" "We feed you," said the program chairman, "and we let you sit on the chair with the cushion."

1090.   I lost my voice just before I came to this meeting. I just borrowed this one to make the talk.

Sports

1091.   A chap who spent most of Sunday in front of his TV watching one football game after another finally fell asleep and spent the night in his chair. When his wife arose in the morning, she was afraid that he would be late to work. "Get up, dear," she said. "It's 20 to 7." In an instant, the man was fully awake. "In whose favor?" he asked.

1092.   A young lad was doing his homework while his father was watching TV. "Dad, there are three basic rules of hygiene to keep you from losing your teeth. Two of them are to brush your teeth twice a day and see your dentist twice a year. But I can't remember the third. Can you?"

"Yes," replied the father, "Don't ask your Dad questions when he's watching a football game."

1093.   An English girl arrived in Berkeley the afternoon that the University of California upset USC in football. She was caught up in the celebrating throngs and wondered what on earth was going on. She asked a Berkeley native and he explained: "This is caused by football, our No. 1 Sport." She sniffed and murmured: "Isn't that revolting?" "No ma'am," he replied. "That's our No. 2 sport."

1094. A football player in a small college was extraordinarily dumb, but to the surprise of everyone he passed all of his work, including a special examination in chemistry. The chemistry professor was asked about it, and he said, "I decided I would let him pass if he answered 50% of the questions. One he answered wrong, one right. Therefore, I let him pass. The first was, 'What color is blue vitriol?' He answered 'Pink.' That time he was wrong. The other was 'How do you make sulphuric acid?' He answered that he didn't know. That time he was right."

1095. A great football coach, on the power of positive thinking: "I want our players to think as positive as the 85-year old man who married a 25-year old woman and ordered a five bedroom house near an elementary school."

1096. Knowing a salary dispute was going on between a super star and his coach, a TV sports announcer asked Mr. Big for a comment on his touchy situation. He tactfully replied, "I've played for a lot of coaches, and I want to say this about Hank—he's certainly one of them."

1097. Did you hear about the man who bought a copy of Ernest Hemingway's "Across the River and Into the Trees," but returned the next day and demanded his money back. He thought it was a book on golf.

1098. The president of an exclusive country club was watching golfers tee off on the first tee. He noticed a man addressing the ball ten feet in front of the markers. "I say there," called the president, "you're supposed to put your ball behind those markers when you tee off."

The golfer ignored him.

"Don't hit the ball there," the president shouted. "Put it behind the markers!"

The golfer looked up and said, "Mister, I've been a member of this snooty club for 3 years, and you are the first person who's spoken to me. But if you're going to talk to me, I wish you wouldn't do it while I'm addressing the ball . . . And lastly, for your information, although it's none of your business, this is my second shot."

1099. Bob Hope on golf: "Golf is for fellows who are too old for girls but still want to get in a trap."

"I play alot of golf with Billy Graham. He prays and I cheat."

"I pray, too, but HE's got a hot line! Once I putted at the hole and it healed over. And once Billy hit it in a trap and grass grew under it."

1100.   I'm not going to say he cheats at golf. Let's just put it this way: Last year he wore out three clubs and six erasers. You have to be a little suspicious of anyone who writes down their golf score and then wipes his fingerprints off the pencil.

1101.   A male foursome was being held up by two slow lady players, one of whom was searching in the rough. Growing impatient, one of the men called to the other woman as she rested casually in the middle of the fairway: "Why don't you help your friend look for her ball?" "Oh, she didn't lose her ball," the woman explained. "She's looking for her club."

1102.   Irate motorist to golfer, "You sliced that golf ball, and it broke my windshield! What do you intend to do about it?"

Golfer, "Probably the best thing to do would be to move my thumb up and change my grip."

1103.   A wife came home from playing golf with her husband and she was very depressed. She said to her neighbor, "I did everything wrong, wrong, wrong! I hit into the woods. I got caught in a sand trap. I hooked every drive. I missed three easy putts. And worst of all—I won!"

1104.   A golfer had a terrible day on the links. At the last hole, he fell into a tantrum. Cursing and swearing, he beat on the ground with his club. "I have to give it up," he moaned. "I have to give it up."

"Give up golf?" encouraged his caddy.

"No," snapped the golfer, "The ministry."

1105.   A golfing person badly beaten by an elderly parishioner, returned to the clubhouse depressed.

"Cheer up," said the opponent. "Remember, you win eventually. You'll be burying me some day."

"Yes," said the person. "But even then it'll be your hole."

1106.   The fellow on the golf tee said to his companion, "I've got to do well here. That's my mother-in-law on the clubhouse porch."

"Don't be silly," said his friend. "That's over 200 yards—you'll never hit her from here."

1107. A golfing duffer finally made a hole-in-one. He came home and joyfully told his wife about it. "What's so wonderful about a hole-in-one?" she sneered.

"Let me explain, honey. I usually make double bogeys, and that means that on a par three hole, I usually make a five-sometimes a six or seven. This time I only took one stroke."

"Then," said she, utterly unimpressed, "why weren't you home earlier for dinner?"

1108. After one Dallas Cowboys' loss, their coach told them a story. He said a sheik, informed that a dozen new oil wells had been drilled on his land and all were gushers, celebrated by calling in his three sons and announcing that he would grant the fondest wish of each.

"O great and gracious father," said the 22-year-old, "I have just received this magazine with a picture in the center of a beautiful maiden and this is what I desire."

The shiek motioned to an aide and ordered: "Buy him one for each month of the year."

The second son, 16, said "This car magazine I take says the (he named a brand) convertible is the best in the world. . . ."

The shiek told the aide: "Buy him 12 cars in each color of the rainbow."

Then the shiek turned to his 8-year-old son and spoke: "Now, my young son, what is your desire?"

"Well, Daddy," exclaimed the child, "I have been watching television on Sunday and there is this Mickey Mouse outfit. . . ."

"You need say no more, the shiek interrupted. He turned again to his aide. "Buy him the Dallas Cowboys."

1109. Fortune magazine was challenged to a baseball game by Business Week, which laid down strict ground rules: "50% women; men batting opposite-handed; no sliding, stealing, bunting, fistcuffs or swearing, and the loser buying the beer." Fortune says that about 60 Staffers showed up. Some had not played in years. Others not at all. Manager Chuck Whittingham, Fortune's assistant publisher, wanted to give everyone a chance.

"You be the catcher," he told one member.

"What do I do?" she asked.

"You catch the ball and throw it back to the pitcher."

"Right," she said. "Where will he be?"

Fortune bought the beer.

1110. Al Lopez was one of the game's greatest managers at Chicago and Cleveland. One afternoon when the White Sox were playing the Yankees, Lopez had a rookie from the deep South sit next to him in the dugout "To watch, ask questions and learn."

Nellie Fox, attempting to go from first to third on a single to right was cut down on a great throw by Roger Maris.

"He was right to try for third," Lopez told the rookie. "You won't see another throw like that for 100 years."

1111.   Bob Uecker (lifetime batting average: .200) was recalling his major league career: "I set records that never will be equalled—in fact, I hope 90% of them don't even get printed," he said. "When I looked to the 3rd base coach for a sign, he'd turned his back on me. When I went to bat with 3 men on and 2 out in the 9th, I looked over in the other team's dugout, and they were already in street clothes. The manager once told me to go to plate without a bat—and hope for a walk.

"They said I was such a great prospect that they were sending me to a winter league to sharpen up. When I stepped off the plane, I was in Greenland."

1112.   During a faculty meeting, several professors were discussing a star basketball player who was on the verge of flunking out of college. "The boy is certainly a great player," commented one teacher. "He can do anything with a basketball—except autograph it."

1113.   A 6'10" player applied for a summer job as a lifeguard. When asked if he could swim fast he said, "I can't swim."

"Then, how could you be a lifeguard?" asked the swimming coach.

"I'm a heck of a wader," he replied.

1114.   Fritz Crisler, former longtime athletic director at Michigan, told about once receiving a doleful letter from a former player who was coaching a woefully weak high school football team. "What do you do," he implored, "when you come to halftime with the score 54–0 against you?"

Said Crisler: "I told him it's very simple. Just refuse to show up for the second half. Then you would forfeit the game 1–0, and who could be mad at you for losing by such a close score?"

1115.   However "Speedy" must rank as one of the steady golfers of all time. For example, he has spent nearly 40 years on the links and still is playing with the same ball. He never hit it hard enough to hurt it or far enough to lose it.

1116.   A coach was explaining the assets of his football team specifically his star quarterback. "He is aggressive, cunning, with deceptive speed . . . He's a lot slower than he looks."

1117. He's really a pro-football nut! He refers to his wife as his first draft choice.

1118. Wife to husband in front of TV: "You never talk to me during halftime any more."

1119. Our football coach is a real winner and a scholar with a master's degree. The subject of his thesis was "What college done for me." Our coach knows nothing but sports. He thinks a dope ring is three officials holding hands in a circle.

1120. Hear about the strange oakie? He thought more about girls than he did about football.

1121. One fellow who can smile while everything goes wrong around him is a golf caddie.

1122. Golf is what gives you something to do while taking a walk.

1123. Our coach has never gone in much for frills. But, he says, "I'm thinking about wearing those headphones. You can't hear the crowd boo. . . ."

1124. A wife, standing on a ladder to paint the ceiling, called to her husband who was watching a TV football game: "If I fall off, will you call an ambulance at half-time?"

1125. An assistant coach and scout, discussing "Too Tall" Jones: "We're not afraid of him. He puts his pants on the same as we do—except four feet higher."

1126. After importing kickers from Austria and Yugoslavia, American pro football is eyeing a tackle from East Germany. They say she's terrific.

1127. One theory on coaching: "It's the only profession in the world where people pay $8 to come and watch you work and then tell you how stupid you are."

1128. Fellow said he shot golf in the low 70's and that he'd quit if it got any colder.

1129. The celebrity golfer had a long putt and asked his caddy for advice. "Just keep the ball low," the caddy replied.

1130. A small college at an athletic meet had an erratic javelin thrower—he didn't win any medals but he kept one guy pinned to his seat and cured several of hiccups.

1131. My neighbor says he'll be hearing any day now whether

his son made the starting basketball five at State University or the coach intends to play favorites again this year.

1132. A National Hockey League goalkeeper took two faithful fans, a father and his son, out to dinner. Therefore, seated around the table that night were the father, the son, and the goalie host.

1133. The Houston Astros were standing around in the airport waiting for their flight to Philadelphia when a young lady approached.

"Excuse me," she said, "are you fellows with some group or something?"

Tommy Helms, always quick on the uptake said, "Yes, lady, we're part of a group. We're caddies on the golf tour."

Five minutes later, the same woman was back.

"You're not caddies," she said, realizing she had been put on.

"That's right," Helms said. "We play for the Houston Astros."

The woman smiled and nodded understandingly.

"If I were in your place," she said, "I wouldn't tell anyone either."

1134. The coach called the Little Leaguer in from center field for a conference. "See here, Eddie," said the coach, "you know the principles of good sportsmanship that the Little League practices. You know we don't tolerate temper tantrums, shouting at the umpire, or abusive language. Do I make myself clear?"

"Yes, sir," replied the Little Leaguer.

"Well, then, Eddie," sighed the coach, "Would you please try to explain it to your mother?"

1135. 1st Boy: "She said that she would be faithful to the end."
2nd Boy: "What's wrong with that?"
1st Boy: "Nothing except that I'm the quarterback."

Streakers

1136. A marketing executive bought some land and planned to use it, with friends, for fish and game. But he was bothered by poachers. Finally, he posted this warning: "Anyone Entering This Property Without Protective Clothing May Sustain Radiation Burns."

The city council of a moderate-size town nearby discussed it and decided it was a threat to life. They sent an investigator to the executive.

"It means," he told him, "that anybody who comes on this property naked is liable to get sunburned."

1137. "My uncle's sure glad that streaking fad is over."
"Really? He's a cop?"
"No—a pickpocket."

Students

1138. A pupil looked at the examination question which read: "State the number of tons of coal shipped out of the United States in any year."
Then his brow cleared and he wrote:
"1492, none."

1139. A young agriculture student wanted to go to college and study to be a tree surgeon but had to give it up cause he couldn't stand the sight of sap.

1140. Sometimes the student misunderstands a slight bit, as shown by answers given to test questions.
Matrimony is a place where souls suffer for a time on account of their sins.
Where was the Declaration of Independence signed? At the bottom.
Where is Cincinnati? First place in the league.
Denver is just below the O in Colorado.
The soil of Prussia was so poor the people had to work hard just to stay on top of it.
The climate of Bombay is such that its inhabitants have to live elsewhere.

1141. A teacher was explaining to a class of teenagers about the Old West and said that Billy the Kid had killed 20 men before he was 20 years old.
A girl who had been listening open-mouthed asked: "What make of car did he drive?"

1142. Freshman: "Hey, you got your long hair cut off? How much weight did you lose?"
Second freshman: "About 200 pounds—I got my Dad off my back."

1143. "Who discovered America?" the teacher asked. When one pupil answered, "Ohio," she said: "Ohio. Goodness, no! America was discovered by Columbus." The pupil replied "Oh, yeah, I just forgot his first name."

1144. A teacher, whose specialty is English, asked her class to write a theme on the subject of royalty.

One student's paper began: "The Queen swept down the staircase in her flowing gown, tripped on the third step and fell prostitute on the floor."

The teacher scribbled in the margin: "You really must learn the difference between a fallen woman and one who has temporarily lost her balance!"

1145. Students in the ninth grade were asked to select the 11 greatest Americans. All promptly complied except for one boy who failed to complete the assignment.

"What happened?" the teacher asked.

"I got hung up," he replied, "on who should be at right tackle."

1146. Did you know that according to a recent survey, the average college student goes through 265 books in four years—261 textbooks and four bank books.

1147. Some students drink from the fountain of knowledge, other just gargle.

1148. Foster Brooks said, "Not too many people know this, but Paul was a brilliant student at Miami. He made straight A's—although his B's were a little crooked."

1149. The new foreign student, invited to a social gathering, was a bit hesitant about attending. His English still gave him trouble. But his friend loaned him a book of etiquette, and he memorized certain handy phrases. The hostess served ice cream, and he expressed his appreciation this way: "Thank you, Miss, Mrs. or Mr., whatever the case may be."

Success

1150. If at first you don't succeed, drop in another coin and kick the machine.

1151. Behind every successful man is a family that didn't keep him waiting to get into the bathroom.

1152. Redd Foxx: "I became a somewhat successful comedian by starving a lot and having nothing to lose by making one more stab at it—over and over again. If I had to do it again, I'd get a regular job and be the funniest guy on the job and eat every day."

1153. To be a financial success nowadays, you have to be a contortionist, with your ear to the ground, your shoulder to the wheel, your nose to the grindstone, and your hand in the till.

1154. Snappy outfits for girls on the "chorus line" are now cited as the reason for several Broadway successes. And especially, I guess, when you have only 10 outfits for 20 girls.

1155. A high school guidance counselor advised a young student: "Your tests indicate that your chances for success are greatest in a field where your family has some influence."

1156. Al Hamburg reports a Texas oil man heard of a car pool and ordered one installed in his car!

1157. One of the biggest troubles with success is that its recipe is about the same as for a nervous breakdown.

1158. Mark Twain was once asked the reason for his success. He replied, "I was born excited."

Talking

1159. A talkative worker spent most of his time bemoaning the fact that fortune seemed to smile on everybody but him. When another employee with less seniority was promoted, he complained: "It's the same old story. The other guys get all the breaks."

1160. "When is my ship ever going to come in?"
"Perhaps," suggested a fellow worker, "it will when you learn that steam has replaced wind."

1161. "Why does Sam talk so fast?"
"It's an inherited trait."
"How could fast talking be a genetic trait?"
"His father was an auctioneer and his mother was a woman."

1162. A high ranking White House official, in an interview, made this reply to a query from a newsman: "I'll answer that question quickly and directly . . . unlike my opponent who's fuzzy, complex, vague, waffling, equivocal, indecisive, indistinct . . . too sophisticated, overly complicated, unperceptible, drawn-out, rambling, and . . . what was that question again?"

1163. Man, can my brother-in-law talk. You couldn't get a word in edgewise if you folded it.

1164. While ordering his luncheon, an American tourist in Paris was using some of his high-school French. "Garcon," he said, studying the menu, "je desire consoome royal, et un piece of pang et burr—nom hang it—une piece of burr—"

"I'm sorry, Sir," said the tactful waiter, "I don't speak French."

"Well, then," snapped the tourist, "for heaven's sake, send me someone who can."

1165. Rookie police officer's report of his first traffic accident: "Miss Jones was involved in the accident which bruised her somewhat and injured her otherwise but apparently did not hurt her elsewhere."

1166. One advantage of talking to yourself is you know at least somebody's listening.

Taxes

1167. See how your tax dollars are being spent. It's educational, enlightening, and probably the best cure for hiccups you'll ever find.

1168. We're coming up to April 15, also known as Sherlock Holmes Day—because that's when we use our powers of deduction.

1169. We're coming up to April 15, which is also known as Mayflower Day—because that's when the whole country comes across.

1170. Chemistry has provided the panacea for every affliction—save one. It has not produced a remedy for the pain in the fleshy area at the base of a taxpayer's spine suffered when the Legislature is in session.

1171. Said the king: "Levy a tax. Then everybody will have to cough up." The treasurer replied: "Alas, sire, the coughers are empty."

1172. Tax collector: A guy who tells you what to do with the money you've already done something with.

1173. Reading those income tax guides is educational. Sometimes you discover that something you've been deducting for years really is deductible.

1174. "What is the difference between a taxidermist and a tax collector? The taxidermist takes only your skin." MARK TWAIN

1175. There is one difference between a tax collector and a taxidermist—the taxidermist leaves the hide. MORTIMER CAPLAN, former IRS Director

1176. "An income tax form is like a laundry list—either way you lose your shirt." FRED ALLEN

1177. "Some taxpayers close their eyes, some stop their ears, some shut their mouths, but all pay through the nose." EVAN ESAR

1178. "Tax reform is when you take the taxes off things that have been taxed in the past and put taxes on things that haven't been taxed before." ART BUCHWALD

1179. It's a good thing the IRS doesn't put a tax on talent. If they did, most of us would get off scott free.

1180. Ask not what your country can do for you, because if you do, you're bound to be taxed for it.

1181. A taxpayer received a strongly worded "Second notice" that his taxes were overdue. Hastening to the collector's office, he paid his bill, saying apologetically that he had overlooked the first notice. "Oh," confided the collector with a smile, "we don't send out first notices. We have found that second notices are more effective."

1182. What would be a good way to raise revenue and still benefit the people? Tax every political speech made by a Democrat in this country.

Teachers

1183. Russian school teacher: "Who were the first human beings?"
Student: "Adam and Eve."
Teacher (smiling indulgently): "And what nationality were they?"
Student: "Russian."
Teacher (more seriously): "How do you know?"
Student: "They had no roof over their heads, no clothes to wear, only one apple for the two of them, and they called it Paradise."

1184. The value of assembling a do-it-yourself project is that after you're through you can understand the instructions.

1185. While there has been great progress in communications in recent years, there's still a lot to be said for paying attention.

1186. Education is what you get from reading the small print in the contract. Experience is what you get from not reading it.

1187. A Latin teacher at Washington High School in Tulsa constructed this interpretation of a very well-known saying in the U.S.: "Duo fragmenta absolute bubulae, condimentum peculiare, lactuca, caseus, salsurae, caepae, in sesamisemine pane!" Or "two all beef patties, special sauce, lettuce, cheese, pickles, onions, on a sesame-seed bun!"

1188. Our favorite teacher got a migraine yesterday. She asked a kid on the front row how he spelled "enough" and he said, "e-n-u-f-f."

"That's strange," she told him, "the dictionary spells it "e-n-o-u-g-h."

"Maybe so," the kid said, "but you asked me how I spelled it."

1189. "What does HNO_3 mean?"

"I've got it right on the tip of my tongue."

"Well, you better spit it out. It's nitric acid."

1190. A teacher says her first grade class was being particularly unruly recently and finally she slammed a ruler down on her desk and said, in a loud voice: "I'm tired of this, children. Do you hear me, I'm tired. I'm tired of telling you to be quiet and I'm tired of telling you to sit down and I'm tired of telling you to pay attention to what you're doing. I'm tired of it, children, I'm tired of it." There were several moments of silence before one little boy raised his hand tentatively and helpfully suggested: "Why don't you go take a nice nap?"

1191. "When Lot's wife looked back," the Sunday School teacher asked the class, "what happened to her?" Albert, who had a high I.Q., replied, "She was transmuted into chloride of sodium."

1192. World history would have been changed, argues a first grade teacher I know, if only famous people had been given different first names. "Who, for example, would have feared Percy the Hun?" she inquires. "And doesn't Billy Joe Hitler have a nice ring to it? Or how about Floyd and Debbie Sue Roosevelt?"

1193. Three little boys had their heads together at the back of the room, and they were whispering. "What's going on back there?" inquired their teacher. "We're telling dirty stories," one of the boys said. "Oh, thank goodness," said the teacher. "I was afraid you might be praying."

1194. Two school teachers vacationing in Taxco, Mexico were approached by a street peddler with a tray of lovely silver bracelets. When told that the price was 3,000 pesos, one lady became discouraged but the other school teacher who had been in Mexico before entered into spirited negotiations with the bracelet vendor. She watched with fascination as her friend matched wits with the peddler and finally bought the bracelet for 1,000 pesos. Then, she stepped in and said, "I'll take one also, at the same price. "No, no

Madame, that is impossible," said the vendor, "for you we start over again."

1195. "Teaching is . . . telling your students that you like them, even though it is sometimes a lie . . . learning never to ask open-ended questions of your students, 'Just how stupid do you kids think I am?' . . . being sad when you learn that a student of yours is dropping out at the age of 16 . . . feeling relieved when you learn the drop-out has found a job . . . becoming sad again when you learn that the drop-out is making more than you are."

1196. Our favorite teacher was encouraged, though. She has a kid in her geometry class that not only described a triangle, he named the people involved.

1197. The teachers don't keep the kids after school these days. When 3:30 comes, they're afraid to be alone in the same building with them.

1198. The teacher was glad to see Friday roll around. She asked for the definition of a grandmother and one kid put down: "that's someone who comes to visit and keeps your mother from hitting you."

1199. My English teacher graded my first theme and remarked, "He should never write anything more ambitious than a grocery list."

1200. Filling out a series of reports at the end of the school year, one tired teacher came upon this line: "List three reasons for entering the teaching profession." Without hesitation she filled in: (1) June; (2) July; (3) August.

1201. One time a pupil told his teacher his pa wuz a-going to kill hogs an the teacher could expect some fresh meat. But days went by, no meat for the teacher. Finally the teacher said to the boy, "how come yer pa didn't send me some meat, like you said?" And the boy said, "Well, you see, the hog got well."

1202. A teacher recently passed out evaluation forms in which students grade their teachers. After a protracted silence, one student raised his hand and asked, "How do you spell INCOMPETENT?"

1203. In a big elementary school, a teacher had given a lesson in a kindergarten class on the Ten Commandments. In order to test their memories, she asked: "Can any child give me a Commandment with only four words in it?"

A kid replied, "Keep off the grass."

1204. A wise old teacher said there are three things to remember when teaching:
1. Know your stuff.
2. Know whom you are stuffing.
3. Then stuff them elegantly.

1205. Nowadays, when Johnny brings an apple to the teacher, she dumps it in water and calls the bomb squad.

1206. "Teacher: Who invented the light?"
Pupil: "Schlitz."

Telephones

1207. One fun loving citizen of Chicago called Illinois Bell and asked why New York has jokes and Chicago doesn't.

"Frankly, nobody has asked for Dial-A-Joke here," was the reply.

"That figures," commented the city dweller. "New York is desperate for laughs. Chicago has City Hall."

1208. Almost 100 years ago, Alexander Graham Bell, working with Thomas Watson on experiments that were to lead to the invention of the telephone, excitedly listened to the first sound over their experimental wire: "I'm sorry, the number you have dialed. . . ."

1209. A painful lesson for phone addicts: Doctors are reporting a new malady among people who talk on the phone for long periods of time. They call it "telephoner's ear" and it consists of a staph infection in the upper curl of the ear. The infection is not caused by the telephone, but it seems to thrive under conditions created when a telephone receiver is clamped to the ear for long stretches. The condition is easily treated with compresses and antibiotics. In extreme cases, ear specialists recommend removal of the telephone.

1210. "You've got it all wrong," said the third. "Prestige is when you are in the Oval Office talking to the President, and the phone rings. He picks it up, listens for a minute, and then says, "It's for you!"

1211. Did you hear about the guy who bought an antique telephone because he loved to make crank calls?

1212. A friend of mine dialed a busy office downtown Houston and heard a voice say "Our automatic answering device is away for repairs. This is a person speaking."

Television

1213. The first night when Harry Reasoner signed off for both of them, saying, "Goodnight from Barbara Walters and I," there is a rumor that Barbara gave Harry a polite but firm English lesson by commenting, "I am sorry, Mr. Reasoner, but you have created a most grievous grammatical faux pas, using the first person, nominative case, when in reality the accusative was in order, as the preposition 'from' calls for the first person singular objective in apposition with the proper name Barbara also being the object of the same preposition. I feel that our association will be more lasting and fruitful if you would exercise due care. In other words, watch it, boy."

1214. This is obviously an election year. The TV networks are devoting more time to politicians than to detergents.

1215. Houston Astros traveling secretary Donald Davidson, describing pitcher Joe Niekro's relaxed attitude: "It takes him an hour and a half to watch '60 minutes.'"

1216. A couple of fellows down in W. Va., were talking about a very rich mutual acquaintance who had just built a new house. "He even had television sets built into the bathrooms," one of the fellows said. "I don't know if I'd care for that," said the other guy. "Where could you go during commercials?"

1217. Andrea Kirby, Baltimore television sportscaster, on why she feels females definitely have been an asset in her occupation: "We smell better than the other sportscasters."

1218. The person who says crime doesn't pay never wrote for television.

1219. Even if you think television is perfect, you've got to admit that 30 years ago, people didn't sit in their living rooms watching 30-year old movies.

1220. Television is the device that acquaints you with all the things going on in the world that you could be a part of if you weren't sitting there watching television.

1221. I just got my TV set insured. If it breaks down they send me a pair of binoculars so I can watch my neighbor's set. HENNY YOUNGMAN

1222. "Maybe one reason the Russians get so confident is they've watched our TV programs and figure all Americans have tired blood, indigestion, and nagging backaches." BOB GODDARD

1223. Television is educational. It teaches you how late you'll sit up to watch something you thought you wouldn't want to see in the first place.

1224. If the Lord had expected us to watch so much TV, he'd have given us square eyeballs.

Texans

1225. Texas is home of the greatest men there are. Half of Texans, however, came to the state from some other place. But even though a man was born somewhere else, if he gains distinction as a banker, lawyer, bank robber or other public figure, he is of course a Texan. By this logic, Texas can claim about everybody. Perhaps the most pitiful case of extreme insanity ever told was a guy who went to a Dallas psychiatrist. "What's your trouble?" asked the shrink. "Well, Doc, I'm from Texas and I'm ashamed of it."

1226. This rancher from Texas wanted to buy his wife a sexy night-gown for her birthday. "What size?" asked the little lady at the lingerie department. "I dunno," the Texan admitted. "But she wears size 30 chaps."

1227. One of "them liars" is a man down in West Texas who told about the winter it got so cold, all the rattlesnakes froze up straight and solid. He said he picked them up and hammered them into the ground for fence posts, and it was the biggest mistake he ever made. When spring came, those snakes thawed out and crawled away with 16 miles of barbed wire.

1228. California is too far from Texas ever to amount to much.

1229. "How many people work in the Texas Senate?"
"About ½ of them."

1230. A Texas rancher had some boots made, and they turned out to be too tight. The bootmaker insisted on stretching them. "Not on your life!" exclaimed the rancher. "Every morning when

I get out of bed, I got to corral some cows that busted out in the night and mend fences they tore down. All day long, I watch my ranch blow away in the dust. After supper, I listen to the radio tell about the high price of feed and the low price of beef; and all the time my wife is nagging me to move to the city. Man, when I get ready for bed and pull off these tight boots, that's the only pleasure I get all day!"

1231. One Texas rancher was talking to another. "What's the name of your spread?" asked the first.

"The XWK Lazy R. Double Diamond Circle Q Bar S," replied the second.

"How many head do you have?"

"Only a handful. Not many survive the brandings."

1232. A Texas girl was practicing her drawl:

"Do you know why my hand is like a lemon pie? 'Cause it's got mahrang on it."

1233. Eastener, "What's the birth rate out here?"

Texan, "One to a person."

1234. A Texas newspaper conducted a contest. They offered a prize for the best essay on "Why I Am Glad to Be a Texan"—in 50,000 words or more."

1235. How about the Texan who boasted he had 5,000 head of cattle.

"Is that a lot?" a visitor asked.

The Texan answered, "In the freezer?"

1236. How about the Texan who was so poor the telephone in his Cadillac was on a party line?

1237. The tall Texas tycoon dashed down the hotel steps and flopped down in the back seat of a cab. "Where to?" the driver asked over his shoulder.

"Anywhere!" said the Texan. "I got business everywhere."

1238. A sign in a Texas restaurant recently advertised: "Wanted: Man to wash dishes and two waitresses." It was reported that applications poured in from thirteen counties.

1239. "Were you born in Texas?"

"Yes."

"What part?"

"All of me."

1240. The guy at the next desk says he never realized how big Texas is until he tried to unfold a map of the state in his car.

1241. One of the favorite stories of President Lyndon B. Johnson concerned a Texan who joined the rebels in 1861 and declared the Southerners could "lick those dam yankees with broomsticks." Upon his return two years afterwards, bedraggled, neighbors asked him about his condition, and he told them: "The trouble was, the dam yankees wouldn't fight with broomsticks."

1242. A visitor in Dallas asked, "What's the quickest way to get to the hospital?" "Say something bad about Texas!" came the reply.

Truck Drivers

1243. The old truck driver passed the cute redhead, popped on the brakes and yelled, "Hi ya babe!" The redhead threw back her head and said, "I beg your pardon. That's no way to talk to a girl whose telephone number is 258–8087."

1244. Flossie overheard a customer talk about a man who was afraid to venture out on the street.

"What's he afraid of?" he was asked.

"Well," was the reply, "seems a truck driver ran off with the man's wife. Now everytime he hears a horn, he's afraid the guy is bringing her back."

1245. There is the story of the fellow who went to buy a new pickup truck. Three of his friends went along with him. After the deal was made, the owner and one fellow climbed into the cab of the truck and the other two got into the back. They were going around a curve at a bit more speed than the law allows where they hit a slick spot on the pavement and the truck slid off the road, down an embankment and into the river. The two fellows in front managed to climb out the open windows and swim to shore. They ran up and down the bank, looking for their friends but couldn't find a trace of them. "Lordy, Lordy," said the driver, wringing his hands. "I bet I know what happened. I bet they couldn't get the tailgate down."

1246. A haggard looking fellow with big dark bags under his eyes went to see a psychiatrist and told the shrink his problem: "Everynight I have the same dream. I'm a truck driver and all night I dream I'm driving the truck, New York to Chicago, and then Chicago to Denver. I drive all night and in the morning, when I wake up,

I'm exhausted. You've got to help me, Doc." The doctor puts the patient into deep hypnosis and tells him: "Listen to me carefully. Tonight, when the truck reaches Chicago, you will call me. I'll come and take over the truck and you will fall into a deep and peaceful sleep. Remember, every time you reach Chicago, call me, and I'll take the truck on to Denver for you." The doctor wakes the patient up and he goes away. In a week, he calls the doctor to report, joyfully, that he's cured, sleeping beautifully every night. Another week goes by. Then the patient turns up in the psychiatrist's office looking more worn out than he did before. "Are you following my instructions?" asks the doctor. "Are you calling me every time you get to Chicago?"

"Yes, Yes," says the exhausted patient, "but now it's a new dream. Every night I dream I go out with one girl and then another girl and then another girl and in the morning I'm so tired I can hardly lift my head off the pillow."

So once again the doctor hypnotizes the man. "Tonight," the psychiatrist instructs him, "after you've gone out with the second girl, you call me and I'll take over from there. Do that each and every night. After you've been with the second girl, call me."

The patient wakes up and goes home. He's back the next week and looking worse than ever. "It's terrible, doc," he moans. "Now it's up to six and seven girls a night and I'm feeling worse every morning."

"But are you following my instructions?" asks the doctor. "Are you calling me before you get to the third girl?"

"Yes, certainly," says the patient. "But it doesn't do any good. You're always on the truck between Chicago and Denver."

1247. In Ireland, they tell the story of Tyrone, the truck driver who drove his 14-foot-high vehicle beneath a 12-foot bridge with noisy results. Jammed tighter than a boot in an Irish bog, Tyrone tried reversing his truck. The only result was smoking rubber. Fifteen bystanders tried shoving. It produced three hernias. Tyrone deflated tires to their rims. The weight of the truck split the sidewalls which stalled the truck firmer than ever. Finally, a police constable rolled by on a bicycle. He stared at a 600-yard traffic jam and frowned at Tyrone. "Are you stuck then?" asked the officer.

"Not a bit of it," seethed Tyrone. "Oi was deliverin' this damned bridge but oi lost the address."

1248. A strong spirit of fraternity prevails among drivers of pickups equipped with campers. As a for-instance, a highway patrolman received a radio call to apprehend three men in a red pickup with a white camper-boat tied on top. They were suspected narcotics dealers. The patrolman intercepted the pickup-camper, ordered the occupants out and up against the side of the camper. Just then, says Probst, along came another camper. They're always eager to help one another. It slid in front of the stopped truck, an old boy jumped out, ran around, put his hands up against the side of the camper with the other three guys and said, "Which way is it falling?"

Vacations

1249. A tourist is a person who on vacation travels thousands of miles just to get a snapshot of himself standing beside his car.

1250. In the next scene, we see a couple who have been married 20 years. He says to her, "Honey, let's go on a vacation." As he says this, he looks in the next room where he sees a little old lady knitting. He says, "If you don't mind, let's go without your mother this time." She says, "My mother . . . I thought she was your mother all this time." HENNY YOUNGMAN

1251. The man who said, "you can't take it with you" never saw a camper truck packed for a vacation.

1252. A man went to New York City for his vacation, and one day while he was riding a taxi he noticed that the driver slowed down a little to miss a pedestrian. Noting his passenger's puzzled expression, the driver explained: "If you hit 'em, you gotta fill out a report."

1253. The conversation around the coffee table had turned to holidays. "Well," said one fellow, "this year about all I can afford is a Scottish vacation." Someone else asked, "What is a Scottish vacation?"

"That's when you stay home and let your mind wander," the first fellow explained.

1254. A vacationing lady mailed postcards to her friends back home each day. To her psychiatrist, she wrote: "Having a wonderful time. Wish you were here to tell me what's wrong."

1255. Despite jets and missiles, they still haven't come up with anything that goes faster than a two-week vacation.

1256. Hot-selling T-shirt: "I $pent My Vacation in A Gas $tation."

1257. I know a doctor who took a vacation and left his son in charge of his practice. His son had only been licensed for two weeks. He told his father when he got back that he had cured a rich elderly lady of chronic indigestion. "I've got news for you, son," the doc said. "That case of chronic indigestion helped put you through medical school."

1258.   The jr. executive arrived back at the office after his vacation, tired and haggard. "What's the matter," asked his secretary, "vacation too much?" "I guess so," was the reply. "With the kids taking vitamins and me taking tranquilizers, it was a losing battle all the way."

1259.   A friend at a vacation resort asked a guest where her husband had disappeared to. With a good deal of anger in her voice and pointing toward the fishing pier, she answered, "There's a fishing pole at the end of that pier, and it's got a worm on either end."

1260.   Hear about the tourist vacationing in Las Vegas? He didn't have any money to gamble so he just watched the games and bet mentally. In no time at all, he'd lost his mind.

Veterinarians

1261.   I know some newlyweds. He claims her cooking never has improved. The vet says her cat has only four lives left.

1262.   A waitress at the Playboy Club became ill, and a young man pushed through the crowd to her. "Let me get to that Bunny." he said, "I'm a veterinarian."

Weight Watchers

1263.   When fat men go on diets sometimes the only thing they lose is their sense of humor.

1264.   A local shop for middleweight women is advertising a "Stock Market Dress." When it reaches 130 it splits.

1265.   Even if you don't have scales at home, you can tell you're gaining weight when the hostess steers you away from the antique chairs.

1266.   Ralph says his wife has an "in between" figure. He says it's in between "oh boy" and obese.

1267.   The easiest way to have a schoolgirl figure is by being a schoolgirl.

1268. Many a go-go mind is attached to a so-so body.

1269. Her figure used to be a legend—but now the legend is beginning to spread.

1270. She has an hourglass figure—but her hips have accumulated time and a half.

1271. The surest way to lose weight is to stop eating. Remember, nothing dentured, nothing gained.

1272. Manufacturers are producing a new reducing belt—which you tie around the refrigerator.

1273. With wry humor, Dr. Joseph Arends, a strong advocate of running for health, suggest some guidelines that indicate you are carrying too much blubber: If, when lying on the beach, some kid paints Goodyear on your belly . . . if you are taller when you lie down than when you stand up . . . if children offer you peanuts at the zoo . . . if you call for an ambulance and they send a crane . . . if you go to the store for a suit and the salesman asks if you want a tent . . . if you get harpooned while swimming. MARK BELTAIRE

1274. Art Donovan, former 310-lb. Baltimore Football Colt's defensive lineman, describing himself as a light eater, said, "As soon as it's light, I start to eat."

1275. A friend is losing weight on what is called the all-wet diet. You're allowed to eat whatever you want, but first you must run water over it. Who wants to eat wet bread and pastry or wet mashed potatoes or wet french fries?

1276. A woman joining a physical fitness class was told to wear loose clothes. When she appeared the instructor said: "Remember, I told you to wear loose clothes?"
    "If I had any clothes that were loose," the applicant replied, "I wouldn't have joined this class."

1277. Jim Morrissey, who is involved in the weight-reducing business, tells about a woman member of a class who has lost 71 pounds, ending a life-long obesity problem. At a recent class meeting she was telling about coming home from work the other afternoon with her arms full of packages, unlocking the door and having her unmentionables fall off. "It was," she sighed, "the happiest day of my life!" Louisville Courier-Journal

1278. There are little telltale signs that warn you when you're gaining weight. Like, your appendix scar is now 14 inches wide.

Wives

1279. I miss my wife's cooking as often as possible.

1280. Nothing helps a woman to keep her chin up as much as having only one.

1281. The reason women are indecisive is because they live longer than men. They have more time to make up their minds.

1282. If medical science has done so much to add years to our lives, how come you never meet a woman who's past 40?

1283. The weaker sex is the stronger sex because of the weakness of the stronger sex for the weaker sex.

1284. Behind every great man is a woman with nothing to wear.

1285. A guy returned from a Safari. He had a few trophies. His wife bagged a huge lion and has the head mounted.
"She got it with that new Enfield 447?" asked a friend?
"No, she got it with the front tire of a rented station wagon."

1286. The wife next door got her husband a beach house tie for Christmas. That's a tie with a bay window at the end of it.

1287. A lady complained that her husband was about to work himself to death.
"How come?" asked her neighbor.
"He's so near-sighted," said his wife, "he can't tell when the boss ain't looking."

1288. Two friends, both recently married, were having lunch together and comparing merits of their wives. One said, "Ah, my Mary is an angel. She could not tell a lie to save her life." The other sighed: "You lucky man. Helen can tell a lie the minute I open my mouth."

1289. A well-informed man is one whose wife has just told him what she thinks of him.

1290. In a certain college, the trustees thought it would be smart to hire the wives of some of the faculty members, as these women often were well qualified. The trustees did so and the plan worked quite well for a while. Then they began having trouble with pregnancies. Wives in an expectant state all wanted to go on teaching right up to immediacy of delivery. So the board of trustees made a rule. All wives were to stand facing a wall with their toes touching the baseboard. If they stood erect, and their tummies didn't touch the wall, they could go on teaching. The wives accepted the rule, but they insisted it must apply to male faculty members as well. When the trustees put the men to the test, they lost five professors and three department heads.

1291. "Good news!" the wife said excitedly. "I've saved enough money for us to go to Europe!"

Her husband responded, "Wonderful! When do we leave?"

"As soon as I've saved enough for us to come back," explained the wife.

1292. A man who had just bought a plane was giving his wife her first ride in it. "What I like about traveling this way," he said, "is that there are no road signs to watch and no pedestrians. So I don't think I'll be bothered by backseat drivers up here." Peering through the windshield, his wife snapped at him, "Watch out for those birds!"

1293. Wife, reading husband's fortune card to him: "You are a leader of men. You are brave, handsome, strong, and popular with the ladies." She paused. "It has your weight wrong, too."

1294. Some say their wife is an angel and others say theirs is a she-devil. Well, a wife is a woman who will stick by you in all the trouble you wouldn't have gotten into if you hadn't married her in the first place.

1295. "Tiptoe down the steps in your bare feet," said the wife who was convinced she heard a midnight prowler beneath the couple's bedroom. "Don't turn on any lights. Sneak up on him before he knows what happened."

The dutiful husband swallowed hard and began following his wife's orders. Just as he reached the bedroom door, she added: "And if you don't get mugged, bring me back a glass of milk."

1296. A man was bending over to tune his radio when he felt a sudden twinge of pain in his back. "I believe I'm getting lumbago," he observed to his wife. "What good will that do," she said. "You won't be able to understand a word they say."

1297. "Why is it," one man asked another, "That wives always remember wedding anniversaries and their husbands don't?"

"I can explain that very easily," replied his friend. "Do you remember the biggest fish you ever caught in your life?"

"Of course," was the speedy answer.

"Do you think the fish remembers?" his friend asked.

1298. The man was coming out of delirium. "Where am I?" he asked. "Am I in Heaven?"

"No, dear," whispered his wife. "I'm still with you."

1299. "I wouldn't want to say that my wife always gets her way and does everything that she wants to do, but she does write her diary a week ahead of time." HENNY YOUNGMAN

1300. My wife and I have a perfect understanding—I don't try to run her life . . . and I don't try to run mine.

1301. He put his wife on a pedestal. Now she can't reach down to clean the floors.

1302. "Your wife is gargling with Absorbine Jr.!"

"She talked so fast, she sprained her tongue!"

1303. "Does your wife find you entertaining?"

"Not if I can help it."

1304. One fellow said his wife was such a bad driver that, if she lived in Egypt, she'd be driving around with a dented camel. The second man said, "That's nothing. My wife has such a terrible sense of direction she even goes the wrong way on an escalator."

1305. My wife will buy anything that's marked down. Yesterday, she brought home an escalator!

1306. "My wife talks to me positively awful."

"That's nothing. Mine talks to me awfully positive."

1307. Wife, discussing husband: "He doesn't smoke, drink, or go out with women—including me."

1308. A plaque on the office wall of a Peace Justice in Dallas contains this thought-provoking message: "If a man has enough sense to treat his wife like a thoroughbred, she will never turn into an old nag."

1309. A man said his wife had such a big mouth that she got lipstick on her ears when she smiled.

1310. A businessman thought his wife would look good in something long and flowing so he pushed her into the Mississippi.

1311. I like to sleep with the windows open. My wife doesn't complain in so many words but she keeps adding anti-freeze to our waterbed.

1312. "I get no respect at all. I took my wife to a tunnel of love, and she told me to wait outside." RODNEY DANGERFIELD

1313. Does my wife spend? I'm sending her Christmas list to the Guiness World Book of Records.

1314. Husband about wife's driving: "You can't miss our house. It's the one with all the tire marks on the curb."

1315. "There are certain things I don't understand. Like, take my wife, we've been married 10 years. We've moved 14 different times to different states and we always have the same milkman." RODNEY DANGERFIELD

1316. Don't tell your wife a "thing or two." Tell her one thing and stick to it.

1317. He puts his wife on a pedestal—so he won't have to look her in the eye.

1318. My wife's a good driver. She just has minor problems—like starting and stopping.

1319. I heard of a housewife, who just before her husband comes home, puts a dab of floor wax behind each ear so that she will smell tired.

1320. "My wife is always trying to get rid of me. The other day she told me to put the garbage out. I said to her I already put out the garbage. She told me to go and keep an eye on it." RODNEY DANGERFIELD

1321. I first knew that I needed psychiatric help when my wife's political views started making sense to me.

1322. Husband to wife: "OK. I'll admit I'm wrong and you were right."
"It won't do any good. I've changed my mind."

1323. Man at racetrack: "I don't have a cent to bet. My wife blew it all in on the rent."

1324. "Do you permit your wife to have her own way?"
"I should say not. She has it without my permission."

1325. "My wife first saw me on the screen . . . then she opened the window and let me in."

1326. The office Milquetoast heard a still small voice telling him what to do the other day. His wife has laryngitis.

1327. "Where did you meet your wife?"

"At a travel bureau. I was looking for a vacation spot and she was the last resort."

1328.   The reason Solomon had so many wives was because he wanted at least one to be in good humor when he came home.

1329.   "Use your imagination," suggested Mai Fuller to her husband at dinnertime. "Don't think of it as hamburger, but as a filet mignon that's come unglued."

1330.   Two old friends got together and were discussing their husbands' faults.

"We've been married 15 years," one said, "and every night after dinner he complains about the food."

The other wife said, "Terrible—does it bother you?"

She said, "Why should it bother me if he can't stand his own cooking?"

1331.   Budnick had a fight with his wife and went to the Turkish baths to steam out. Later in the evening, he decided to phone home and maybe apologize. So he called her up. "Hello, sweetie," he said. "What are you makin' for dinner?"

"What I'm makin', you bum? Poison, that's what I'm makin'. Poison!"

"So make only one portion! I'm not comin' home."

1332.   His wife was always nagging him to take her out to eat— so he built a fireplace in the back yard.

1333.   Nothing is quite so gratifying to a wife as seeing a double chin on her husband's old girlfriend.

1334.   "Daddy, what's polygamy?"

"Having more than one wife. Having one wife is called monotony."

1335.   After extensive research, Fred has discovered how to avoid hitting your thumb while driving a nail. "Hold the hammer in both hands," Fred suggests, "and let your wife hold the nail."

1336.   The most effective consumer protection agency ever devised is the wife who goes with her husband to pick out a new suit.

1337.   Wife to marriage counselor: "That's my side of the story. Now let me tell you his."

1338.   The trouble with having a perfect wife is there's never any hope for improvement.

1339. Man on phone: "Doc, my wife dislocated her jaw. If you're out this way in the next few weeks, drop in."

1340. A fellow was stopped by a police officer who said, "You're going to get a ticket for speeding."

The motorist said, "Well, I was only doing 40 miles an hour."

The patrolman replied, "No, you were doing 50 in a 30-mph zone."

"No," said the motorist, "I was only doing 40!"

Then his wife popped up and snapped, "Don't argue with my husband when he's been drinking."

1341. At 5 o'clock every day my neighbor washes his car in his driveway. I said, "Harry, you pay more attention to your car than you do to your wife. Pay some attention to her." I came home the other night and there he was in the driveway, washing his wife.

1342. The retiree was asked what he was doing now that he is completely retired.

"Not much of anything 'cept working for my wife," the fellow said. "She pays me three and a half a day."

"Three and a half a day?"

"Yeah! Three meals and half the bed."

1343. Max was leaving for the office one morning when he found a note under the front door. "Unless you deliver $10,000 to us by 2:00 p.m. this afternoon at the spot indicated on the map, we shall kidnap your wife. Max went immediately to the spot and left the following reply: "Gentlemen, I haven't got $10,000, but keep in touch, your proposition interests me."

1344. My wife is on a health food kick. Whatever she gets her hands on, she throws into the blender. Last week I drank a chicken. Now I'm on carrot juice. My wife said: "Drink carrot juice. It'll make your eyes very strong." So I've been drinking it till it's coming out of my ears. But it works. My eyes are very strong, except I can't sleep at night—I see through my eyelids.

1345. "What would you like for your birthday?" a man asked his spouse.

"I'd like something that's hard to break," she replied.

"Like what?" he asked.

"Like a hundred-dollar bill," she declared.

1346. Housewife on telephone: "Come quickly, our house is on fire!"

Fireman: "How do we get there?"

Housewife: "Gee, don't you have your little red truck anymore?"

1347. Some women can drop a hint to their husbands before things get out of control. Two old drinking companions were discussing the situation and one remarked to the other, "On the way to a party the other night my wife said, 'If it turns out to be a dull party—leave it that way.'"

1348. My wife fed me so much saccharine that I'm developing artificial diabetes.

1349. Husband: "I'm not working today. Our union went on strike."
Wife: "Strike?"
Husband: "Yeah, we're trying to get shorter hours."
Wife: "That's a good idea. I always did think 60 minutes was too long for an hour."

1350. But how about the florist's wife who delighted in showing her bloomers.

1351. The other night we got in an argument and I had my wife on her hands and knees.
"Really?"
"Yeh, she was yelling, Come out from under that bed and fight, you coward!"

1352. My wife now has a phone in her car—she crashed it into a telephone booth!

1353. "Daddy, does bigamy mean that a man has one wife too many?"
"No, son. A man can have one wife too many and still not be a bigamist."

1354. Husband: "I've changed my mind."
Wife: "Thank Heavens! I hope it works better than the other one."

1355. You've heard of strapless and backless gowns? My wife's is shapeless and hopeless.

1356. My wife's wardrobe consists of summer clothes. Summer paid for—summer not.

1357. How did I meet my wife? I just opened my wallet and there she was.

1358. The guy in the next office keeps a picture of his wife on his desk. It's a great likeness except for the darts sticking in it.

1359. The kind of wife I'm looking for is one who can sew. The kind you can give a handful of buttons to and say: Here—sew some shirts on these.

1360. I believe in women's rights, but they overdo it. My wife hasn't let me work the controls on our electric blanket since the honeymoon.

1361. I wish I could figure out some way to retire and not have my wife find out.

1362. Bigamy would never work in the U.S. Can you imagine six wives in a mobile home?

1363. More wives would learn from their mistakes if they weren't so busy repeating them.

1364. My wife bought three cartons of cigarettes, four albums, a case of beer, a garden hose and remarked, "Food prices are getting higher every day."

Women

1365. One of the new perfumes for women has a secret ingredient—it makes a man imagine he can support a wife.

1366. A woman told an ear specialist: "I've never had any trouble hearing, but lately I've had a little trouble overhearing."

1367. A soap opera is where it takes eleven months for a woman to have a premature baby.

1368. Some women resist a man's advances, others block his retreat.

1369. A NASA scientist says he is sure there are women on Mars. "NASA shot a communications satellite up there and got a busy signal."

1370. A woman I know had $50 of groceries stolen . . . right out of her glove compartment.

1371. A women's libber says, "If God had meant women to stay in the kitchen, he would have made them out of Reynolds Wrap."

1372. One of the go-go girls claims she has performed cosmetic brain surgery on several fellows and now they think only beautiful thoughts about her.

1373. The women's book club voted unanimously to have a review on the *Charge of the Light Brigade.* Women always get interested fast when they hear the word charge.

1374. Speed limits are getting ignored every day. Isn't it shocking the way some women drivers push their carts through supermarkets at speeds in excess of $55 an hour?

1375. A woman in slacks usually gives you the impression she's living beyond her jeans.

1376. First woman: "Last year we went to Majora on vacation."
Second woman: "Where's that?"
First woman: "I don't know, we flew."

1377. A woman asked to cash a check at Neiman-Marcus. The clerk asked, "Can you identify yourself?" She whipped out a mirror, looked in it and said, "Yep, it's me alright."

1378. People are going nuts. One woman shot her husband with a bow and arrow—claimed she didn't want to wake the kids.

1379. "I went with my woman for six months and then she gave me the air. I said to her, 'What's the matter, is there somebody else?' She looked at me and said, 'There must be.' "

1380. Fifty-one percent of the nation's drivers are women and that's only counting the front seats.

1381. Horse sense is what keeps a woman from becoming a nag.

1382. A recent survey reported that one of three women have wrinkled pantyhose.

1383. Did you hear about the modern day Cinderella? At the stroke of midnight she turns into a motel.

1384. Woman: "I'd like a winter coat."
Clerk: "How long?"
Woman: "For the whole winter."

1385. Some women are regular magicians at Christmas time. They're able to get mink coats out of old goats.

1386. The average woman should concentrate on beauty rather than brains, because the average man can see much better than he can think.

1387. Anita Loos, 80 year old author: "The people I'm furious with are the women's liberationists. They keep getting up on soapboxes and proclaiming that women are brighter than men. It's true, but it should be kept quiet or it ruins the whole racket."

1388. A woman went on a very expensive ocean voyage and was asked if she got to eat with the captain. She said, "No, for that kind of money, why should I eat with the help?"

1389. Know how women are sure their stretch pants are the right size? They put a dime in the back pocket. If the salesclerk can tell if it's heads or tails—that's the right size.

1390. A lady motorist from the hills of Arkansas was stopped by the local fuzz who accused her of doing 45 miles an hour. "45 miles an hour? That's ridiculous," she said, "I haven't been out an hour."

1391. Comedienne Joan Rivers recently gave a command performance for Queen Elizabeth II and reports: "I was very nervous. I spent all week curtseying to the Princess phone to get in shape. I didn't know what to do when I met her. The only time I had ever seen her was on a stamp. So I went over and licked her head."

1392. "I'm at a bad time in my life," she said.
  "Why?"
  "I am too young for medicare and too old for men to care."

1393. Two young women discussing their financial condition: "I live from one paycheck to another," said the first.
  "Huh!" shrugged the second. "You're lucky. I wish I could get by that easy."

1394. Two women were discussing ways of controlling the nocturnal wanderings of their spouses. One said she had the perfect cure for her late husband. When she heard him fumbling around downstairs, she called out, "Is that you Harold?"
  "So, how does that cure him?" asked her friend.
  "His name is Joe."

1395. A night parachute jumper missed his mark and landed in a remote parking lot. With lights still flashing and crash helmet turned crossways he asked, "Where am I?" A woman swallowed hard and said, "Earth?"

1396. You think it's been windy here—out in California it blew so hard that Ann Miller's hair moved.

1397. Here's a form of the old Trojan War story:
  A handsome young soldier broke into a house where he found two luscious maidens and their Aunt Kate.

Chuckling with glee, he roared, "Prepare thyselves to be taken away as wives my pretties."

The lovely girls fell to their knees and pleaded with him. "Do with us as you must, but spare our faithful old aunt."

"Shut your mouth," snapped Kate, "war is war."

1398. "Recently, on the subway, I got up and gave my seat to a lady who was holding on to a strap. She was rather surprised and said to me, 'Why did you do that?' Seeing that she was incapable of understanding a spiritual reason, I said to her, 'Madame, I tell you, ever since I was a little boy, I have had an infinite respect for a woman with a strap in her hand.' "

1399. Heard from a young woman to her escort in a Birmingham hotel bar: "Of course there's no one else, Arnold! That's why I'm out with you."

1400. An unmarried woman well beyond ever being a child bride was asked if her relations with a certain man were platonic. "Well," she said, "it may be play for him, but it's tonic for me."

1401. A reporter was interviewing Winston Churchill. "What do you think of the prediction that in the year 2050 women will be ruling the world?"

Churchill smiled, "They still will, eh?"

1402. Women drive about as well as men. They don't seem ashamed of it either.

1403. A caged snake, a prop for an amateur theatrical show, got out one night and wrapped itself around another stage prop—a telephone. The leading lady walked on stage, prepared to answer the ringing phone. She spotted the snake and froze, allowing the phone to ring and stopping the action of play. The stage manager sent the actress who played the maid—and wasn't particularly afraid of reptiles—to fetch the snake. The actress barged across the stage and snatched up the reptile. But standing there with the snake in her hand, she thought she ought to say something to explain herself to the audience.

"Pardon ma'am, she said to the leading lady, "I forgot to tidy up this morning."

1404. A woman who suffers in silence probably can't get a word in edgewise.

1405. It is said that a woman's mind is cleaner than a man's because she changes it more often.

1406. An exhaustive study of police records shows that no woman has ever shot her husband while he was doing the dishes.

1407. "Many girls would be willing to marry a man who is tall, dark and has some." GLORIA PITZER

1408. "It's not true that women change their minds frequently. Ask a woman her age and she'll give you the same answer for years." EARL WILSON

1409. A low neckline is about the only thing a man will approve of and look down on at the same time.

1410. A subway rider overheard a pretty young thing exclaim: "I slapped Tom's face when I found a blond hair on his jacket. Then I had to apologize when I learned it was his wife's!"

1411. Mary had a little skirt,
And it was very tight,
Who gives a hoot for Mary's lamb
With Mary's calves in sight?

1412. If we had more women Senators, Congress would be in better shape.

1413. Most women don't want a go-getter; they want an already-gotter.

1414. Buy your girl a bikini. It's the least you can do for her.

1415. Cupid makes a lot of wild shots. He aims at the heart while staring at the kneecap.

1416. Nowadays it costs so much for wine, women and song, there's very little left over for luxuries.

1417. "Pardon me, Miss, are you unattached?"
"No, just put together sloppy."

1418. "Peek-a-boo gown" is a dress that isn't all there for women who are.

1419. Women are a problem, but they're the kind of problem I like to wrestle with.

1420. Two women were preparing to board the airliner. One of them turned to the pilot and said: "Now, please don't travel faster than sound. We want to talk."

1421. By the time a fellow is able to read a woman like a book, his eyes go bad.

1422.   A woman's life is spent straightening out her two most important possessions, her handbag, and her husband.

1423.   After man came woman—and she has been after him ever since.

1424.   A true music lover can be defined as a man who puts his ear to the keyhole when he hears a girl singing in the bathtub.

1425.   There are two kinds of women—those who'll argue over nothing, and those who'll argue over anything.

1426.   The greatest job in the world is in gynecology. Who else can tell a beautiful woman to take off all her clothes, lie down, look her over thoroughly, at leisure, and then send the bill to her husband.

1427.   "I told my girl the truth. I told her I was seeing a psychiatrist. She told me the truth. She was seeing a psychiatrist, 2 plumbers, and a bartender. RODNEY DANGERFIELD

Index

T

U

V

W